The Chartered Institute of Marketing

Professional Certificate in Marketing

STUDY TEXT

Marketing Information and Research

2010 edition

Second edition August 2010
First edition July 2008

ISBN 9780 7517 8937 9
(Previous ISBN 9780 7517 4864 2)

e-ISBN 9780 7517 9145 7

British Library Cataloguing-in-Publication Data
A catalogue record for this book
is available from the British Library

Published by

BPP Learning Media Ltd
Aldine House, Aldine Place
London W12 8AA

www.bpp.com/learningmedia

Printed in the United Kingdom

We are grateful to the Chartered Institute of Marketing for
permission to reproduce in this text the syllabus, tutor's
guidance notes and past examination questions.

Author: Dr Kellie Vincent
With thanks to Kate Machattie for her input to this second
edition.

Your learning materials, published by BPP Learning Media Ltd,
are printed on paper sourced from sustainable, managed
forests.

Contents

Introduction

Chapters

Review form & free prize draw

1 Aim of the Study Text

This book has been deliberately referred to as a 'Study Text' rather than text book, because it is designed to help you though your specific CIM Professional Certificate studies. It covers Unit 3 Marketing Information and Research.

So, why is it similar to but not actually a text book? Well, the CIM have identified key texts that you should become familiar with. The purpose of this workbook is not to replace these texts but to pick out the important parts that you will definitely need to know in order to pass, simplify these elements and, to suggest a few areas within the texts that will provide good additional reading but that are not absolutely essential. We will also suggest a few other sources and useful press and CIM publications which are worth reading.

We know some of you will prefer to read text books from cover to cover whilst others amongst you will prefer to pick out relevant parts or dip in and out of the various topics. This text will help you to ensure that if you are a 'cover to cover' type, then you will not miss the emphasis of the syllabus. If you are a 'dip in and out' type, then we will make sure that you find the parts which are essential for you to know. Unlike a standard text book which will have been written to be used across a range of alter native qualifications, this Study Text has been specifically written for your CIM course, so if a topic appears in this book then it is part of the syllabus and therefore will be a subject the examiners could potentially test you on. Throughout this Study Text you will find real examples of marketing in practice as well as key concepts highlighted.

2 Studying for CIM qualifications

There are a few key points to remember as you study for your CIM qualification:

(a)   You are studying for a **professional** qualification. This means that you are required to use professional language and adopt a business approach in your work.

(b)   You are expected to show that you have 'read widely'. Make sure that you read the quality press (and don't skip the business pages), read Marketing, The Marketer, Research and Marketing Week avidly.

(c)   Become aware of the marketing initiatives you come across on a daily basis, for example, when you go shopping look around and think about why the store layout is as it is; consider the messages, channel choice and timings of ads when you are watching TV. It is surprising how much you will learn just by taking an interest in the marketing world around you.

(d)   Get to know the way CIM write their exam papers and assignments. They use a specific approach which is (the Magic Formula) to ensure a consistent approach when designing assessment materials. Make sure you are fully aware of this as it will help you interpret what the examiner is looking for (a full description of the Magic Formula appears later and is heavily featured within the chapters).

(e)   Learn how to use Harvard referencing. This is explained in detail in our CIM Professional Certificate Assessment Workbook.

(f)   Ensure that you read very carefully all assessment details sent to you from CIM. They are very strict with regard to deadlines, completing the correct paperwork to accompany any assignment or project and making sure you have your CIM membership card with you at the exam. Failing to meet any assessment entry deadlines or completing written work on time will mean that you will have to wait for the next round of assessment dates and will need to pay the relevant assessment fees again.

3 The Professional Certificate Syllabus

The Professional Certificate in Marketing is aimed at anyone who is employed in supporting marketing role such as Marketing Co-ordinator or Executive. You may also be a manager with a senior role within in a small or medium sized company where marketing only forms part of a wider work remit. Or you may be looking to move into your first marketing role or to specialise.

The aim of the qualification is to provide a strong foundation of marketing knowledge. You will develop the breadth of knowledge of marketing theory but also appreciate issues faced within the organisation as CIM qualifications concentrate on applied marketing within real work-places.

The complete qualification is made from four units:

- Unit 1 Marketing Essentials
- Unit 2 Assessing the Marketing Environment
- Unit 3 Marketing Information and Research
- Unit 4 Stakeholder Marketing

CIM stipulate that each module should take 40 guided learning hours to complete. Guided learning hours refer to time in class, using distance learning materials and completing any work set by your tutor. Guided learning hours do not include the time it will take you to complete the necessary reading for your studies.

The syllabus as provided by CIM can be found below with reference to our coverage within this Study Text.

Unit characteristics

This unit focuses on the importance of marketing information in gaining a more in-depth understanding of both the market in which the organisation operates and the customers it seeks to serve.

It aims to provide an understanding of how marketing information supports marketing decisions within the organisation and how information contributes to the overall marketing process. The unit explores different research methodologies and encourages consideration of complementary approaches to collecting a range of market and customer information.

The unit also considers the role of databases in information management, the nature and scope of the research industry, and of various research methodologies linked to the collection of primary and secondary data.

By the end of the unit, students should be able to demonstrate a thorough knowledge and understanding in the ways of collecting and manipulating information to support and justify key marketing decisions.

Overarching learning outcomes

By the end of this unit, students should be able to:

- Identify appropriate information and marketing research requirements for marketing decision making

- Evaluate the importance of customer databases and their contribution to providing detailed market information to support marketing decisions

- Review the processes involved in establishing an effective database

- Explain the nature and scope of the research industry and discuss the importance of working in line with the industry's code of conduct

- Explain the process for selecting a marketing research supplier, in domestic and international markets, developing the criteria to support that selection

- Explain the process for collecting marketing and customer information, utilising appropriate primary and secondary sources

- Appraise the appropriateness of different qualitative and quantitative research methodologies to meet different research situations

SECTION 1 – The importance of marketing information (weighting 20%)

		Covered in chapter(s)
1.1	Discuss the need for information in marketing management and its role in the overall marketing process: • Information on customers • Information on competitors and other organisations • Information on the marketing environment • Descriptive v comparative v diagnostic role of information	1
1.2	Evaluate the impact of information technology on the marketing function and discuss the challenges facing organisations in collecting valid, reliable and measurable information to support the decision making process: • Growth in information sources (The Information Explosion) • The Internet/Intranet • Consumer generated media eg, on-line communities/blogs • Customer databases • Internal reporting system, scanning/inventory control etc • Validity and reliability of different information sources	2
1.3	Explain the concept of a marketing decision support system and its role in supporting marketing decisions: • Definition • Components (data storage, reports and displays, analysis and modelling) • Types of information held • Manner in which it can assist decision making	2
1.4	Review the key elements and formats when reporting or presenting marketing information to decision makers: • Understanding the audience/audience thinking sequence • Physical and On-line Research Report Format • Oral presentation format • Using tables and graphs	11

SECTION 2 – The role of databases in information management (weighting 20%)

		Covered in chapter(s)
2.1	Demonstrate an understanding of the role, application and benefits of customer databases in relation to customer relationship management (CRM): • Types of customer data (behavioural data, volunteered data, attributed data) • Role in profiling customers • Role in marketing intelligence testing campaigns/forecasting • Role in determining life-time value • Role in personalising offerings and communications • Role in building relationships	3
2.2	Identify and explain the different stages in the process of setting up a database: • The importance of evaluating software and what is needed to ensure it works properly • Evaluating software • Identifying needs of users of a database • Processing data (formatting, validation, de-duplication)	3
2.3	Explain the principles of data warehousing, data marts and data mining: • Understanding how databases can be used to select, explore and model large amounts of data to identify relationships and patterns of behaviour	3
2.4	Explain the relationship between database marketing and marketing research and explain the legal aspects of data collection and usage, including the Data Protection Legislation: • Data protection legislation • List brokers • Profilers and their offerings (eg, Acorn, Mosaic etc) • Issues involved in merging marketing research and customer database information (transparency, aggregation of data, using customer databases for marketing research purposes)	3

SECTION 3 – The nature of marketing research (weighting 25%)

		Covered in chapter(s)
3.1	Discuss the nature and structure of the market research industry: • Marketing Research Departments v Marketing Research Agencies • Types of Marketing Research Agency • Scale of Industry • Professional Bodies and Associations in the Marketing Research Industry	4
3.2	Explain the stages of the market research process: • Identification of problems and opportunities • Formulation of research needs/the research brief • Selection of research provider/the proposal • Creation of research design • Collection of secondary data • Collection of primary data • Analysis of data • Preparation and presentation of research findings and recommendations	4
3.3	Evaluate a range of procedures and criteria used for selecting a market research supplier in domestic and international markets: • Short-listing criteria • The research proposal • Supplier assessments (Pitch) • Selection criteria	4
3.4	Explain how best to liaise with the research agency on a day to day basis to leverage best levels of service, support and implementation and high quality information to support the business case development: • Monitoring working arrangements using quality and service standards	4
3.5	Explain the stages involved in order to develop a full research proposal to fulfil the brief which support the information needs of different marketing projects: • Content of proposal covering background, objectives, approach and method, reporting and presentation procedures, timing, personal CVs, related experience, contract details	5 & 6
3.6	Evaluate the ethical and social responsibilities inherent in the market research task: • Need for goodwill, trust, professionalism, confidentiality • Codes of marketing and social research practice (eg, Market Research Society code of conduct) • Responsibilities to respondents (Use of information/protection of vulnerable groups such as children, etc) • Responsibilities to clients (transparency, data reporting, etc)	4

SECTION 4 – Research methodologies (weighting 35%)

		Covered in chapter(s)
4.1	Evaluate the uses, benefits and limitations of secondary data: • Benefits • Limitations • Sources of secondary data • Internet search strategies • Integrating secondary data with primary data	7
4.2	Evaluate the various procedures used for observing behaviour: • Categories of observation (natural v contrived, visible v hidden, structured v unstructured, mechanised v human, participant v non-participant) • Audits and scanner based research • Television viewing measurement • Internet monitoring • Mystery shopping	10
4.3	Identify and evaluate the various techniques for collecting qualitative data: • Types of research most suited to qualitative research • Individual depth interviews • Group discussions (including basic guidelines on group moderation, stimulus material and projective techniques) • Using the Internet for qualitative research (online group discussions, chat rooms, blogs) • Overview of approach to the analysis of qualitative research	8
4.4	Identify and evaluate the various techniques for collecting quantitative data: • Face to face survey methods • Telephone interviews • Postal surveys • Online surveys • Omnibus surveys • Forum voting (pressing voting buttons)	9
4.5	Identify and evaluate the various techniques for undertaking experimentation: • Hall tests • Placement tests • Simulated test markets	10
4.6	Design a basic questionnaire and discussion guide to meet a project's research objectives: • Discussion guide format • The questionnaire design process • Question and response formats • Scaling techniques (Likert and semantic differential) • Sequence and wording • Design layout and appearance • Questionnaire generating software	8 & 9
4.7	Explain and evaluate different **basic** sampling approaches designed to maximize the benefit of market research activities: • The sampling process • Difference between probability and non-probability samples • Knowledge of convenience, judgement and quota samples • Determining sample size • Sampling and non-sampling error • Panels	6

The unit covered by this study text (Unit 3 Marketing Information and Research) is assessed by an assignment. In order to help you focus specifically on your assignment we have also written a Professional Certificate in Marketing Assessment Workbook which is available either through your usual book retailer or our website www.bpp.com/learningmedia.

4 The Magic Formula

The Magic Formula is a tool used by CIM to help both examiners write exam and assignment questions and you to more easily interpret what you are being asked to write about. It is useful for helping you to check that you are using an appropriate balance between theory and practice for your particular level of qualification.

Contrary to the title, there is nothing mystical about the Magic Formula and simply knowing it (or even mentioning it in an assessment) will not automatically secure a pass. What it does do however is to help you to check that you are presenting your answers in an appropriate format, including enough marketing theory and applying it to a real marketing context or issue. After passing the Professional Certificate in Marketing, if you continue to study for higher level CIM qualifications, you would be expected to evaluate more and apply a more demanding range of marketing decisions. As such the Magic Formula is weighted with an even greater emphasis on evaluation and application as you move to the Professional Diploma and Postgraduate CIM levels.

Graphically, the Magic Formula for the Professional Certificate in Marketing is shown below:

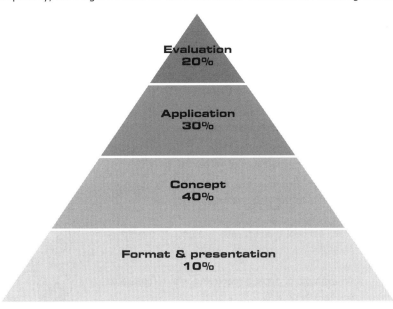

Figure 1 The Magic Formula for the Professional Certificate in Marketing

You can see from the pyramid that for the Professional Certificate marks are awarded in the following proportions:

- ## Presentation and format – 10%

    Remember, you are expected to present your work professionally which means that it should ALWAYS be typed and attention should be paid to making it look as visually appealing as possible. It also means that the CIM will stipulate the format that you should present your work in. The assessment formats you will be given will be varied and can include things like reports to write, slides to prepare, emails, memos, formal letters, press releases, discussion documents, briefing papers, agendas, and newsletters.

- ## Concept – 40%

    Concept refers to your ability to state, recall and describe marketing theory. The definition of marketing is clearly a core CIM syllabus topic. If we take this as an example, you would be expected to recognise, recall, and write this definition to a word perfect standard to gain the full marks for concept.

- ## Application – 30%

  Application based marks are given for your ability to apply marketing theories to real life marketing situations. For example, you may be asked to discuss the definition of marketing, and how it is applied within your own organisation. Within this sort of question 40% of the marks would have been awarded within the 'concept' aspect of the Magic Formula. You will gain the rest of the marks through your ability to evaluate to what extent the concept is applied within your own organisation. Here you are not only using the definition but are applying it in order to consider the market orientation of the company.

- ## Evaluation – 20%

  Evaluation is the ability to asses the value or worth of something sometimes through careful consideration of related advantages and disadvantages or weighing up of alternatives. Results from your evaluation should enable you to discuss the importance of an issue using evidence to support your opinions.

  Using the example of being asked whether or not your organisation adopts a marketing approach. If you were asked to 'evaluate' this, you should provide reasons and specific examples of why you think they might take this approach, as well as considering why they may not take this approach, before coming to a final conclusion.

5   A guide to the features of the Study Text

Each of the chapters will contain specific features (see below) which will help you to break down the content into manageable chunks and ensure that you are developing the skills required for a professional qualification.

Chapter feature	Relevance and how you should use it	Corresponding icon
Chapter topic list	Study the list, each numbered topic denotes a numbered section in the chapter.	–
Introduction	Shows why topics need to be studied and is a route guide through the chapter	–
Syllabus linked Learning Objectives	Outlines what you should learn within the chapter based on what is required within the syllabus	–
Format & Presentation	Outlines a key marketing presentation format with reference to the Magic Formula	
Concept	A key concept to learn with reference to the Magic Formula	
Application	An example of applied marketing with reference to the Magic Formula	
Evaluation	An example of evaluation with reference to the Magic Formula	
Activity	An application based activity for you to complete	
Key text links	Emphasises key parts to read in a range of other texts and other learning resources	
Marketing at work	A short case study to illustrate marketing practice	
Exam/ Assessment tip	Key advice based on your assessment	
Quick quiz	Use this to check your learning	
Objective check	Use this to review what you have learnt	

6 A note on Pronouns

On occasions in this Study Text, 'he' is used for 'he or she', 'him' for 'him or her' and so forth. Whilst we try to avoid this practice it is sometimes necessary for reasons of style. No prejudice or stereotyping according to sex is intended or assumed.

7 Additional resources

7.1 The CIM's supplementary reading list

We have already mentioned that CIM requires you to demonstrate your ability to 'read widely' . CIM issue an extensive reading list for each unit. For this unit they recommend supplementary reading. Within the Study Text we have highlighted in the wider reading specific topics where these resources will help. CIM's supplementary reading list for this unit is:

Brace, I (2004) <u>Questionnaire design: how to plan, structure and write survey material for effective market research</u> Kogan Page, London.

Bradley, N. (2007) <u>Marketing research: tools and techniques</u>, Oxford University Press, Oxford.

Chisnall, P. (2004) <u>Marketing research,.</u> 7th edition, McGraw Hill, Maidenhead.

ESOMAR (2007) <u>Market research handbook,</u> 5th edition, John Wiley, Chichester.

Gordon, W. (1999) <u>Good thinking: a guide to qualitative research</u>, NTC Publications Henley on Thames.

Humby, C., Hunt, T. and Phillips, T. (2008) <u>Scoring points: how Tesco continues to win customer loyalty</u>, 3rd edition, Kogan Page, London [Due June 2008].

Proctor, T. (2005) <u>Essentials of marketing research.</u> 4th edition, Prentice Hall, Harlow.

Stone, M., Bond, A. and Foss, B. (2004) <u>Consumer insight: how to use data and market research to get close to your customer,</u> Kogan Page, London.

Tapp, A. (2005) <u>Principles of direct and database marketing. 3rd Edition.</u> Harlow, FT Prentice Hall.

7.2 Assessment preparation materials from BPP Learning Media

To help you pass the entire Professional Certificate in Marketing we have created a complete study package. The **Professional Certificate Assessment Workbook** covers all four units for the Professional Certificate level. Practice question and answers, tips on tackling assignments and work-based projects are included to help you succeed in your assessments.

Our A6 set of spiral bound **Passcards** are handy revision cards and are ideal to reinforce key topics for the Marketing Essentials and Assessing the Marketing Environment exams.

8 Your personal study plan

Preparing a Study Plan (and sticking to it) is one of the key elements to learning success.

CIM have stipulated that there should be a minimum of 40 guided learning hours spent on each unit. Guided learning hours will include time spent in lesson, working on fully prepared distance learning materials, formal workshops and work set by your tutor. We also know that to be successful, students should spend *at least* an additional 40 hours conducting self study. This means that for the entire qualification with four units you should spend 160 hours working in a tutor guided manner and at least an additional 160 hours completing recommended reading, working on assignments, and revising for exams. This study text will help you to organise this 40 hour portion of self study time.

Now think about the exact amount of time you have (don't forget you will still need some leisure time!) and complete the following tables to help you keep to a schedule.

	Date		Duration in weeks
Course start			
Course finish			Total weeks of course:
Submission date for research project	Draft	Final	Total weeks to complete:
Task 1			
Task 2			
Task 3			
Complete project			

Content chapter coverage plan

Chapter	To be completed by
1 The importance of marketing information	
2 The role of IT and marketing decision support systems	
3 CRM and databases	
4 The market research industry	
5 Information requirements, research projects, briefs and proposals	
6 An overview of research methods	
7 Secondary data	
8 Collecting qualitative data	
9 Collecting quantitative data	
10 Observation and experimentation	
11 Reports and presentations	

Chapter 1

The importance of marketing information

Topic list

1 The need for information
2 Marketing information requirements
3 Descriptive, comparative, diagnostic and predictive information
4 Information technology and marketing

Introduction

To be truly marketing orientated the organisation needs to process a large amount of information to check that it is satisfying and meeting customer needs and that customers are at the core of their business.

Without **information**, no-one in an organisation could take effective action. Managers **gather** information about tasks or problems, **process** the information to decide what needs to be done, and then **communicate** their decisions in the form of instructions to their staff. This goes on constantly throughout the organisation, from the very top levels to the most junior.

This chapter sets the scene for the remainder of the text. The first section defines information and assesses the need for information. It also addresses the questions of why marketers need information, how the need for information fits into the marketing process, the concept of an information age and what we mean by knowledge management. How the need for information fits into the marketing process is also discussed.

The second section of the chapter concentrates on the nature of different types of marketing information and where this information may come from. Specifically we investigate the need for information about customers, other organisations and the marketing environment. In addition, we consider potential sources of this information.

The final section looks at the different nature of marketing information and compares descriptive, comparative, diagnostic and predictive information.

Syllabus linked learning objectives

By the end of the chapter you will be able to:

Learning objectives	Syllabus link
1 Discuss the need for information	1.1
2 Identify the nature of marketing information in helping to make decisions	1.1
3 Explain what information is needed about customers	1.1
4 Explain what information is needed about other organisations	1.1
5 Explain what information is needed about the marketing environment	1.1
6 Compare the nature of information as descriptive, comparative, diagnostic or predictive.	1.1

1 The need for information

1.1 Information defined

The term information is often used without any real thought (Wilson, 2006) as it has multiple meanings including gathered facts; communication of facts; computerised data which has been interpreted and definite knowledge which has been acquired.. So what do we mean as marketers when we refer to information? Generally, information will refer to a mixture of all of the above because data and facts should be gathered, organised, processed and interpreted in order to understand markets.

Information is a **marketing asset**. It impacts on performance in several ways.

- It helps to increase **responsiveness** to customer demands.
- It helps to identify **new customer opportunities** and new product/service demands.
- It helps to anticipate **competitive attacks** and threats.

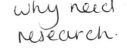
why need research.

Overall, marketers need information to help them to make decisions.

 KEY CONCEPT

concept

In a **knowledge-based economy** organisations compete by obtaining **superior information**. The more information that a firm can obtain about competitors and customers, the more it should be able to adapt its product/service offerings to meet the needs of the market place.

The 'Information Age'

There's nothing new about using information to get things done, but you will often hear that we now live in the **'Information Age'**. That suggests that information is more important than ever before – perhaps **the** most important thing in modern life.

- At one time organisations could be successful simply by investing in physical resources – bigger and better factories, nearer to customers than their competitors' factories, for example. The problem was producing enough to satisfy demand.

- As competition has increased and become more global there is no significant difference between, say, a Ford factory in Chicago and a Nissan factory in Wales. The problem now is creating enough demand in the first place.

research into lines of communication any create new/faster lines of communication.

In a **knowledge-based economy** economic factors such as land and capital are not vital for success. Organisations now compete by **knowing** more about the markets they serve, who the best suppliers are, how to do things, and – above all – by having the best new ideas. In other words they compete by **gathering information** and **using it intelligently**.

Firms are becoming increasingly aware of the competitive advantage that may be achieved through the use of information. Information systems can affect the way the firm approaches **customer service** – the very essence of the **marketing concept** – and can provide advantages over competitor approaches. Superior customer service can only be achieved by being able to anticipate and satisfy customer needs. In order to meet this objective, **information** which is **up-to-date**, **accurate**, **relevant** and **timely** is essential. *Need to give timescale when to be done again?*

1.2 Knowledge management

In a knowledge-based economy knowledge must be actively managed. Knowledge includes **tacit knowledge** in employees' heads as well as **formally recorded facts** (known as codified knowledge), transactions and so on.

Knowledge is information within people's minds. It may or may not be recorded in the form of generally accessible information.

A **knowledge-based economy** is an economy based on application of knowledge. Organisations' capabilities and efficiency in using their knowledge override other, more traditional, economic factors such as land and capital.

As we have noted, modern organisations operate in a **knowledge-based economy**. It is an age in which the competitiveness of organisations depends on the accumulation of knowledge and its rapid mobilisation to produce goods and services.

(a) Producing unique products or services or producing products or services at a lower cost than competitors is based on **superior knowledge**.

(b) Knowledge is especially valuable as it may be used to create **new ideas**, insights and interpretations and for decision making.

(c) However knowledge, like information, is of no value unless it is **applied**.

As the importance of knowledge increases, the success of an organisation becomes increasingly dependent on its ability to gather, produce, hold and disseminate knowledge.

 KEY CONCEPT

concept

Knowledge management entails identifying knowledge and using a variety of organisational and technological means to ensure that it is shared.

Knowledge management involves the identification and analysis of available and required knowledge, and the subsequent planning and control of actions to develop knowledge assets so as to fulfil organisational objectives.

Knowledge assets are the sum of the knowledge regarding markets, products, technologies, resources, skills and systems that a business owns or controls and which enable it to achieve its objectives.

Knowledge management programmes are attempts at:

(a) Designing and installing techniques and processes to create, protect and use **explicit knowledge** (codified knowledge that the company knows that it has). Explicit knowledge includes facts, transactions and events that can be clearly stated and stored in management information systems.

(b) Designing and creating environments and activities to discover and release **tacit knowledge** (explained below).

Tacit knowledge is expertise held by people within the organisation that has not been formally documented.

(a) Tacit knowledge is a difficult thing to manage because it is **invisible** and **intangible**. We do not know what knowledge exists within a person's brain, and whether he or she chooses to share knowledge is a matter of choice.

(b) The **motivation to share** hard-won experience is sometimes low; the individual is 'giving away' their value and may be very reluctant to lose a position of influence and respect by making it available to everyone.

For these two reasons **an organisation may never fully know what knowledge it possesses** and could exploit. Knowledge management is an attempt to address this problem. It attempts to turn all relevant knowledge, including personal knowledge, into corporate **knowledge assets** that can be easily and widely shared throughout an organisation and appropriately applied.

1.2.1 Where does knowledge reside?

There are various actions that can be taken to try to determine the prevalence of knowledge in an organisation.

One is the **identification and development of informal networks** and communities of practice within organisations. These self-organising groups share common work interests, usually cutting across a company's functions and processes. People exchange what they know and develop a shared language that allows knowledge to flow more efficiently.

Another means of establishing the prevalence of knowledge is to look at knowledge-related business **outcomes**. One example is **product development and service innovation**. While the knowledge embedded within these innovations is invisible, the products themselves are tangible.

Some organisations produce guides to enable employees to easily locate the information they are searching for. Sometimes intranets are used to help with this but you should remember that the existence of an intranet does not automatically mean

[handwritten margin notes: "how are the findings of research going to be effectively communicated throughout organisation?"; "could we look @ CRM systems as ? making research to investigate what transactions/ comms currently take place?"; "How has the service that is already there come about?"]

that knowledge is well organised and shared. A quote from Martin Archer from the knowledge consultancy Stratagem was featured in a special report on 'The Art of Knowledge Management' within Research magazine. Archer, believes that the context of knowledge has to be personal and states 'It's only when I understand how information can be applied by me as an individual that it has any tangible meaning and becomes knowledge'.

Within the special report, Wain (2007) identifies some key notes in creating a strong knowledge management system, they are:

(a)   Information is not knowledge... and an intranet, in isolation is not a knowledge management system

(b)   As knowledge is personal and tacit focus on enabling rather than managing it

(c)   Technology can enable knowledge sharing but let the human lead and the technology follow

(d)   Stocks of knowledge are far less powerful than flows, so don't just store it in stagnant pools, actively encourage it to burst its banks

(e)   To convert your human into intellectual capital, concentrate on generating social capital... and ensure that your organisational capital is supporting , not constraining the sharing of knowledge

(f)   Manifestly foster a 'knowledge' culture- reward those who share, not those who hoard

(g)   Simply give people the means, motivation and opportunity to share.... ideas, stories, mistakes, successes. Don't direct or control the input, just observe and codify it

(h)   Trust and risk-taking are essential to knowledge development, between agency and client, but also within a single organisation

(i)   Ensure the way you recruit, manage, develop, deploy, measure and reward your people deliberately and transparently supports knowledge-sharing

1.2.2 Customer knowledge within the organisation

Many business functions deal with customers, including marketing, sales, service, logistics and financial functions. Each function will have its own reasons for being interested in customer information, and may have its own way of recording what it learns and even its own customer information system. The diverse interests of different departments make it **difficult to pull together** customer knowledge in one common format and place and the problem is magnified because all have some political reason to keep control of what they know about customers.

While much of this book is about the processes of **market research** (which generates **explicit knowledge**, often by going outside the organisation), it is also worth remembering the necessity to **motivate employees to record, share and use** knowledge gained in a **less formal** manner. This includes experiential observations, comments made, lessons learned, interactions among people, impressions formed and so on.

Organisational means of encouraging sharing include emphasising it in the corporate **culture**, **evaluating** people on the basis of their knowledge behaviour and **rewarding** those who display good knowledge-sharing practice.

On a more practical level, **information and communications technology** can be of great assistance too, as we will see in the next chapter.

The more information that a firm can obtain about competitors and customers, the more it should be able to adapt its product/service offerings to meet the needs of the market place through strategies such as **differentiation**. For example, mail order companies that are able to store data about customer buying habits can exploit this data by recognising patterns of buying behaviour, and offering products at likely buying times that are in line with the customer's profile.

Good information systems may alter the way business is done and may provide organisations with **new opportunities**.

The term information has strong links with IT and the role of IT in helping marketers to make decision is every growing. Marketers often face 'information overload' where they have too much information thrown at them from multiple sources. IT systems can help alleviate this by helping to store and structure the information to hand. The key point to remember however is that technology alone does not help to cut through the sheer amount of information. Marketers need to understand the decisions that have to be made, define them well and then clearly identify the information that is then required. No IT system to date has been able to do that: human intervention and planning is always required.

KEY CONCEPT

Information is required by marketing and sales management for **analysis**, **planning**, **implementation** and **control**: APIC.

1.4 Analysis, planning, implementation, control: APIC

Kotler (1994) outlined that the process of marketing involves stages of analysis, planning, implementation and control.

To carry out marketing management activities, **marketing managers need information**. They need to:

- Anticipate changes in demand
- Introduce, modify or discontinue products or services
- Evaluate profitability
- Set prices
- Undertake promotional activity
- Plan budgets
- Control costs

Marketing management activities have been summarised using the acronym **APIC** (Kotler *et al, 1994*).

Analysis	**P**lanning	**I**mplementation	**C**ontrol

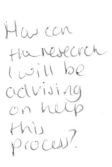

How can the research I will be advising on help this process?

(a) **Analysis**. 'Managing the marketing function begins with a complete analysis of the company's situation. The company must analyse its markets and marketing environment to find attractive opportunities and to avoid environmental threats. It must analyse company strengths and weaknesses, as well as current and possible marketing actions, to determine which opportunities it can best pursue. Marketing analysis feeds information and other inputs to each of the other marketing management functions.'

(b) **Planning**. 'Through strategic planning, the company decides what it wants to do with each business unit. Marketing planning involves deciding on marketing strategies that will help the company attain its overall strategic objectives.'

(c) **Implementation**. 'Good marketing analysis and planning are only a start toward successful company performance – the marketing plans must be carefully implemented. It is often easier to design good marketing strategies than put them into action.

People at all levels of the marketing system must work together to implement marketing strategy and plans. People in marketing must work closely with people in finance, purchasing, manufacturing and other company departments. And many outside people and organisations must help with implementation – suppliers, resellers, advertising agencies, research firms, the advertising media. All must work together effectively to implement the marketing program.'

(d) **Control**. 'Many surprises are likely to occur as marketing plans are being implemented. The company needs control procedures to make certain that its objectives will be achieved. Companies want to make sure that they are achieving the sales, profits, and other goals set in their annual plans. This control involves measuring ongoing market performance, determining the causes of any serious gaps in performance, and deciding on the best corrective action to take to close the gaps. Corrective action may call for improving the ways in which the plan is being implemented or even changing the goals.

Companies should also stand back from time to time and look at their overall approach to the marketplace. The purpose is to make certain that the company's objectives, policies, strategies, and programs remain appropriate in the face of rapid environmental changes. To do this, good quality marketing information is essential.

How do people want to be contacted/appropriate contact now. When is this likely to change again?
→ redo research.

Think about your own organisation and try to think about the following questions for ONE aspect of your job:

(a) What information do you use on a regular basis?

(b) Where does this information come from?

(c) What do you use this information for?

(d) Who else uses the same information?

2 Marketing information requirements

2.1 The organisation's marketing information requirements

Here is a list of questions that marketing managers might need answered.

(a) **Markets**. Who are our customers? What are they like? How are buying decisions made?

(b) **Share of the market**. What are total sales of our product? How do our sales compare with competitors' sales?

(c) **Products**. What do customers think of our product? What do they do with it? Are our products in a 'growth' or 'decline' stage of their life cycle? Should we extend our range?

(d) **Price**. How do our prices compare with others: higher, average, lower? Is the market sensitive to price?

(e) **Distribution**. Should we distribute directly, indirectly or both? What discounts are required?

(f) **Sales force**. Do we have enough/too many salespeople? Are their territories equal to their potential? Are they contacting the right people? Should we pay commission?

(g) **Advertising**. Do we use the right media? Do we communicate the right message? Is it effective?

(h) **Customer attitudes**. What do they think of our product/firm/service/delivery?

(i) **Competitors' activities**. Who are our competitors? Are they more or less successful businesses? Why are they more or less successful?

(j) **Environmental factors**. What factors impact on marketing planning (SLEPT factors)?

Another way of viewing information needs in marketing management is to consider the **four key strategic questions**.

Question	Examples of information needed	Sources of information
Where are we now? Strategic, financial and marketing analysis	Current sales by product/market Market share by product/market Competitors' market shares Customer attitudes and behaviour Corporate image versus competitors' image Company strengths and weaknesses	Accounting system Customer database Market analysis/surveys Competitor intelligence Customer surveys Internal/external analyses
Where do we want to be? Strategic direction and strategy formulation	Market forecasts by segment Environmental changes Growth capabilities Opportunities and threats Competitor response New product/market potentials	Industry forecasts/surveys SLEPT analysis PIMS Competitor research Product/market research

Question	Examples of information needed	Sources of information
How might we get there? Strategic choice and evaluation	Marketing mix evaluation Buying behaviour New product development Risk evaluation Alternative strategic options	Internal/external audits Customer research Concept testing/test marketing Feasibility studies/competitor response modelling/focus groups/marketing mix research
How can we ensure arrival? Strategic implementation and control	Budgets Performance evaluation	Internal accounting, production and human resource systems Marketing information systems Marketing audit Benchmarking External (financial) auditing

2.2 Information on customers, other organisations, competitors and the marketing environment

Although we have looked at information in a strategic framework, put another way we can think about it in terms of three key areas where marketing decisions are required. Three key questions exist:

1. How can we satisfy customer needs?
2. How do we ensure we are competitive within the market?
3. What external factors are likely to affect us?

To address these questions we need to gather information on customers, competitors and the marketing environment. The table below outlines the broad issues and then focuses on some of the detail that marketers will need to consider.

Customer Information required	Information required on competitors and other organisations	Information required about the marketing environment
Who are our customers? Can our customers be segmented in any way? Are customers B2B or individual consumers or both? Do we have groups of key customers or a broad market appeal?	**Competitor activity** Who are competitors? What are their core competences? What share of the market do they have? What additional threat do they pose?	**Macro Environment** What are the PESTEL factors to impact us? Is our market growing or in decline? Are we likely to remain profitable in the current and future market conditions?
Where are customers found? Location? Frequent visitors to where? Online presence, sites visited? Where can we be available at their convenience?	**Performance benchmarking** Who should we measure ourselves against? What metrics should be used to provide a meaningful analysis?	**Micro Environment** How effective is our internal market? Are we working with the right partners, suppliers etc? Internally are we organised as best as we can be to meet customer needs? Do our people understand our customers and how to best meet their needs?

Handwritten note in left margin: Are there more the more in-depth questions we need to be asking in order to ground the research with as much current customer knowledge as possible? (or irrelevant?)

Customer Information required	Information required on competitors and other organisations	Information required about the marketing environment
How do we build a relationship with customers? Are our customers exclusively loyal? Are we part of a portfolio of brands that our customers purchase? How do our customers like to communicate with us? What is our history with our customers? How do customers perceive us?	**Partner organisations and marketing networks** What referral markets should we belong to? Are we making the most of the networks that we belong to? How can we partner with other organisations for mutual gain?	
How do customers make purchases? What is the decision making process for consumers? What reference groups are important? What decision making units are involved in the purchase? Do customers regard purchases as high or low involvement?		
How do we satisfy customers needs? Have we correctly identified what customer needs are? How does our offering meet their needs? What are satisfaction levels? How can satisfaction levels be improved?		
What are the behaviour patterns of customers? Do customers relate to our product/service individually or within a group? What is the influence of third parties on the behaviour of customers with regard to our product / service?		

Blythe (2006) recognised that there is a degree of confusion about the distinction between market research and market research. He argues that marketing research refers to information about anything that may be of interest to marketers. Market research on the other hand refers to the investigation of customers, competitors, suppliers and market conditions in general. Chapter 7 within his text Principles and Practice of Marketing gives a very broad overview of marketing research and you may find it useful to put this unit in context at an early stage. ■

3 Descriptive, comparative, diagnostic and predictive information

KEY CONCEPT

concept

Marketing information may have four roles: **descriptive**, **comparative**, **diagnostic** and **predictive**.

Alan Wilson (2006) distinguishes four roles for marketing information.

(a) *Descriptive information answers questions such as which products are customers buying and where are they buying them. 'What', 'where' and 'when' questions are addressed.*

(b) *Comparative information looks at how one factor compares with another, for instance how good an organisation's after-sales support is when compared with its* competitors*. 'How' questions are used for performance measurement.*

(c) *Diagnostic information is intended to explain customer behaviour: eg why are they buying less of product A? 'Why' questions are asked.*

(d) *Predictive information attempts to determine the outcome of marketing actions; eg how would customers respond if Product A were made available in larger sized packs? 'What would happen?' questions cover predictive information.* ■

[handwritten margin notes: Need to ensure that the research can provide each of these types of info.]

[handwritten note: Do we need to compare our customer contact to that of our competitors?]

ACTIVITY 2

application

Try to find three examples each for descriptive, comparative, diagnostic and predictive information needs. You can think of your own organisations for the purpose of this activity.

3.1 Information and decision making

KEY CONCEPT

concept

[handwritten note: How will the research we provide fall into the marketing mix? Will it help with tactics?]

Information is required for **strategic**, **tactical** and **operational decisions** relating to matters such as markets and market share, products, prices, distribution, sales force organisation, advertising, customer attitudes, competitors' activities and ~~SLEPT~~ *[handwritten: PESTEL]* factors.

The APIC activities described by Kotler *et al* (1994) culminate in marketing and selling **decisions** being taken. Information is required for all levels of decision making within an organisation, whether **strategic**, **tactical** or **operational**. Decision-making levels, and the types of marketing and selling decisions taken at these levels, are shown in the following table.

Levels of decision making	Marketing and selling decisions
Strategic	Product/market decisions
	Product life cycles
	Product development
	Entry into new markets
	Investment in new technology to provide better information
	Database development
Tactical	Setting short term prices
	Discounting
	Promotional campaigns
	Advertising
	Distribution
	Product service levels
	Customer service levels
	Packaging
	Planning sales territories
	Short-term agency agreements
Operational	Pricing, including discounting
	Competitor tracking
	Customer research
	Consumer research
	Distribution channels and logistical choices
	Sales and marketing budgets and sub-budgets, eg promotion/advertising
	Database management

4 Information technology and marketing

 KEY CONCEPT

concept

Information and communications technology (ICT) is changing the way markets are structured and it has created **new marketing techniques** and **new marketing channels**.

Take the clothing industry as an example. It is now possible for a retail organisation in England to develop designs and production specifications which may be sent electronically to a remote manufacturer off-shore. The manufacturer will put the garments into production, organise transportation, inform the customer, invoice the customer and despatch the goods – all within a matter of days rather than the weeks or months that this might have taken not so long ago.

This not only opens up new market opportunities but may also present competitor threats. New technologies increase the opportunities to develop **global markets** for what once may only have been local products or services.

ICT has also created new **marketing techniques** and new **marketing channels**. As we'll see in much more detail later in this book, **database marketing** allows vast amounts of customer data to be stored and analysed and used to produce more accurate targeting as well as other marketing tactics. This is significant when a firm is able to gain an advantage over competitors by accessing and applying technologies that the competitor has not yet developed, information that the competitor do not possess, and ideas that have not occurred to others.

Accurate database required in order to communicate appropriate + timely info – not bombarded with irrelevant info.

In terms of comms channels – if a competitor does it better, use more appropriate channels

Let us take the example of a theatre which is in a tourist city and which wants to build a **database**. The types of data it may wish to have are as follows.

(a) Analysis of theatregoers by specific **characteristics**: age, sex, home address
(b) How many **performances** each theatre customer sees in the year
(c) How many days visitors stay in the city and how they choose a day or night at the theatre
(d) **Types of production** customers like to watch
(e) **Factors** important to their decision to visit the theatre, such as price, location, play, cast, facilities
(f) Where they obtained **information** on the theatre and its productions: press, hotel, leaflets, mailings and so on
(g) **Other purchases** customers make when visiting the theatre
(h) **Other entertainment** that theatregoers choose to spend their money on

This data could then be used by the theatre marketing management to build relationships with customers and to exploit sales and promotional opportunities.

(handwritten note in left margin): what info would it be good for our database to store.

 Alan Wilson's (2004) text 'Marketing Research and Integrated Approach' Chapter 1 covers similar material to this chapter and would provide additional context for this part of the syllabus including some useful case studies. The Allied Domecq case number 8 on page 300 will give you a good idea of a situation when information was required about a specific group of customers. ■

 ASSIGNMENT TIP

Concept

The December 2008/March 2009 assignment contained a task on the importance of marketing research and database information for your chosen organisation.

Learning objectives	Covered
1 Discuss the need for information	☑ Information for competitive advantage
	☑ Superior information equals competitive power
	☑ Required to meet needs
2 Identify the nature of marketing information in helping to make decisions	☑ Identify and monitor satisfaction of needs
	☑ Marketing information is a much broader concept than market research
	☑ Decisions are made through integrating a range of information from a number of sources
	☑ The careful organisation of information is essential to avoid information overload
3 Explain what information is needed about customers	☑ What satisfies customers
	☑ Who they are
	☑ Where they are
	☑ How they make purchases
	☑ What their needs are
	☑ Their characteristics
	☑ Their behaviour patterns
4 Explain what information is needed about competitors and other organisations	☑ Competitor activity
	☑ Performance benchmarking
	☑ Partner organisations and marketing networks
5 Explain what information is needed about the marketing environment	☑ Macro marketing environment PESTEL factors
	☑ Micro environment marketing audit
6 Compare the nature of information as descriptive, comparative, diagnostic or predictive.	☑ Descriptive - What? , when? , where? questions
	☑ Comparative – How? questions
	☑ Diagnostic – Why? questions
	☑ Predictive – What would happen? questions

Quick quiz

1   Information helps the marketing manager to increase .... to customer demands, identifying ....and new product/service demands, and to anticipate .... and threats.

Fill in the gaps.

2   Information and communications technology only creates opportunities, it does not pose threats. True or false?

3   What are the activities involved in marketing management, in broad terms?

4   What questions might an organisation need to answer under the following headings?

Products ....

Advertising ....

5   The roles of information may be summarised by the acronym DCDP. What do the letters stand for?

6   Effective marketing decision need to be made with information about which three mains areas?

7   Define knowledge management.

8   What are the two main reasons why tacit knowledge is hard to manage?

LEARNING MEDIA

1   Information helps the marketing manager to increase **responsiveness** to customer demands, by identifying **new customer opportunities** and new product/service demands, and to anticipate **competitive attacks** and threats

2   False. If your firm has the technology others can acquire that technology too, or develop better technology. Communications technology has created global competition. Sometimes marketers are also too reliant on technology and don't spent sufficient time reviewing information.

3   APIC: Analysis, Planning, Implementation and Control

4   **Products**. What do customers think of our product? What do they do with it? Are our products in a 'growth' or 'decline' stage of their life cycle? Should we extend our range?

    Advertising. Do we use the right media? Do we communicate the right message? Is it effective?

    You may have thought of other examples.

5   Descriptive, Comparative, Diagnostic, Predictive

6   Information on customers
    Information o other organisations
    Information on the marketing environment

7   Knowledge management involves the identification and analysis of available and required knowledge, and the subsequent planning and control of actions to develop knowledge assets so as to fulfil organisational objectives.

8   Tacit knowledge is hard to manage because the organisation cannot know that it exists (even the possessor of the information may not realise why it is that he or she is better at doing something than others), and because people may be reluctant to share it.

1   You will probably find that the information comes from a number of sources and that it is often quite complex pulling this all together. Think about the following example. A marketing executive of a small group of five private dental practices has been asked by the group managing director to monitor levels of patient satisfaction and to report this at monthly practice meetings. The marketing executive has responded to this activity using this aspect of their job.

    (a)   What information do you use on a regular basis? Patient satisfaction information

    (b)   Where does this information come from?

        (i)   Patient complaints received: online, by letter, verbal complaints recorded on a complaints database, discussions with dentists, nurses, reception staff.

        (ii)   Patient satisfaction cards returned in the comments boxes within the practices.

        (iii)   Feedback left on the group website and individual practice microsites.

        (iv)   Patient numbers including number of visits, returns, length of registration with the practices, number of new patients for each practice.

    (c)   What do you use this information for? Information is processed to lead to direct measures such as the satisfaction cards and complaints received with the rest of the information being used to provide context and less direct indications of satisfaction. Satisfaction levels are monitored to ensure that we are meeting patient needs. As this information is tracked continuously, any issues that may arise within a practice are discovered quickly and the information is also useful to check whether there are any differences in the level of perceived service between practices. Any changes in practices such as redecoration, the introduction of new treatments etc can be monitored and compared with practices which have not undergone any change.

    (d)   Who else uses the same information? Nobody else uses this combination of information as it is processed and presented as a handout and slide to be used within monthly meetings by myself (the marketing executive). The final collation of the information is distributed to all staff members within the five practices via the group intranet. The finance director uses the same source of information used to identify patient numbers as this data also shows sales revenue.

In this example, there are many sources of information used to collect information to address one simple question 'how satisfied are patients each month?'. It is likely that you will have some aspect of your job where you are reliant on a number of diverse sources.

In relation to APIC, the example above this single question will help to analyse the situation with current customers and plan for any changes required to improve satisfaction levels. The information could help with the implementation of specific marketing initiatives for example a refurbishment may have taken place during working hours within one practice, this may have led to a great deal of dissatisfaction with patients and so how these practice improvements are handled for the rest of the group could be altered to take place outside of working hours. Finally, the most obvious use for this information comes into the control stage of the marketing process. Essentially satisfaction measures are a key metric used in order to monitor performance.

2   Using the same dental practice group as Activity 1, the following information needs are plausible examples:

Role of marketing information	Example information needs
Descriptive information	What practice advertising have patients seen in the last six months?
	Where are the nearest competitor practices to our group practices?
	When do patients tend to book appointments?
Comparative information	How similar is the practice equipment compared to our nearest competitor?
	How does satisfaction levels differ between each of the groups practices?
	How regularly do patients attend for checkups compared to NHS patients?
Diagnostic information	Why do patients like to see fish in waiting rooms?
	Why do patients switch between different dentists within the group?
	Why is there not a large uptake of Saturday morning appointment times?
Predictive information	What would happen if we opened until 8pm weekdays?
	What would be the effect of a 10% price increase?
	What would be the perception of patients if we increased our service offering to include physiotherapy?

References

Blythe, J (2009) *Principles and Practice of Marketing*, 2nd edition, South-Western/Cengage Learning.

Dillon, W. Madden, T. and Firtle, N. (1987) *Marketing Research in a Marketing Environment* 3rd Edition, Irwin, Illinois.

Kotler, P. (1994) *Marketing Management: Analysis, Planning, Implementation and Control*, 8th Edition, Prentice Hall, New Jersey.

Wain, D. (2007) 'The art of knowledge management' Research, MRS, December 2007 edition, London.

Wilson, A. (2006) *Marketing Research An Integrated Approach* 2nd Edition, Prentice Hall, Harlow.

Chapter 2

The role of IT and marketing decision support systems

Topic list

1 The growth in information sources
2 IT to support information needs
3 Marketing Information Systems (MkIS)
4 Customer Relationship Management (CRM) systems
5 Designing an effective system

Introduction

A 'marketing decision support system' may be a personal organiser, a communal file or one or two **assistant** personnel who look after matters when the marketing manager can't be in the office or has too much else to do, or even a full **customer relationship management** (CRM) system with dozens of software modules and a customer database spanning most of the world. Each may be equally effective, depending on the circumstances and the size and complexity of the business. The growth in information sources has been referred to as an 'explosion' (Wilson, 2006) and we begin by looking briefly at the effects of this.

Pretty much everything to do with marketing support in medium to large organisations is given the **'CRM' label** these days. No doubt system vendors think it is sexier to add the CRM tag to things that in the late 1980s/early 1990s might have been described with a name like **'executive information system'** (for instance). However, the older **generic names** are still valid, so that is where we begin this chapter. We'll also consider systems that encourage knowledge sharing and collaboration. None of these are **exclusively** for the support of marketing management, of course, but they support marketing management just as much as they support other functions in the organisation.

We will then look at what used to be described as **Marketing Information Systems (MkIS)**: the term is less common these days, perhaps because the customer-focused marketing concept has taken hold, or perhaps because the thought of a system entirely devoted to the marketing function is too insular an approach in a modern organisation. Nevertheless the ideas behind a MkIS provide a good introduction both to the use of databases in marketing and to the broader perspective of CRM systems.

You will often read that the **customer database** is the most important component of CRM, and it is certainly important enough in the context of this syllabus to merit an entire section to itself. However, databases are just the **means**. The really important thing about CRM systems is that they **integrate** systems right across the organisation and facilitate their use as a source of management information from one central point.

Syllabus linked learning objectives

By the end of the chapter you will be able to:

Learning objectives	Syllabus link
1 Evaluate the impact of IT on the marketing function	1.2
2 Discuss the challenges in collecting valid and reliable information	1.2
3 Consider the growth in information sources	1.2
4 Explain marketing information systems	1.3
5 Identify the components and types of information held within a marketing information system	1.3
6 Introduce CRM	2.1

1 The Growth in Information Sources

There is no substitute for effective judgement to be used to make decisions by the marketer. IT solutions cannot and possibly never be capable of making decisions on behalf of a human, it can however, if used appropriately help to store, organise, sort, and assist decision making by enabling easier access to information. The growth in IT has also opened up the accessibility of information and the ability for disparate groups of individuals to publish materials online. The net effect is that we can access information faster, from a wider range of sources and more conveniently than ever before.

Most decisions however are still based on incomplete information. All possible information is not available. Beyond a certain point, the gathering of more information would not be worth the extra time and cost of obtaining and analysing it.

Too much information also makes decision making harder rather than easier as 'information overload' takes effect.

MARKETING AT WORK application 30%

Trout (2008) highlighted the widespread issue of information overload:

'*One of the pitfalls of the multibillion-dollar marketing research industry is that researchers don't get paid for simplicity. Instead, they seem to get paid by the pound. A true story may be in order.*

The scene: The office of a brand manager at **Procter & Gamble**. *The problem is what to do with one of their largest brands. I ask a simple question as to the availability of their research. I'm surprised by the answer: 'Research?' We've got a computer full of it. How do you want it? In fact, we've got so much of it that we don't know what to do with it.*'

You might question the value of this 'research' in terms of the information it provides. Think about the cost and resource implications of being in a situation such as this.

The diagram below shows just some of the information which is available to marketers to assist in decision making.

Published reports
(govt, trade, market)

Internet and intranet
(newsgroups, blogs,
social networks, searches)

Existing ad hoc internal data
(past data, trends, reports,
strategies)

General environmental scanning
(news, exhibitions, trade shows)

Bought research reports
(Mintel, Keynote, Datamonitor)

Retail audits
(consumer panels,
EPOS sales tracking)

Secondary sources of information

Formal marketing research

Internal information

Primary research projects

Qualitative and quantitative
data collection

Ad hoc and continuous projects

Modelling and forecasting

Special analyses of
continuous panels

Sales data (transactions, customer groups,
salesforce analysis, regional data)

Customer databases (enquiries, orders,
complaints, survey responses,
competition entries, product requirements,
credit history, transactions,
personal information)

Internal continuous reports (board reports,
project blueprints, sales productivity,
market share, supplier performance)

HR reports and employee performance

Production reports and capability analysis

Product specs and recipes

Service guarantees/ guidelines

Information to support
marketing decisions

1.1 The information explosion

You will see from the diagram that far from being short of information, the average marketer has a wealth of data at their disposal. The trick however is being able to cut through the data, process it and establish some real meaning. Wilson, (2006) argued that many of the problems associated with the ability to make decision are as a result of the inability of marketers to filter the relevant data from the explosion of information.

Technological advances have fuelled the information explosion. The internet for example has opened a wealth of opportunities not only as a way of gathering information by observing how consumers behave online, recording transactions efficiently to build more powerful databases and opening communications with customers through forums. More recently the use of Web 2.0, online survey tools, voting buttons added to sites, analysis of social networks and virtual worlds have not only enabled new data collection methods but continue to add to the banks of information available to organisations.

Manyika, J. Et a. (2008) identified eight technological trends to look out for. These have contributed and will continue to contribute to the Information Explosion. You can access the article within McKinsey Quarterly through EBSCO. As a CIM studying member you automatically gain access to such articles. Go to the Knowledge Hub and Leading Articles to gain access. The authors outline the potential power of information:

> *'Just as the Internet and productivity tools extend the reach of and provide leverage to desk-based workers, technology is helping managers exploit ever-greater amounts of data to make smarter decisions and develop the insights that create competitive advantages and new business models. From 'ideagoras' (eBay-like marketplaces for ideas) to predictive markets to performance-management approaches, ubiquitous standards-based technologies promote aggregation, processing, and decision making based on the use of growing pools of rich data.*

> *Leading players are exploiting this* information explosion *with a diverse set of management techniques. Google fosters innovation through an internal market: employees submit ideas, and other employees decide if an idea is worth pursuing or if they would be willing to work on it fulltime. Intel integrates a 'prediction market' with regular short-term forecasting processes to build more accurate and less volatile estimates of demand. The cement manufacturer Cemex optimizes loads and routes by combining complex analytics with a wireless tracking and communications network for its trucks.*

> *The amount of* information *and a manager's ability to use it have increased explosively not only for internal processes but also for the engagement of customers. The more a company knows about them, the better able it is to create offerings they want, to target them with messages that get a response, and to extract the value that an offering gives them. The holy grail of deep customer insight--more granular segmentation, low-cost experimentation, and mass customization--becomes increasingly accessible through technological innovations in data collection and processing.'* ■

1.2 The validity and reliability of marketing information

KEY CONCEPT

concept

Valid data is data which represents that which it is supposed to eg. if you were collecting information about the number of cars parked within a town during weekends, data collected during weekdays would not be valid.

Reliable data is data which would look similar if it were collected in exactly the same way in the future. In other words consistent result would be found if there were no other confounding factors eg. if different researchers conducted the count of cars in a different way (cars stopping for less than a minute being considered 'parked' by one research but only cars which stop for more than ten minutes are defined as 'parked' by another researcher) then the data will not be reliable.

All data collected should be evaluated using the following criteria.

(a) Is the data relevant to the purpose for which it was collected?

(b) Is it up-to-date?

(c)   Is it reliable and accurate?

(d)   Is the source of the data credible and objective, or unbiased? Look for the following.

CREDIBILITY

Reputation of source | Internal evidence | Interest, motives, values and purpose of sources

(e)   Is the data subject to confirmation, or comparison with data from other sources? Are you prepared to risk basing decisions on uncorroborated data? The term triangulation refers to the ability to produce similar findings from multiple sources. If once source verifies another, the findings are viewed as more credible.

(f)   Is the data based on a large and representative statistical sample of the relevant population (the group or issue under investigation)?

(g)   Has the data been gathered in a way that makes it meaningful and reliable? Has the same question been put to all respondents? Were all terms consistently defined? Did researchers lead or suggest 'right' answers? Were the respondents influenced by the researcher, or each other, or the desire to be nice?

(h)   Has the data collection and analysis been worthwhile? Has it fulfilled its purposes at a reasonable cost in money, time and effort?

1.3 Analysis and presentation of marketing information

Regardless of the source of information, how it is analysed and presented will ultimately determine how useful it is in helping to make decisions. Chapter 11 within the study text, covers in more detail the presentation of information but we raise it here as an issue to consider from the outset.

Quantitative research quite often presents raw data: lists or tables of numbers, or ticks in boxes. This data must be analysed in order to identify key features, trends, probabilities and averages.

Qualitative research also presents raw data in the form of records of words in narrative form. This data must be analysed in order to summarise, interpret, categorise and measure the frequency of responses, for presentation in quantitative or statistical form.

As the number of sources we utilise as marketers increases, so do the challenges in presenting the information.

The management information, or decision-support information, resulting from data analysis must be formatted for presentation to the target user.

- Printed tables
- Charts
- Graphs
- Narrative reports
- Online and real-time reporting
- Oral presentation with visual aids
- Interpretation and recommendations

The key issue with being able to use the data to be able to make meaningful decisions is the ability to interpret it easily. The usability of information is greatly improved when the data is presented clearly.

KEY CONCEPT

Understanding the **audience thinking sequence** as outlined by Wilson (2006) helps to ensure that information is communicated effectively. The rules of effective research presentation according to the audience thinking sequence are:

1. Respect my (the audience's) importance
2. Consider my (the audience) needs
3. Demonstrate how your information helps me
4. Explain the detail that underpins your information
5. Remind me of the key points
6. Suggest what I should do now

1.4 Information systems

KEY CONCEPT

In general terms information systems in organisations consist of **transaction processing systems**, **expert systems**, **decision support systems** and **executive information systems**.

We are **not**, of course, talking about **hardware components** (keyboard, mouse etc) in this section, although it is worth noting in passing that there is an ever wider range of devices that can be used in conjunction with an information system, thanks largely to developments in **communications technology** such as mobile telephony and wireless technologies.

Information systems in all but the smallest organisations are conventionally divided into several broad categories.

(a) **Transaction processing systems** do the essential number crunching.

(b) **Expert systems** are used principally at the **operational** level and assist in structured problems that can be solved by applying the relevant business rules.

(c) **Decision support systems** are used by **middle managers** for routine modelling, but also to analyse unstructured problem situations where there is no precedent that can be used as a universal guideline.

(d) **Executive information systems** are used at **strategic** level, for unstructured problems, or to identify new opportunities.

ACTIVITY 1

How much do you know about information systems used in your organisation? You may have access to only a part of the system, but you should appreciate the range of marketing and sales related information it contains and hopefully know how to get reports on matters of relevance to your job. Find out as much as you can because this may help you to relate to the assessment.

1.5 IT influenced data collection

(a) The capture of transaction data via **barcodes** and scanners is commonplace these days. The combination of Electronic Point of Sale (**EPOS**), Electronic Funds Transfer at Point of Sale (**EFTPOS**) and possibly a **loyalty card** scheme enables individual transactions and individual purchasers to be tracked, identified and linked. This helps to build up a very detailed picture of the buying habits of individual customers, as well as serving the practical purpose of updating stock records and financial accounts.

Barcode technology is well-established and is especially suitable for retailers, but the capture of data is still so time consuming and expensive for many organisations that new applications and developments will continue to emerge.

(b) The **Internet** offers the possibility for customers to do all the data entry themselves as well as allowing organisations to track browsing behaviour. You may think that the Internet is a familiar tool, but Tim Berners-Lee, the 'inventor' of the World Wide Web, still considers the technology and the possible applications to be at infant stage. Certainly, the developments in web use are one of the key areas to impact businesses and management consultants McKinsey identify it as one of the eight business technological trends to continue to watch (Manyika, 2008). Web 2.0, social networks and online collaboration are all examples which will be covered later in the text.

Communicating via social networks with customers [handwritten margin note, arrow pointing to paragraph (b)]

(c) **Voice recognition software** already enables computers to interpret and respond to human speech to a limited extent and the technology is steadily improving.

(d) Better 'seeing' devices and software will capture **visual information** in ways that computers can understand. This will enable machines to carry out surveillance, checking and inspection activities with less human supervision.

MARKETING AT WORK

application

There is already an 'Internet fridge' on the market:

'Watch TV, listen to music or surf the Internet using this titanium finish, state-of-the-art fridge freezer. It's the ultimate in kitchen technology with a built-in MP3 player for downloading and playing music from the Internet, email and video mail using a built-in camera and microphone. It even has full Internet access so you can restock the refrigerator online or check on the latest news and weather – all without leaving the kitchen. And it's great for storing food too ...'

ACTIVITY 2

evaluation

How could voice recognition be used in marketing research? → *post - phone call 'yes'/'no' survey, (or) touch keypad one - can use this for my research?* [handwritten answer]

2 IT to support information needs

2.1 Systems

KEY CONCEPT

concept

Knowledge management is **aided by software** that encourages and facilitates collaboration and sharing of information. Examples range from basic 'Office' and e-mail packages on a network, to formal groupware such as Lotus Notes or Microsoft Exchange, which aids scheduling and workflow as well as communication.

Any system – even a basic e-mail system – that helps and encourages people to work together and share information and knowledge will aid knowledge management. We have already covered expert systems, which may help to solve specific marketing problems, but marketing management is also likely to have the support of more general information sharing tools.

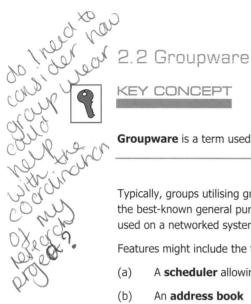

do I need to consider how groupware could help with the coordination of my research project?

2.2 Groupware

concept

Groupware is a term used to describe software that provides functions for the use of collaborative work groups.

Typically, groups utilising groupware are small project-oriented teams that have important tasks and tight deadlines. Perhaps the best-known general purpose groupware product is **Lotus Notes**. However, the components of **Microsoft Exchange** used on a networked system could also be considered to be a form of groupware, as could a CRM system.

Features might include the following.

(a)   A **scheduler** allowing users to keep track of their schedule and plan meetings with others

(b)   An **address book**

(c)   '**To do**' lists

(d)   A **journal**, used to record interactions with important contacts, record items (such as e-mail messages) and files that are significant to the user, and record activities of all types and track them all without having to remember where each one was saved

(e)   A **jotter** for jotting down notes as quick reminders of questions and ideas

(f)   File sharing and distribution utilities

There are clearly advantages in having such information available from the desktop at the touch of a button, rather than relying on scraps of paper, address books, and corporate telephone directories. However, it is when groupware is used to **share information** with colleagues that it comes into its own. Here are some of the features that may be found.

(a)   **Messaging**, comprising an **e-mail** in-box which is used to send and receive messages from the office, home, or the road and **routing** facilities, enabling users to send a message to a single person, send it sequentially to a number of people (who may add to it or comment on it before passing it on), or sending it to everyone at once.

(b)   Access to an **information database**, and customisable **'views'** of the information held on it, which can be used to standardise the way information is viewed in a workgroup.

(c)   **Group scheduling**, to keep track of colleagues' itineraries. Microsoft Exchange Server, for instance, offers a 'Meeting Wizard' which can consult the diaries of everyone needed to attend a meeting and automatically work out when they will be available, which venues are free, and what resources are required.

(d)   **Public folders**. These collect, organise, and share files with others on the team or across the organisation.

(e)   One person (for instance a secretary or a stand-in during holidays or sickness) can be given **'delegate access'** to another's groupware folders and send mail on their behalf, or read, modify, or create items in public and private folders on their behalf.

(f)   **Conferencing**. Participation in public, online discussions with others. Further IT developments in this area include the use of virtual world conferences. Some IT experts suggest that virtual worlds such as Second Life are likely to be used by global organisations to hold virtual meetings and seminars. The ability to transpose personal identities onto virtual characters to act out our role is increasing capabilities in this area. What seems futuristic now is likely to become commonplace in the near future.

(g)   **Assigning tasks**. A task request can be sent to a colleague who can accept, decline, or reassign the task. After the task is accepted, the groupware will keeps the task status up-to-date on a task list.

(h)   **Voting** type facilities that can, say, request and tally responses to a multiple-choice question sent in a mail message (eg 'Here is a list of options for this year's Christmas party').

(i)   **Hyperlinks** in mail messages. The recipient can click the hyperlink to go directly to a Web page or file server.

(j)   **Workflow management** (see below) with various degrees of sophistication.

BPP
LEARNING MEDIA

Workflow is a term used to describe the defined series of tasks within an organisation to produce a final outcome. Sophisticated workgroup computing applications allow the user to define different **workflows** for different types of jobs. For example, when preparing a brochure, a document might be automatically routed between writers and then on to an editor, a proof-reader and finally the printers.

At **each stage** in the workflow, **one individual** or group is **responsible** for a specific task. Once the task is complete, the workflow software ensures that the individuals responsible for the **next** task are notified and receive the data they need to do their stage of the process.

ACTIVITY 3

application

What kind of systems do you use to collaborate with colleagues? How could they be improved?

2.3 Intranets

KEY CONCEPT

concept

An **intranet** is a mini-version of the Internet accessible only within a company. Intranets can be used for a wide variety of information-sharing purposes.

An **intranet** is an internal network used to share information. Intranets utilise Internet technology and protocols. The firewall surrounding an Internet fends off unauthorised access.

Intranets use a combination of the organisation's own networked computers and Internet technology. Each employee has a browser, used to access a server computer that holds corporate information on a wide variety of topics, and in some cases also offers access to the Internet.

Potential applications include company newspapers, induction material, online procedures and policy manuals, employee web pages where individuals post details of their activities and progress, and **internal databases** of the corporate information store.

Most of the **cost** of an intranet is the **staff time** required to set up the system.

The **benefits** of intranets are diverse.

(a) Savings accrue from the **elimination of storage**, **printing** and **distribution** of documents that can be made available to employees on-line.

(b) Documents on-line are often **more widely used** than those that are kept filed away, especially if the document is bulky (eg training manual) and needs to be searched. This means that there are **improvements in productivity** and **efficiency**.

(c) It is much **easier to update** information in electronic form.

(d) Wider access to corporate information should open the way to **more flexible working patterns**, eg material available on-line may be accessed from remote locations.

2.4 Extranets

KEY CONCEPT

An **extranet** is an intranet that is accessible to designated authorised outsiders.

could use an extranet for customers to put into an ⟨or⟩ *offer for the agency to show the client how the research is going.*

Whereas an intranet is accessible only to people who are members of the same company or organisation, an extranet provides various levels of accessibility to outsiders.

Only those outsiders with a valid username and password can access an extranet, with varying levels of access rights enabling control over what people can view. Extranets are becoming a very popular means for **business partners to exchange information** for mutual benefit.

Extranets therefore allow better use of the knowledge held by an organisation – by facilitating access to that knowledge.

MARKETING AT WORK

Continuous market research providers such as AC Nielsen and IRI rely on extranets to provide faster information as part of an added-value service proposition. Retailers and grocery product manufactures who make up these organisations core clients log onto dedicated extranet sites using bespoke passwords. Once logged onto the system, they are able to access information based on scanned EPOS data and responses from panels of consumers who scan products they purchase and then proceed to complete lifestyle surveys.

Log onto the general IRI and AC Nielsen websites and look at the types of services that these organisations offer.

www.acnielsen.co.uk
www.iriuk.infores.com

3 Marketing Information Systems (MkIS)

For task 3 ↳ Need to consider how the findings of the research would be supported by MkIS + whether there are tools to do it and put recommendations into place

KEY CONCEPT

A **marketing information system** is built up from several different systems which may not be directly related to marketing. Typical components are an **internal reporting system**, a **marketing intelligence system**, a **marketing research system** and a decision and **analytical marketing system**.

In today's environment marketing managers cannot operate unless there is lots of information coming into the organisation from a wide variety of sources such as commissioned research, third-party continuous research, databases, secondary sources of all descriptions, sales figures, customer surveys, environmental scanning and so forth.

KEY CONCEPT

The collection, organisation and analysis of marketing information is the responsibility of a **marketing information system** (MkIS), which in itself is part of the hierarchy of information systems that exist within an organisation. The information collected, organised and analysed by an MkIS will typically include the following.

- Details on consumers and markets
- Sales – past, current and forecast

- Production and marketing costs
- Data on the operating environment: competitors, suppliers, distributors and so on

Kotler (1994) defines a marketing information system as a 'continuing and interacting structure of people, equipment and procedures to gather, sort, analyse, evaluate, and distribute pertinent, timely, and accurate information for use by marketing decision makers to improve their marketing planning, implementation and control.'

Three aspects of the information-gathering system are of special significance here.

(a) **The speed of feedback**. The sooner the information is collected, the more accurate and useful it will be.

(b) **The length of the planning horizon**. The planning horizon is getting shorter and there is no value in having quicker response times in the marketing function if these are not matched by quicker response times in other parts of the organisation. In the retail world, for example, scanning and EPOS systems mean that retailers know very quickly if a product on the shelves is selling or not.

(c) **Planning how to do it** is becoming more important than planning **what to do**. To be able to react quickly to change, it is important to have a clear picture of how to respond in various eventualities so that when any given scenario emerges, action can be initiated rapidly.

3.1 Components of a MkIS

A MkIS is therefore built up from several different systems which **may not be directly related to marketing**. It is likely to contain the following **components**.

Despite being designed a long while ago, Kotler's (1994) model of a marketing information systems remains true to this day because it is simple and clear.

The marketing information system

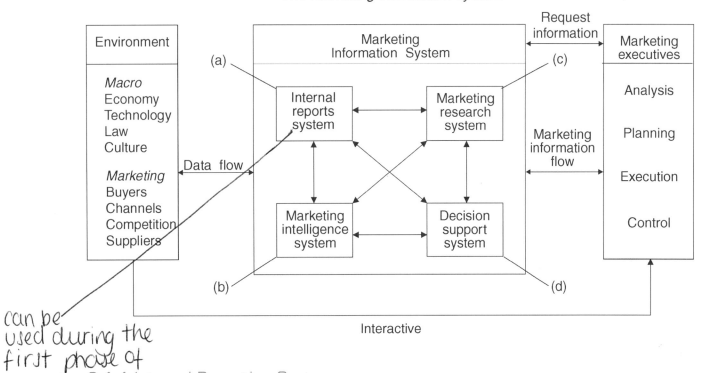

can be used during the first phase of research

3.1.1 Internal Reporting System

This part of the MkIS utilises internal records of the company – information on costs, production schedules, orders, sales and some types of financial information relating to customers (such as credit ratings).

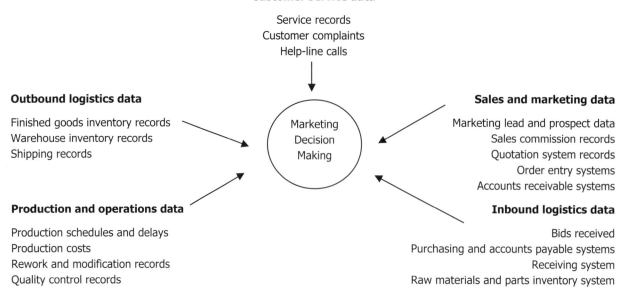

Customer service data

Service records
Customer complaints
Help-line calls

Outbound logistics data

Finished goods inventory records
Warehouse inventory records
Shipping records

Marketing
Decision
Making

Sales and marketing data

Marketing lead and prospect data
Sales commission records
Quotation system records
Order entry systems
Accounts receivable systems

Production and operations data

Production schedules and delays
Production costs
Rework and modification records
Quality control records

Inbound logistics data

Bids received
Purchasing and accounts payable systems
Receiving system
Raw materials and parts inventory system

Although these records have been generated for some other purpose, they provide an invaluable insight into the current activity and performance of the company. Data such as sales records, invoices, production records and accounts are used in a system of this type. Many of these records are stored in computerised databases and therefore storage, retrieval and analysis of such records is relatively quick and easy.

The current operations of a business can be analysed and understood. It is good marketing practice to build any strategy or plan from an understanding of 'where we are now' and this system provides that understanding. For example, these records may be used to provide an understanding of size and growth of customer segments, buying patterns, product profitability and many other areas.

3.1.2 Marketing Intelligence System

 KEY CONCEPT

concept

A **marketing intelligence system** is a set of procedures and sources used by managers to obtain everyday information about pertinent developments in the marketing environment.

This system collects and stores everyday information about the external environment – information such as industry reports, competitors' marketing materials and competitors' quotes. Information collected here allows a company to build a more accurate profile of the external environment. The data may take the form of press cuttings and information derived from websites, but can also incorporate subscriptions to external sources of competitive data.

This could allow a company to calculate market sizes and growth patterns, competitor positioning and pricing strategy. This information may help in decision making in many areas such as gap analysis, segmentation and targeting, market development and pricing strategy.

Managers can scan the environment in four ways.

(a) **Undirected viewing**: having general exposure to information with no specific purpose in view
(b) **Conditional viewing**: directed exposure
(c) **Informal search**: an unstructured effort to obtain specific information
(d) **Formal search**: a deliberate effort with a plan, procedure, or methodology to obtain specific information

As part of the environ scanning process (task 3) suggest conducting mystery shopping on competitors to improve the marketing intelligence system.

BPP
LEARNING MEDIA

Can you think of any dangers inherent in a marketing intelligence system?

3.1.3 Marketing Research System

This system uses marketing research techniques to gather, evaluate and report findings in order to minimise guesswork in business decisions. The system is used to fill essential information gaps which are not covered by the other components of the MkIS system. In this way it provides targeted and detailed information for the decision making problem at hand.

A company might use marketing research to provide detailed information on new product concepts, attitudes to marketing communication messages, testing advertising effectiveness and understanding customer perceptions of service delivery. This would include both primary research collected to address a specific problem and secondary date from other sources. Primary data is collected from scratch with appropriate data collection tools such as surveys, for example.

3.2 Decision support systems

 KEY CONCEPT concept

Decision support systems help managers to consider and evaluate alternative answers to problems that cannot be reduced to rules.

Decision support systems are used by management to assist them in making decisions on issues which are not clear-cut. The objective is to allow the manager to consider a number of **alternatives** and **evaluate** them under a variety of potential conditions.

 KEY CONCEPT concept

A **marketing decision support system** is a coordinated collection of data systems, tools and techniques with supporting **software and hardware** which is used for gathering and interpreting relevant information from the business and its environment, which may be used as a basis for marketing decisions and action. It is used by management to aid decision making on unstructured, complex, uncertain or ambiguous issues.

A Marketing Decision Support System

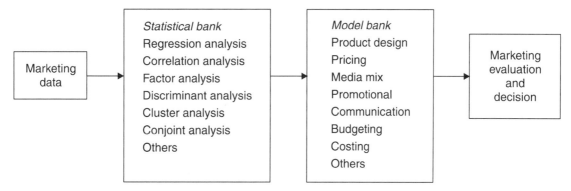

In fact a simple **spreadsheet** 'what if' model, using data extracted from an accounting package, is one form of decision support tool: you may have devised one of your own without realising how clever you were being! However, there are also many specialised software packages that enable **computer modelling** of **complex marketing management problems**. We'll look at some recent examples later in this chapter.

3.3 Executive information systems

 KEY CONCEPT

concept

Executive information systems offer summary level data that is easy to access, manipulate and understand at a glance.

An **executive information system** (EIS) is an 'information system which gives the executive easy access to key internal and external data'.

An EIS is likely to have the following features.

(a) Provision of **summary-level data**, captured from the organisation's transaction processing or other systems.

(b) A facility which allows the executive to **'drill down'** from higher to lower levels of information for more details, usually using hyperlinks and clickable images, as on a website.

(c) **Data manipulation facilities** (such as comparison with budget or prior year data, trend analysis).

(d) **Graphics**, for user-friendly presentation of data.

The basic design philosophy of executive information systems is that they should:

(a) Be **easy to use** as an EIS may be consulted during a meeting

(b) Make **data easy to access**, so that it describes the organisation from the executive's point of view, not just in terms of its data flows

(c) Provide **tools for analysis** such as forecasts and trends

(d) Provide **presentational aids** so that information can be converted into graphs, charts and tables at the click of the mouse

3.3.1 Analytical Marketing System

This comprises analytical techniques that enable marketing managers to make full use of the information provided by the other sources. This analysis may range from simple financial ratios and projections of sales patterns to more complex statistical models, spreadsheets and other exercises in extrapolation.

An example would be a price sensitivity analysis tool using internal data from sales records together with market share and pricing information on competitors to calculate the price sensitivity of products.

4 Customer Relationship Management (CRM) systems

 KEY CONCEPT

concept

CRM software integrates the entire marketing and sales process, bringing together all customer facing systems.

As noted at the beginning of this chapter **the label 'CRM'** now tends to be applied (especially by software vendors) to **any and all systems** designed to support marketing and sales.

Traditional 'vertical' organisation structures tended to create stand-alone systems developed for distinct functions or departments, which were responsible for the four main types of interaction with the customer: marketing, sales, fulfilment and after sales. The modern philosophy is that these systems need to be integrated into (or replaced by) central facilities that allow data to be accessed from and fed into the central system from other departments and applications (including Internet applications), so that all customer information can be kept up-to-date and shared.

A CRM system is above all an **integrated system,** covering the entire sales and marketing process. It brings together a number of marketing and customer facing systems within one strategy or homogeneous software application. The following features are usually associated with CRM:

- Data warehouses
- Customer service systems
- Call centres
- E-commerce
- Web marketing
- Operational systems (eg invoicing and payment)
- Sales systems (eg mobile communications)

 MARKETING AT WORK

application

You will find that there are many vendors of CRM software. Some of the best known packages are SAP, Sage CRM, Oracle and Goldmine.

4.1 Self-support?

With an effective CRM system, each time a customer contacts a company – whether by telephone, in a retail outlet or online – the customer should be recognised and managed in the appropriate way, receiving appropriate information and attention. CRM software provides advanced personalisation and customised solutions to customer demands and gives marketing management a range of key information about each customer which can be applied to the transaction and future transactions.

However some commentators would argue that it is now **customers** who **manage** the relationship with **companies**, and not the other way around.

The rapid growth of online communities, blogs and permission marketing has contributed to this trend.

5 Designing an effective system

 KEY CONCEPT

concept

Design considerations include ease of access and use, cost, flexibility, the purity of data, reporting capabilities, and training needs.

When marketing management support systems are being designed the following factors should be considered.

(a) Users should **understand** the systems and be in a position to evaluate and control them. Management's **access** to the information must be **easy and direct** and the true meaning of the information provided must be clear.

(b) The **cost** of data/information **gathering** should be **minimal**.

(c) **Data gathering** should not cause excessive inconvenience to information sources. Preferably the data will be gathered without customers having to make any extra effort (for example through analysis of supermarket checkout receipts which show consumer purchase patterns).

(d) **Data gathering should be regular and continuous** since a small amount of data gathered regularly can build a considerable database. Regular data gathering produces more reliable results because it reduces the likelihood of bias of one kind or another.

(e) The system must be **flexible**. It should be regularly **reviewed** and **improved** where possible.

Obviously the system needs to produce useful information in a useable format and it will only do so if the following matters are addressed.

(a) **Irrelevant and/or inaccurate content** must be eliminated. (This is discussed in more depth in the next chapter). In particular a system that suggests **answers** that are clearly **nonsense** (for instance because business rules are badly defined) will not be trusted and not be used.

(b) The system must allow for the easy and effective **storage and retrieval** of data and so consideration must be given to matters such as the following.

- Manual or computerised data, or both?
- The regularity of back up
- Cross referencing of data
- Data protection legislation considerations

(c) **Dissemination of the information**. Who needs to, or who should, receive information? Newsletters (or email or an intranet) can be used for standardised regular information, but ad hoc reports should be available to senior managers on demand.

There will of course be **cost** and **organisational implications** of any marketing management support system.

- **Training** of all staff will be necessary.
- Staff with **specialist skills** might have to be recruited or contracted from outside.
- **Software** and suitable networking and communications **hardware** may be very expensive.
- Organisational considerations might include the **reallocation of duties** or **redundancies**.

 MARKETING AT WORK

application

As a quick **example** of a marketing management support system in action, let us visualise a company that has identified **quality service** as a strategic priority. To meet this goal, the system must be capable of performing a wide range of tasks, including the following.

(a) Provide managers with **real time** information on how customers and staff **perceive the service** being given
(b) Measure quality of both service and customer care so as to provide evidence that they do matter
(c) Monitor how (if at all) the **customer base is changing**
(d) Perhaps, provide a basis on which marketing staff bonus payments can be determined

These things need to be considered when thinking about how the info from the mystery shopping can be disseminated Task 3.

5.1 Stages of system development

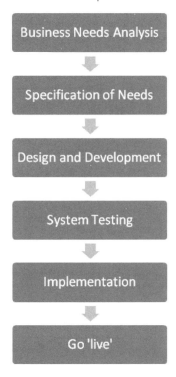

To summarise:

- There has been a massive explosion in the number of information sources.

- In general terms information systems in organisations consist of transaction processing systems, expert systems, decision support systems and executive information systems.

- Knowledge management is aided by software that encourages and facilitates collaboration and sharing of information. Examples range from basic 'Office' and e-mail packages on a network, to formal groupware such as Lotus Notes or Microsoft Exchange, which aids scheduling and workflow as well as communication.

- An intranet is a mini-version of the Internet accessible only within a company. Intranets can be used for a wide variety of information-sharing purposes. Extranets allow access to business partners' information systems.

- A marketing information system is built up from several different systems which may not be directly related to marketing. Typical components are an internal reporting system, a marketing intelligence system, a marketing research system and an analytical marketing system.

- CRM software integrates the entire marketing and sales process, bringing together all customer facing systems.

- Design considerations include ease of access and use, cost, flexibility, the purity of data, reporting capabilities, and training needs.

Learning objectives	Covered
1 Evaluate the impact of IT on the marketing function	☑ Information explosion
	☑ Information overload can be a significant problem
	☑ IT can assist in organising, sorting, formatting, presenting and speeding up the availability of information
2 Discuss the challenges in collecting valid and reliable information	☑ Valid if measures what is intended
	☑ Reliable if consistently collected
	☑ Relevance, bias, source credibility
	☑ Confirmation and triangulation of sources
3 Consider the growth in information sources	☑ IT developments
	☑ Secondary sources
	☑ Internal information
	☑ Marketing research
	☑ Human judgement remains essential
4 Explain marketing information systems	☑ A range of organisational information systems
	☑ Systems to assist knowledge management
	☑ Systems to help make decisions
5 Identify the components and types of information held within a marketing information system	☑ Internal reporting
	☑ Marketing intelligence and research
	☑ Decision support systems
	☑ Executive information systems
6 Introduce CRM	☑ An integrated system covering sales and marketing processes
	☑ Customer contact management

1   Information systems ALWAYS have to be IT based. True or false?

2   Decisions made by a decision support system are likely to be better than decisions made by a manager. True or false? Explain your answer.

3   List six ways in which groupware helps organisations to share information.

4   An extranet cannot be considered to be part of an organisation's marketing management support system because it involves other organisations. True or false? Explain your answer.

5   A marketing information system has four typical components. Fill in the gaps.

I .... R .... System

M .... I .... System

M .... R .... System

A .... M .... System

6   A marketing information system requires a complex statistical analysis package. True or false? Explain your answer.

7   What is the most important thing that is achieved by CRM systems as opposed to earlier types of system?

8   List five 'modules' that might be available in a customer relationship management package.

9   A web-enabled CRM system:

A   Means that a company's employees can take more care of customers
B   Is more impersonal because customers have to serve themselves
C   Empowers customers to define the sort of relationship they want with an organisation

10 What are the possible consequences of failing to eliminate inaccurate or irrelevant information from a marketing management support system?

1   The answer will be specific to your own circumstances. It is a good idea to do it now so that you have a portfolio of information you can add to for your assignment.

2   Voice recognition is not yet advanced enough for any but the simplest applications ('say 'one' if you want option 1') but as the technology develops it could be used to analyse responses made by customers during recorded telephone conversations with live staff and perhaps measure attitude from tone of voice. You may have thought of other answers.

3   Again the answer will be specific to your circumstances. At the very least you probably use e-mail and e-mail attachments to circulate documents or else have common access to documents via a computer network. You may use a program such as Outlook to manage appointments and meetings, and facilities in programs like Word or PowerPoint to add comments to others' drafts.

4   One strong danger is information overload – collecting or receiving more information from the system than you can possibly take in and make use of. Another is the danger that information will be inaccurate or out of date: you have no control over the reliability of external sources.

1   False. Some excellent information systems are actually just well-organised folders. A lack of IT resource doesn't mean the organisations can't have an information system.

2   False. Decision support systems do not make decisions, they help managers to weigh up the options. Managers make decisions.

3   The features mentioned in the text of the chapter are: messaging, access to databases, scheduling, shared public folders, delegate access, conferencing, task assignment, voting, and workflow management.

4   False. If something helps with marketing management it can be considered to be part of the support system, no matter who actually 'owns' it.

5   Internal Reporting System

Marketing Intelligence System

Marketing Research System

Analytical Marketing System

6   False. Much of the analytical work may be done by fairly simple spreadsheets, although there are packages that make things even easier for those not familiar with analytical techniques.

7   Integration of information from all the systems that impact upon marketing.

8   Five possible examples are Field Sales Management, Call Centre Management, Order Capture, Customer Behaviour Modelling, Warehouse Management. Larger systems have modules for practically everything you can think of, so it is hard to get this question wrong!

9   C is the 'most' correct answer, although an argument could be made for options A and B, depending on the circumstances. For instance if the customer is doing most of the data entry this frees up the time of customer service staff, and that may mean that fewer customer service staff are needed or it may mean that they spend more time dealing with problems. Web technology allows the offer to the customer to be highly personalised, but many people still prefer explaining their needs to human beings and being reassured that they are ordering the right product.

10 The obvious immediate consequence is that incorrect data may lead to incorrect decisions and actions. Taking a longer term view just a few pieces of incorrect data may mean that users do not trust the system at all (even if the bad data is the exception) and so do not use it.

References

Kotler, P. (1994) *Marketing Management: Analysis, planning, implementation and control*, Prentice Hall, New Jersey.

Manyika, J., Roberts, Roger P., Sprague, Kara L. (2008) '*Eight business technology trends to watch*'. McKinsey Quarterly, 00475394, 2008, Issue 1.

Trout, J. (2008) '*The Research Trap*' [online] available from: http://www.fores.com/opinions/2008/05/14/trout-marketing-research-oped-cx it014trout.html.

Wilson, A. (2006) *Marketing Research An Integrated Approach* 2nd Edition, Prentice Hall, Harlow.

Chapter 3
CRM and databases

Topic list

Introduction

All the topics that we have studied so far have assumed that useful marketing information is stored somewhere and that it can be retrieved, analysed and manipulated as and when required. We looked at Marketing Information Systems and briefly at CRM in Chapter 2.

It is now very easy and relatively cheap to store vast amounts of data about customers using a computer **database** and appropriate software. This chapter looks at databases in more detail.

Database marketing holds that the whole point of finding out about a customer is to **attach information to a name and address** to which offers, product information and special deals can later be sent to develop a **relationship** that leads to **repeat purchasing**.

This rather long, but **very important chapter** deals with all of the syllabus requirements relating to customer databases.

Syllabus linked learning objectives

By the end of the chapter you will be able to:

Learning objectives	Syllabus link
1 Define customer databases	2.1
2 Consider the benefits of customer databases	2.1
3 Link databases and CRM	2.1
4 Consider the benefits of customer databases	2.1
5 Explain the process of setting up a database	2.2
6 Identify the uses of databases	2.1, 2.4
7 Explain data warehousing, data marts and data mining	2.3
8 Explore the relationship between databases and marketing research	2.4

1 Customer databases

KEY CONCEPT

[Handwritten note: → for task 1, bullet 1 'different customer groups' → CRM could provide this information or needs to be implemented post-research to enable recommendation to be effective.]

concept

Customer databases can contain a wide variety of information about the customer such as **contact details**, **transaction history**, **personal details** and **preferences** and so on. Information may come from a variety of sources besides transaction processing systems, including specialist geodemographic data and lifestyle information.

A **customer database** is *'A manual or computerised source of data relevant to marketing decision making about an organisation's customers.'* (Wilson 2006).

Database marketing has been defined as *'an interactive approach to marketing, which uses individually addressable marketing media and channels to extend help to a company's target audience, stimulate their demand and stay close to them by recording and keeping an electronic database memory of customer, prospect, and all communication and commercial contacts, to help them improve all future contacts and to ensure more realistic planning of all marketing.'*

A marketing database can provide an organisation with much information about its customers and target groups. **Every purchase a customer makes has two functions**.

- Provision of **sales revenue**
- Provision of **information** as to future market opportunities

A typical customer database might include the following.

Element	Examples
Customer or company details	Account numbers, names, addresses and contact (telephone, fax, e-mail) details; basic 'mailing list' data, relationship to other customers. For business customers these fields might include sales contact, technical contact, parent company or subsidiaries, number of employees
Professional details	Company; job title; responsibilities – especially for business-to-business marketing; industry type
Personal details	Sex, age, number of people at the same address, spouse's name, children, interests, and any other relevant data known, such as newspapers read, journals subscribed to
Transaction history	What products/services are ordered, date, how often, how much is spent (turnover), payment methods
Call/contact history	Sales or after sales service calls made, complaints/queries received, meetings at shows/exhibitions, mailings sent, etc
Credit/payment history	Credit rating, amounts outstanding, aged debts
Credit transaction details	Items currently on order, dates, prices, delivery arrangements
Special account details	Membership number, loyalty or incentive points earned, discount awarded), where customer loyalty or incentive schemes are used

The **sources** of information in a customer database and the **uses** to which it can be put are outlined in the diagram below.

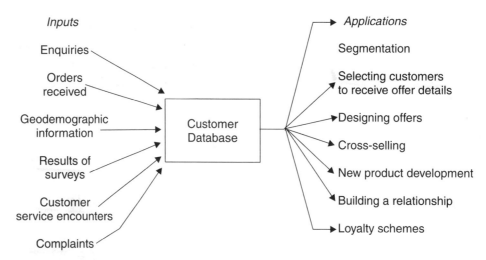

(a) The **majority** of customer information will be gleaned from the orders they place and the enquiries that they make. A relatively recent development in this area is the combination of cookies or user log-ins and server logging software, which enables **tracking and recording** of a customer's progress through a **website**, perhaps revealing interests that would otherwise have gone unnoticed.

(b) **Geodemographic** information relates to the characteristics of people living in different areas. Even simple post-code information can contain a lot of data about the customer.

(c) **Customer service** can be used to indicate particular concerns of customers. For example, in a DIY store, if customers have to ask service staff where items are stored, the volume of complaints might indicate poor signage and labelling.

(d) **Complaints** also indicate deficiencies in the product or the fact that customer expectations have been poorly communicated.

(e) The specific information held may **vary by type of market**. For example, an industrial database will hold data on key purchasers, influencers and decision makers, organisational structure, industry classification (SIC codes), and business size.

Customer data can be categorised into four groups :

(a) **Behavioural data** which is collected by the organisation as a result of their interactions with the customer eg. contact records, letters, complaints, competition entries, orders, payments, online enquiries, tracked web pages visited , discussion forums used, loyalty or membership cards swiped etc

(b) **Volunteered data** is generated when customers complete forms, register with websites, request more information and provide their own details, respond to calls for more information, agree to be contacted by relevant third parties and update their online profiles.

(c) **Attributed data** is data generated as a result of a specific research project. This information is confidential and therefore individual respondents cannot be added to a database using their personal identity. The results of a research study however can be used to add more detail to your database. For example, a charity may have conducted some research into the type of communications message that is most likely to illicit a response from different groups of potential donors. If for example they found that a plea for help worked well with mothers aged between 20 and 40 years of age then they could place a code next to individuals within that group on their database to show that they are best communicated using that type of message, professional men aged 40 – 50 may have been found to respond more to altruistic appeals and therefore males fitting this profile could be tagged accordingly. The next time the charity sent a piece of direct mail, they could then adapt their tone and send more targeted messages to the individuals on their database.

Relevant!

(d) **Profile data** is collected when it is linked with data prom another source eg. lifestyle databases purchased, corporate databases, geodemographic profiles. Profiling is explored in more detail later in the chapter.

Databases may be populated by information that the organisation collects for themselves or through information that is hired or purchased from data providers.

There are a number of large data providers who sell or rent their lists for organisations to use in marketing activities or to populate their information systems. Look at some of the following companies website:

Geodemographic profilers:

CACI – uses ACORN geodemographic profile based on postcode (www.CACI.co.uk)

Experian – A portfolio of segmentation models under the MOSAIC brand which can pinpoint global and UK postcode linked lifestyle variables (www.business-strategies.co.uk)

Lifestyle profilers:

A number of large lifestyle databases exist in the UK. The agency Prime Prospects uses a combination of these and outlines on their website a few example case studies showing how they use the data (www.primeprospects.co.uk)

Company databases:

Dun & Bradstreet are one of the largest suppliers of company information (www.dnb.co.uk) ▪

1.1 The benefits of customer databases

Databases can provide **valuable information** to marketing management.

(a)   Computer databases make it easier to collect and store more **data/information**.

(b)   Computer software allows the data to be **extracted** from the file and **processed** to provide whatever information management needs.

(c)   In some cases businesses may have access to the databases of **external organisations**. Reuters, for example, provides an on-line information system about money market interest rates and foreign exchange rates to firms involved in money market and foreign exchange dealings, and to the treasury departments of a large number of companies.

Other benefits of database systems might include:

(a)   Increased **sales and/or market share** (due to enhanced lead follow-up, cross-selling, customer contact)
(b)   Increased **customer retention** (through better targeting)
(c)   Better use of **resources** (targeting, less duplication of information handling)

Databases enable marketing managers to improve their **decision making**. *of contact.*

- **Understanding customers** and their preferences
- Managing **customer service** (helplines, complaints)
- Understanding the **market** (new products, channels etc)
- Understanding **competitors** (market share, prices)
- Managing **sales operations**
- Managing **marketing campaigns**
- **Communicating** with customers

A database built for marketing purposes will, like the marketing function itself, be **future orientated**. It will be possible to **exploit** the database to **drive future marketing programmes**, not just glory in what has happened in the past.

KEY CONCEPT

Databases provide valuable **information** to assist with many marketing management tasks and decisions and can play a key part in **customer relationship management** because they permit **mass customisation**.

Customer relationship management (CRM) describes the methodologies, software, and usually Internet capabilities that help an enterprise to manage customer relationships.

We mentioned 'CRM' in the previous chapter because it is now so commonly used as a label for marketing management software products. More precisely, however, customer relationship management consists of:

(a)   Helping an enterprise to **identify** and **target** its **best customers**, manage marketing campaigns with clear goals and objectives, and generate quality leads

(b)   **Allowing** the **formation of relationships** with **customers**, with the aim of **improving customer satisfaction** and **maximising profits**; identifying the most profitable customers and providing them with the highest level of service

(c)   **Providing employees** with the **information** and **processes necessary** to know their customers, understand their needs, and effectively build relationships between the company, its customer base, and distribution partners

(d)   Assisting the organisation to improve **sales**, **account**, and **sales management** by **optimising information shared**, and **streamlining existing processes** (for example, taking orders using mobile devices)

(e)   Measuring and anticipating the life-time value of customers

The **database** is clearly key to CRM. For example, an enterprise might build a database about its customers that describes relationships in enough detail to allow management, salespeople, service staff and maybe customers themselves to access information, match customer needs with product plans, remind customers of service requirements and know what other products a customer had purchased, and so on.

The result is something called **mass customisation**, in which a large number of customers can be reached, but simultaneously these customers can be treated **individually**. It has been remarked how the traditional values of the 'corner shop' are returning with the resurgence of relationship marketing and customer focus.

MARKETING AT WORK

'*Newcomers to database marketing have to make a mental leap from viewing the database as a collection of names to seeing it as an engine for driving truly personal marketing*', says Melanie Howard, head of direct marketing studies at the Henley Centre. '*Companies must understand the database is not a way of marketing, but it facilitates the personal marketing approach. They must be careful. If they think they are doing personal marketing just because they have a name and address they have a problem.*' They must understand what will win consumer loyalty.

'*Analysing the data properly and using it effectively will separate the winners from the losers*', argues Edwina Dunn of Dunn-Humby, the company involved in running Tesco ClubCard. '*Manufacturers have learned that data about purchasing is valuable and if they can link it to names and addresses that is even more valuable. Not many are grasping the deeper meaning of that. The few that do are forward-thinking and visionary,*' she says.

She puts Tesco in that category. Its ClubCard collects purchasing information at the swipe of the card. The card can be used at any store, enabling marketers to build a picture of individual habits. Because the Tesco system is about collecting points then sending out vouchers, the retailer has a valid reason to write to customers.

'*Being in the forefront of database marketing will take more than up-to-date technology and marketing skills*', Dunn says. It will demand a third skill which she thinks has been left out of the database equation: statistical analysis. '*We are not bringing statisticians into the world of marketing. The bridge building is being done between marketing and IT. The big bridge that*

needs to be built now is between statisticians and marketing. That will separate out people who know what to do with the data.'

Marketing Business

Companies such as Tesco, who use their database effectively, do so because they specifically target individual customers based on their behaviour. If you purchase anything through Amazon.com, note how quickly they are able to suggest other products you may like.

2 Setting up a database

KEY CONCEPT

concept

Modern business databases are maintained on a central computer to enable **sharing of data** and avoid duplication. A typical relational database consists of a number of inter-related tables of records and fields.

A database need not be computerised. A paper address book that you keep in your briefcase is a form of database and so is a card index. However most modern business databases will be created and maintained **centrally on a computer**. This is obviously the most efficient method where **large amounts of data** are involved and for several important additional reasons.

(a)   **Common data** for all users to share

(b)   Avoidance of **data duplication** in files kept by different users

(c)   **Consistency** in the organisation's use of data, and in the accuracy and up-to-dateness of data accessed by different users, because all records are centrally maintained and updated

(d)   **Flexibility** in the way in which shared data can be queried, analysed and formatted by individual users for specific purposes, without altering the store of data itself

(e)   **Speed** of data retrieval

The collection of computer programs that process data is more properly referred to as a **database management system (DBMS)**.

Basic features of database packages allow you to readily perform the following activities.

(a)   **Find particular records**, using any data item you know

(b)   **Sort records alphabetically**, numerically or by date, in ascending or descending order

(c)   **Interrogate records**, generating the selection of records based on a complex set of criteria, from one or more linked tables. (For example, you might specify that you want all customer records where the field 'City' equals London or Birmingham and where the field 'Product' equals Widget and where the field 'Purchase Date' is between January 2008 and January 2009. The query would generate a table consisting of customers in London and Birmingham who purchased Widgets in 2008.)

(d)   **Calculate and count** data entries. For example if you wanted to find out how many customers had purchased each product, you could run a query that asked the database to group the data by the field 'product' and then count by field 'customer ID': it would count the number of distinct customer ID numbers linked to each product. You could also ask to 'sum' or add up all the values in a field: total number of purchases, or total purchase value.

(e)   **Format** selected data for a variety of uses, as reports, forms, mailing labels, charts and diagrams.

Find out what type(s) of database your organisation (or college) uses, and for what applications. If possible, get access to the database and browse through the index, directory or switchboard to see what databases/catalogues contain what database files or tables, queries, reports and forms, with what fields. If you can't get access to a database at work, try the local library, where you may find that the 'index card' system has been computerised as a database. Or use an Internet search engine or browser to interrogate some on-line databases. This is not really something you can learn from books – have a go!

2.1 User requirements and evaluating software

There may be a number of different users of the database management system possibly within different departments. For example a telecommunications company may have a basic marketing database with details of their home broadband customers. This database may have details such as:

- Name and contact details
- Duration of contract
- Interactions with the company such as calls to helpdesk, customer complaints, enquiries, changes in package
- Details of phone, mobile, mobile broadband suppliers used
- Payment details

From looking at just this one brief example you may have noticed that a number of departments within the organisation will find the information useful. The sales department may find it helpful to see if they could cross sell other products. The customer services department may need the information to maintain customer satisfaction levels. The finance department may need the information to ensure that payments are processed efficiently. It is important therefore that from the outset, the objectives, needs and uses of the database is made clear and the software available is able to meet user demands. Frequently also information is available within a database, the format that it can be obtained in may not be useful for all users and so an agreed **specification of requirements** should be made.

Software used for database applications should be evaluated for;

- Compatibility with existing software applications (eg you may wish to import and export data between applications)

- Ability to provide the required reporting formats

- Ease of use bearing in mind the users of the system

- Software support and training

- Impact of the implementation of the software (eg will it be easily integrated into the existing working practices or will it be a complete change in procedures causing significant disruption for a period)

- Ease of ongoing maintenance, updates and future proofing

2.2 Key components

There are two basic kinds of **computerised** database.

(a) A **flat file system** lumps all the data into single file. A single worksheet in a spreadsheet is an example.

(b) A **relational database system** allows greater flexibility and storage efficiency by splitting the data up into a number of tables, which are linked and can be integrated as necessary. For example, one table may contain customer names and another customers' payment histories. A linking field such as a customer ID number would allow the user to interrogate both tables and generate an integrated report on a particular customer's purchases and payments, or a list of customers who had made multiple purchases, or a list of those with a poor payment record.

Flat systems are easy to build and maintain, and are quite adequate for applications such as mailing lists, or membership databases. **Relational systems** integrate a wider range of business functions, for invoicing, accounting, inventory and marketing analysis: they are, however, complicated to develop and use properly. If your organisation already operates a relational system, learn how to use it. If you are required to set up or build a relational system, get help: use a 'wizard' or template (in the database package) or ask an expert, at least the first time.

All databases have some kind of structure, otherwise you would never be able to retrieve information from them. For instance a telephone directory stores entries in alphabetical order. Computer database packages store data as follows.

(a) **Fields** are the labels given to types of data. A simple customer database, for example, might include fields such as: Title, First name, Last name, Address fields, and other contact details. The fields are the **columns** in a tabular database.

(b) **Records** are the collection of fields relevant to one entry. So all the above data fields for a particular customer make up one customer record. The records are the **rows** in a tabular database.

ID	Title	First name	Last name	Address 1	Address 2	Address 3	City	County	Postcode	Country	Telephone	Fax	Email
1	Mr	Kieran	Davies	25 Dill Street	Merton		London		SW17 4QF	UK	020 7884 1122		kieran.davis@virgin.net
2	Mrs	Shagura	Jumal	37 Nelson Road	Trafford		Manchester		M41 2BD	UK	01584 452291		sjumal@freeserve.com

(c) **Tables** are collections of records that describe similar data. All the customer records for a particular region or product may be stored in one table.

(d) **Databases** are collections of all the tables relating to a particular set of information. So your customer database may include tables for various regions, products and customer contacts.

 ACTIVITY 2

application

Why are records stored as rows rather than columns?

2.3 Data cleansing

 KEY CONCEPT

concept

A key issue in setting up a database is **data cleansing**: ensuring that the information is correct, up-to-date and not duplicated. Much can be done at the data entry stage, but where data is imported from other systems a good deal of preparatory work may be needed to ensure that it is in the correct format.

Data cleansing is the process of amending or removing data in a database that is incorrect, out of date, incomplete, improperly formatted, or duplicated.

As mentioned in the previous chapter information systems are only valuable if they give **good** information, and that depends crucially on the accuracy of the data.

A typical organisation will have many years' worth of potentially valuable information and this will have got into the system in a variety of ways.

(a) It may have been typed in by hand – correctly or incorrectly

(b) It may have been scanned in from paper documents, but this depends on how good the scanning process is (accurate scanning of ordinary text has only been possible for a few years)

(c) It may have arisen from EPOS and EFTPOS systems

(d) It may have been imported from other systems in other parts of the organisation – perhaps in an incompatible format.

(e) It may have been purchased from another organisation (for instance a mailing list broker) or have arisen as a result of a merger between two organisations.

[handwritten margin note: when contacting customer for research need to ensure that current CRM has been cleansed + is appropriate for use.]

All of these methods are liable to lead to incorrect, out of date, incomplete, improperly formatted, or duplicated data that needs to be 'cleansed'.

ACTIVITY 3

concept

Would data from EPOS/EFTPOS systems need to be cleansed?

MARKETING AT WORK

application

Benjamin (2008) reviewed the nature of the data cleansing industry within the UK for Marketing Direct magazine. and looked at the issues associated with poor quality data. Key issues found by the journalist were:

'Ask any direct marketer to pinpoint what makes a successful campaign and the likely answer will be the quality of the data. It sounds simple in theory, but in reality it's a different story, if recent research is anything to go by. A survey from data services provider QAS revealed that the UK is the worst performing country when it comes to data quality, with the retail and financial services sectors named as the biggest culprits.

What's more, in separate findings, only eight per cent of the UK organisations polled validate the information they collect, while 34 per cent admitted that they fail to validate any of the data they gather, despite recognising the negative impact this has on their businesses, brands and budgets.

More than half of those surveyed said they validated address and postcode information prior to putting it on their systems, but admitted that most other customer contact information is stored unchecked.

Evidence of such poor data quality is inevitably putting a strain on the data-cleaning sector, as the increasing inaccuracy of name and address information is becoming harder to match against a base source of data. Martin Doyle, managing director of data-cleaning software provider DQ Global, believes the biggest challenge facing the sector is a general apathy and abdication of responsibility for data quality.'

need to be able to guarentee data validation as part of research process.

Within this example, data cleansing was regarded from a direct marketing perspective however if you are looking at it from a research perspective, in order to comply with the data protection principles in operation within the UK and Europe then individuals records should be aggregated so that no one individual can be highlighted for further analysis. When we consider data quality issues, it is even more important to ensure that data is robust because if a large proportion of the information is incomplete or incorrect, once it is aggregated errors in the information may magnified and therefore highly misleading.

Source for quote: Benjamin, K. (2008) '*Strategy: Data Cleansing – A fresh approach*' Marketing Direct, 5th March 2008

Be mindful of data protection issues throughout research

The article by Benjamin (2008) highlighted in the Marketing at Work example above was published in Marketing Direct. You can gain access to this article through the CIM's Knowledge Hub when you sign in. The article addresses the impact of poor data quality and considers whether marketers should be able to access the UK Death Register in order to cleanse data further. The article is well worth a read because it highlights the nature of the data cleansing industry and may help you to put the issue of customer databases into context.

2.4 Cleansing new data

2.4.1 Form elements

A great deal can be done to ensure that **new data is clean** at the time when it is initially entered into a system. For instance computerised forms for data entry can contain a variety of elements that help to avoid human error and bad data.

These **pre-define the acceptable responses** and simply require the user to select the appropriate option rather than type anything.

(a)   **Radio buttons** force the user to choose one and only one of a number of options.

Would you like to receive further information?

○ Yes

○ No

could you look @ using an organisation's current CRM system to conduct the research? eg) phone calls from the system and entering the info directly against the record as here

(b)   **Check boxes** allow more than one choice, but still from a limited range of options

Which newspaper(s) do you read every day?

☐ Financial Times

☐ Guardian

☐ Telegraph

☐ Mirror

(c)   **List boxes** operate in a similar way to either radio buttons or check boxes, but the selectable option or options drop down instead of being written out (this saves space on screen).

Title

2.4.2 Validation

Validation is the application of pre-programmed tests and rules by the data entry program to make sure that **typed data input** is reasonable.

There are a number of different types of computer controls for validating a user's typed entries. Here are some examples.

(a)   **Format checks** test the data in each input area against rules governing whether it should be numeric, alphabetic or a combination of the two and whether it should have a minimum or maximum number of characters. For example the software would not allow alphabetic characters to be entered in a box designated for a telephone number. It would check an e-mail address to ensure that it contained the @ symbol and at least one full stop.

(b)   **Range checks** test that the data is within an appropriate range, for example no products are priced at less than £10 or more than £100. This will prevent somebody keying in the price of a customer purchase for £22.99 as £2,299 in error. These checks can also be applied to dates: for instance you should not be able to enter a date of birth of 31 February, or enter an 'account opened' date in 2007 if it is 2006.

(c)   **Existence checks** compare the input data with some other piece of data in the system, to see if it is reasonable. For example a customer code might be compared with an existing list of customer records. If the code exists there will be no reason to duplicate data already entered. If the code does not exist the computer would give you the options of amending the code you entered (in case you typed it wrongly) or of creating a new customer account. Deliberately incorrect entries can also be prevented, or at least discouraged, by this means: for instance the system may query a customer name entered as 'Mickey Mouse', although some kind of override will be necessary, in case that really is the customer's name.

(d)   **Completeness checks** ensure that all required data items have been entered. For example if the system requires a contact telephone number you will not be able to save a record until you provide one.

Checks like these are very common when filling in forms on websites. Watch out next time you fill in one of these. Ideally fill one in wrongly, deliberately, and try to work out how (or if) the computer knows you have made an error or given incorrect information. The amount of checking will vary from site to site.

2.4.3 Verification

Verification is the **comparison** of **input** data with the **source** document. Computers can't yet see in the way that humans can but they can encourage the person entering the data to check the accuracy of their inputs. For instance if the user enters a post code the computer may automatically display a street name and a range of house numbers. If the displayed information is not the same as the information that appears in the data source this should alert the user that either he or she has made a mistake or the source data is unreliable.

2.5 Cleansing data that is imported

2.5.1 Format and consistency

Suppose you **acquire an existing database** of customer addresses arranged with fields for:

Title, Last Name, First Name, House Number, Street Name, Town, City, Post Code

Your own database may have fields for:

Title, First Name, Last Name, Address1, Address2, Address 3, Post Code

On the face of it the information is the same in both databases but there are small differences that will make it **impossible to 'cut and paste'** the acquired data into your existing data without some cleansing work.

In this example the order of the fields is slightly different, and the acquired database has two fields for your 'Address1' field. Even if you succeed in importing the new data much of it will end up in the wrong field as far as your database is concerned and produce nonsense results when analysed.

Similar problems will arise if the data you want to import includes options that are **not allowed** in your database (a title of 'Prof.' or 'Lord', say), or if the **maximum size** of the Last Name field is 100 characters in one database and 50 characters in the other, or if **dates** are in US format (MM/DD/YYYY) in the new data but UK format (DD/MM/YYYY) in yours, or even if tiny things like **spacing** or **punctuation** (eg DD.MM.YYYY) are different or if **foreign characters** are used.

Computerised databases are sensitive to differences in format in a way that human beings are not because they need to **store** information as **efficiently** as possible for subsequent **high-speed analysis**. Before you can import data into your own database you need to ensure that it is in a format (the same order, the same field size and so on) that is consistent with your existing data. This can often involve a **considerable amount of preparatory work**.

A technology called **XML** is likely to alleviate many formatting problems, but most organisations have only just started down this path.

2.5.2 Deduplication

Duplication of entries in your database is one of the best ways of annoying your customers! Suppose your database contains a record for Mrs Jane Wordingham and another for Ms J. Wordingham. If you send 'both' of these people the same mailshot you may successfully reach two different customers ... or you may strongly irritate one.

Duplication can occur for a variety of reasons.

(a)   The data may have been **acquired** from another part of the organisation, or from another organisation such as a list broker, and be recorded slightly differently. Different systems ask for different information (eg 'Initial' as opposed to 'First Name').

[handwritten margin note: Need to ensure that this has been done in order to create the list of customers that we will contact as part of the research.]

BPP
LEARNING MEDIA

(b)   **People are inconsistent** in the data they provide. For instance they may generally include their 'Town' when providing their address, but leave it out if they are in a hurry.

(c)   Even if data is read in **automatically**, from a credit card, say, there is nothing to prevent someone using **more than one credit card** and having slightly different versions of their personal information on each.

Fortunately, it is usually a fairly simple matter to **identify duplicates**. The software should be able to **compare a common field** such as post code and either **delete** duplicates **automatically** or **generate a report** for further investigation. This may be more problematic in business-to-business marketing, where several different businesses may operate out of the same location, or the same business may operate out of multiple locations.

Some organisations deal with duplicates by deleting information relating to all but the most recent transaction ('overkill'). Others seem to rely on customers to tell them about duplicate entries but are otherwise happy to send mailshots to everyone on their database, even if some customers get two or more copies ('underkill').

What sort of organisations would be keen to avoid overkill?

2.6 Database maintenance

as more information via research is obtained.

A customer database should be **regularly and systematically maintained.**

(a)   **New fields** can be added to the database design as new types of information become available.

(b)   Any **up-dated, altered or new information** should be entered in the database: changes of address, customer status, product interests.

(c)   Names which have received **no response** after a certain period of time or number of contacts, should be **deleted**.

(d)   If mailshots are **returned to the sender**, they will often be marked with the reason for non-delivery: no longer at this address, not known at this address. Whenever this happens addresses and names should be checked, and amended if possible (common errors include misspelt names, missing lines of the address, or the wrong company name).

(e)   **Requests from customers** to have their **details erased** from the database should be honoured. This is a **legal requirement**: see Chapter 4.

(f)   Maintaining the functionality of the database as it grows will also need careful consideration and significant IT support. Over time, if new applications are found or additional inputs from alternative sources are available, the database may require restructuring. For this reason, making sure requirements are well defined from the start can help to future-proof the database and ensure compatibility between software programs.

3   Database applications

The range of database applications include:

- focusing on **prime prospects**
- evaluating **new prospects**
- **cross-selling** related products
- **launching new products** to potential prospects
- identifying **new distribution channels**

- building **customer loyalty**
- converting **occasional users to regular users**
- generating **enquiries** and **follow-up sales**
- **targeting niche markets**.

The most valuable information in a customer-focused organisation is its knowledge of its customers. The customer database has two uses in such an organisation:

both of these can be used for research purposes.

(a) **Operational support** (for example, when a telephone banking employee checks that the password given by a caller is correct before giving out details of the account)

(b) **Analytical uses** (the analysis by the same bank of the customers who receive a certain amount into their account each month and so may be targeted with personal loans or other offers)

The database may be applied to meet a variety of objectives with numerous advantages over traditional marketing methods.

- Focusing on prime prospects
- Evaluating new prospects
- Cross-selling related products
- Launching new products to potential prospects
- Identifying new distribution channels
- Building customer loyalty
- Converting occasional users to regular users
- Generating enquiries and follow-up sales
- Targeting niche markets

3.1 Identifying the most profitable customers

The Italian economist Vilfredo Pareto was the first to observe that in human affairs, 20% of the events result in 80% of the outcomes. This has become known as Pareto's law, or the 80/20 principle. It shows up quite often in marketing. For example, twenty percent of the effort you put into promotion may generate eighty percent of the sales revenue. Whatever the precise proportions, it is true that in general a small number of existing customers are 'heavy users' of a product or service and generate a high proportion of sales revenue, buying perhaps four times as much as a 'light user'.

A customer database which allows purchase frequency and value per customer to be calculated indicates to the marketer who the potential heavy users are, and therefore where the promotional budget can most profitably be spent.

3.2 Identifying buying trends

By tracking purchases per customer (or customer group) you may be able to identify:

(a) **Loyal repeat customers** who cost less to retain than new customers cost to find and attract

(b) **'Backsliding'** or lost customers, who have reduced or ceased the frequency or volume of their purchases. These may be a useful diagnostic sample for market research into declining sales or failing customer care.

(c) **Seasonal** or local purchase patterns (heavier consumption of soup in England in winter, for example).

(d) **Demographic purchase patterns**. These may be quite unexpected. Lower income consumers might buy top-of-the-range products, which they value and save for. Prestige and luxury goods, which marketers promote largely to affluent white-collar consumers, are also purchased by students, secretaries and young families, who have been dubbed 'Ultra Consumers' because they transcend demographic clusters.

(e) Purchase patterns in response to **promotional campaigns**. Increased sales volume or frequency following promotions is an important measurement of their effectiveness.

3.3 Identifying marketing opportunities

More detailed information (where available) on customer likes and dislikes, complaints, feedback and lifestyle values may offer useful information for:

(a) **Product** improvement

(b) **Customer care** and quality programmes

(c) New **product development**

(d)   **Decision-making** across the marketing mix: on prices, product specifications, distribution channels, promotional messages

Simple data fields such as 'contact type' will help to evaluate how contact is made with customers, of what types and in what numbers. Business leads may be generated most often by trade conferences and exhibitions, light users by promotional competitions and incentives, and loyal customers by personal contact through representatives.

Customers can be investigated using any data field included in the database: How many are on e-mail or the Internet? How many have spouses or children? Essentially, these parameters allow the marketer to **segment** the customer base for marketing purposes.

⤷ into groups that prefer certain contact

 MARKETING AT WORK

application

Synovate's electronic footfall counting technology, begins by answering the retailer's most basic question 'What is actually driving our business: are changes in the volume of sales the consequence of a rise / fall in footfall levels or changes in the percentage of shoppers that make a purchase?' With the highest level of accuracy, we measure and report upon customer numbers entering stores, building a factual picture of footflow for the retailer, hour by hour, week by week, month by month, year-on-year.

www.synovate.com

3.4 Using database information

The following is a summary of the main ways in which database information can be used.

(a)   **Direct mail** used to:

- Maintain customer contact between (or instead of) sales calls
- Generate leads and 'warmed' prospects for sales calls
- Promote and/or sell products and services direct to customers
- Distribute product or service information

(b)   **Transaction processing**. Databases can be linked to programmes which generate order confirmations, despatch notes, invoices, statements and receipts.

(c)   **Marketing research and planning**. The database can be used to send out market surveys, and may itself be investigated to show purchasing patterns and trends.

(d)   **Contacts planning**. The database can indicate what customers need to be contacted or given incentives to maintain their level of purchase and commitment. A separate database may similarly be used to track planned and on-going contacts at conferences and trade shows and invitation lists to marketing events.

(e)   **Product development and improvement**. Product purchases can be tracked through the product life cycle, and weaknesses and opportunities identified from records of customer feedback, complaints and warranty/guarantee claims.

4   Profiling customers and prospects

 KEY CONCEPT

concept

Building **accurate** and **up-to-date profiles** of customers enables the company to **extend help** to a company's **target audience**, to stimulate further demand, and to stay close to them. The company's own information can be enriched by collating it with geodemographic and lifestyle information from sources such as ACORN.

As we have seen, a database is a collection of available information on past and current customers together with future prospects, structured to allow for the implementation of effective marketing strategies.

Database marketing is a customer-oriented approach to marketing, and its special power lies in the techniques it uses to harness the capabilities of computer and telecommunications technology. Building **accurate and up-to-date profiles** of customers enables the company:

- to extend **help** to a company's target audience
- to **stimulate further demand**
- to **stay close** to them.

Keeping an electronic database of customers and prospects (and of all communications and commercial contacts) helps to improve all future contacts.

4.1 Customer intelligence – why is it so important?

For years the rhetoric of marketing has been that of **warfare**: targets, campaigns, offensives. The approach has been one of trying to beat the 'enemy' into submission and 'win' new customers. Many organisations now realise that there is more to be gained from **alternative strategies**.

(a) Investing in activities which seek to **retain existing customers**, based on the argument that it costs more to attract new customers

(b) Encouraging existing customers to **spend more**

Retaining customers is the basis of such relationship marketing techniques. Customers are seen not only in terms of what they are buying today, but also in terms of their **potential for future purchases**.

Although it is clear that **added services** and **quality of service** are the key to retaining customers, this still begs questions: precisely what services to add, for instance?

To be effective at **retention marketing**, the organisation has to have a good database **profiling past, present and prospective customers**, with details of the nature of the relationship; it has to know about their attitudes, their perceptions of the organisation's products and service, and their expectations. Just as importantly, the organisation must know, from systematically-acquired **customer feedback**, precisely what it is doing wrong.

A well-developed customer database will use **postcodes** to overlay specialist **geodemographic data** from **ACORN** (see below) or other sources , or include **lifestyle information** allowing rich customer profiles to be developed.

MARKETING AT WORK

application

CACI (www.caci.co.uk) is a company which provides market analysis, information systems and other data products to clients. It advertises itself as 'the winning combination of marketing and technology'.

As an illustration of the information available to the marketing manager for incorporation into corporate databases, here is an overview of some of their products.

Paycheck	This provides data about income levels for all the millions of individual post codes across the UK. This enables companies to see how mean income distribution varies from area to area.
People UK	This is a mix of geodemographics, life stage and lifestyle data. It is person rather than household specific and is designed for those companies requiring highly targeted campaigns.
eTypes	eTypes is a tool for understanding online consumer behaviour. It can tell organisations who their online customers are, and what they use the internet for – whether it's finding holidays, buying CDs, managing their stocks & shares or just chatting.
ACORN	This stands for A Classification of Residential Neighbourhoods, and has been used to profile residential neighbourhoods by post code since 1976. ACORN classifies people in any trading area or on any customer database into more than 50 different types.
Lifestyles UK	This database offers over 300 lifestyle selections on 44 million consumers in the UK. It helps with cross selling and customer retention strategies.
Monica	This can help a company to identify the age of people on its database by giving the likely age profile of their first names. It uses a combination of census data and real birth registrations.

[handwritten margin notes:] rationale for research

can code new customers based on current ones in an attempt to market to them in this way from the beginning

You can use ACORN yourself for free when you use the website www.upmystreet.com

This site uses geodemographic profiling from ACORN to give a neighbourhood profile. You can enter your postcode (or one where you are familiar with the area) and then go to 'read neighbourhood profile'. You may be initially shown a short version but click on 'real full profile' . The type of information you will find included will be:

- Education levels
- Social activities
- The type of TV watched and newspapers and magazines read
- Typical family composition
- Level of interest in current affairs and social issues
- Types of shops visited

4.2 Customer segmentation

Organisations with a large customer base, a wide range of products, a global market, and several discrete product/brand names may be tempted to treat customers as if they were all alike, all wanting much the same things, all applying similar criteria when judging the product, the service, or the organisation as a whole.

In practice, this is bound to be a misleading assumption. Customer A may want reliability of delivery on an hourly basis; Customer B may want an unusual range of financial options; Customer C may want the highest possible standards of after-sales support; Customer D is only interested in one product.

Research shows that there are differences in customers' expectations which can be exploited, if they are identified and recorded, by offering levels of service which match the needs of particular sectors, possibly withdrawing from some or increasing prices/charges to an economically-justified level.

5 Data warehousing and data mining

communication with customers is part of the extended marketing mix and so need to be considered and done appropriately for each group

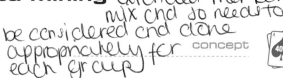
Data warehousing involves extracting information from disparate organisational sources to build a coherent set of information available to be used across the organisation for management analysis and decision making. On-line analytical processing (OLAP) techniques allow the data to be viewed from many different perspectives.

Two techniques designed to utilise the **ever-increasing amounts of data** held by organisations are data warehousing and data mining.

5.1 Data warehousing

Data warehousing involves a centrally stored source of data that has been extracted from various organisational databases and standardised and integrated for use throughout an organisation. Data warehouses contain a wide variety of data that present a coherent picture of business conditions at a single point in time.

Could store the info in this form (or) use this form to see where the business is currently, if have this info.
→ Could compare the two from pre to post research

A data warehouse contains data from a range of internal (eg sales order processing system, nominal ledger) and external sources. If necessary, the user can drill-down to access transaction level detail. Data is increasingly obtained from newer channels such as customer care systems, outside agencies or websites.

Components of a data warehouse

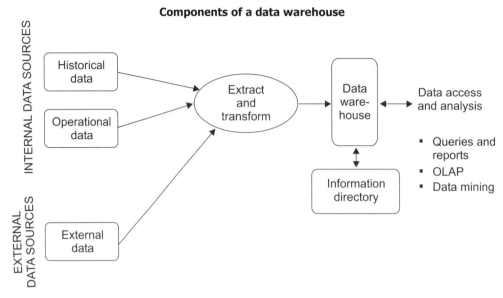

Data is copied to the data warehouse as often as required – usually either daily, weekly or monthly. The process of making any required changes to the format of data and copying it to the warehouse is usually automated.

The result should be a coherent set of information available to be used across the organisation for management analysis and decision making. The reporting and query tools available within the warehouse should facilitate management reporting and analysis.

The reporting and query tools should be flexible enough to allow multidimensional data analysis, also known as on-line analytical processing (**OLAP**). Each aspect of information (eg product, region, price, budgeted sales, actual sales, time period etc) represents a different dimension. OLAP enables data to be viewed from each dimension, allowing each aspect to be viewed and in relation to the other aspects.

The website http://www.dwinfocenter.org will give you a general overview of data warehouses including their advantages and disadvantages. Unlike some other resources which cover this topic, the site is written in plain, easy to understand and fairly jargon free language. ◼

5.1.1 Data marts

data mart could be a cost-effective option for Tech4events.

Organisations may build a single central data warehouse to serve the entire organisation or may create a series of smaller **data marts**. A data mart holds a selection of the organisation's data for a specific purpose.

A data mart can be constructed more quickly and cheaply than a data warehouse. However, if too many individual data marts are built, organisations may find it is more efficient to have a single data warehouse serving all areas.

5.1.2 Advantages of data warehouses and data marts

Advantages of setting up a data warehouse or data mart include the following.

(a) Decision makers can access data without affecting the use of operational systems.

(b) Having a wide range of data available to be queried easily encourages the taking of a wide perspective on organisational activities.

(c) Data warehouses have proved successful in some businesses for:

- Quantifying the effect of marketing initiatives
- Improving knowledge of customers
- Identifying and understanding an enterprise's most profitable revenues streams

Some organisations have found they have invested considerable resources implementing a data warehouse for little return. To benefit from the information a data warehouse can provide, **organisations need to be flexible and prepared to act on what they find**. If a warehouse system is implemented simply to follow current practice it will be of little value.

 MARKETING AT WORK   application

Dunnhumby is the agency behind the interrogation of the massive Tesco Clubcard database containing purchase behaviour information of 13 million UK households.

When consumers make a purchase in store, online or through Tesco's partners in the scheme, information is stored and analysed in order to make decisions. Dunnhumby also sell analysis to manufacturer brands and will interrogate the data according to a specific brands needs.

Tesco put their customers, your customers, at the heart of their business. Understanding who they are, how they behave and what they want drives the decision making processes.
Having co-developed Clubcard and worked on the world leading loyalty and insight programme for more than ten years, dunnhumby is uniquely qualified to show you how to maximise your opportunities with the third largest retailer in the world. If you can understand customers and talk their language with Tesco, you will get products, prices and offers spot-on for customers.

It's your ability to do that which could create a step change in your relationship with Tesco.

- What could it mean for your business if you really understood Tesco?
- How much more effective could you be if you knew Tesco customers inside out?
- Wouldn't you like to talk the language of Tesco and their customers?

dunnhumby offers you the chance to do just that with a unique training programme.'   http://www.dunnhumby.com

5.2 Data mining

 KEY CONCEPT   concept

Data mining software examines the data in a database or data warehouse and discovers previously unknown relationships using complex statistical techniques. The hidden patterns and relationships the software identifies can be used to guide decision making and to predict future behaviour.

Data mining is a class of database applications that look for hidden patterns in a group of data. For example, data mining software can help retail companies find customers with common interests. The term is commonly misused to describe software that presents data in new ways. True data mining software does not just change the presentation, but actually discovers previously unknown relationships among the data. This can be used to guide decision making and to **predict future behaviour**.

 MARKETING AT WORK   application

(1)   The American retailer Wal-Mart discovered an unexpected relationship between the sale of nappies and beer! Wal-Mart found that both tended to sell at the same time, just after working hours, and concluded that men with small children stopped off to buy nappies on their way home, and bought beer at the same time. Logically therefore, if the two items were put in the same shopping aisle, sales of both should increase. Wal-Mart tried this and it worked.

(2)   Some credit card companies have used data mining to predict which customers are likely to switch to a competitor in the next few months. Based on the data mining results, the bank can take action to retain these customers.

The types of relationships or patterns that data mining may uncover may be classified as follows.

Relationship\Discovery	Comment
Classification or cluster	These terms refer to the identification of patterns within the database between a range of data items. For example, data mining may find that unmarried males aged between 20 and 30, who have an income above £50,000 are more likely to purchase a high performance sports car than people from other demographic groups. This group could then be targeted when marketing material is produced/distributed.
Association	One event can be linked or correlated to another event – such as in the Wal-Mart example above.
Forecasting	Trends are identified within the data that can be extrapolated into the future.

  ACTIVITY 7

application

Why might competitive pressures encourage data mining?

Most data mining models are either:

(a) **Predictive**: using known observations to predict future events (for example, predicting the probability that a recipient will opt out of an e-mail list)

(b) **Descriptive**: interrogating the database to identify patterns and relationships (for example, profiling the audience of a particular advertising campaign)

Some of the key statistical techniques used in data mining are described below.

(a) **Neural networks**: non-linear predictive models or formulas that adjust inputs and weightings through 'training'

(b) **Decision-trees**: paths are followed towards a solution or result, branching at decision points which are governed by rules (is gender male? Yes/No) giving a complex picture of possible outcomes

(c) **Classification techniques**: assigning people to predetermined classes based on their profile data (in complex combinations)

(d) **Clustering**: identifying occurrences in the database with similar characteristics and grouping them into clusters

 MARKETING AT WORK

application

Data mining software

The following is extracted from marketing material for a Data mining product called the NeoVista Decision Series.

Understand The Patterns In Your Business and Discover The Value In Your Data

Within your corporate database resides extremely valuable information – information that reflects how your business processes operate and how your customers behave. Every transaction your organisation makes is captured for accounting purposes, and with it, a wealth of potential knowledge.

When properly analysed, organised and presented, this information can be of enormous value. Conventional 'drill down' database query techniques may reveal some of these details, but much of the valuable **knowledge content will remain hidden**.

The NeoVista Decision Series is a suite of knowledge discovery software specifically designed to address this challenge. Analysing data without any preconceived notion of the patterns it contains, the Decision Series **seeks out relationships and trends**, and presents them in easy-to-understand form, enabling better business decisions.

The Decision Series is being used today by leading corporations to discover the hidden value in their data, providing them with major competitive advantages and organisational benefits.

- A Large Multi-National Retailer uses the Decision Series to **refine inventory stocking levels**, by store and by item, to dramatically reduce out-of-stock or overstocking situations and thereby improve revenues and reduce forced markdowns.

- A Health Maintenance Group uses the Decision Series to **predict which of its members are most at risk** from specific major illnesses. This presents opportunities for timely medical intervention and preventative treatment to promote the patient's well-being and reduce the healthcare provider's costs.

- An International Retail Sales Organisation uses the Decision Series to **optimise store and department layouts**, resulting in more accurate targeting of products to maximise sales within the scope of available resources.

NeoVista's unique software can be applied to a wide range of business problems, allowing you to:

- Determine the **relationships** that lie at the heart of your business.
- Make reliable **estimates of future behaviour** based on sophisticated analyses of past events.
- Make business **decisions** with a higher degree of understanding and confidence.

Data mining is renowned for exposing important facts and anomalies within data warehouses. The NeoVista Decision Series' knowledge discovery methodology has the proven ability to expose the patterns that are not merely interesting, but which are critical to your business. These patterns provide you with an advantage through insight and knowledge that your competition may never discover.

---

6 Database marketing and marketing research

  KEY CONCEPT

concept

Marketing managers must make a **distinction** between **information collected** in the **ordinary course of business** and **information collected via marketing research**. It is not acceptable to incorporate personal information derived from marketing research directly into a customer's record.

As we shall see in the next chapter when we discuss ethical and social responsibilities and codes of conduct, information collected by means of **marketing research** should **not be used** subsequently to create marketing databases that are used for **direct marketing**. Likewise direct marketing initiatives should not be disguised as marketing research, and customers should be given the opportunity to refuse to allow information they give you to be used for direct marketing purposes.

As a slightly frivolous example, let's say you discover, through the responses of willing participants in a **marketing research** study, that 87% of people who are over a certain weight prefer your company's Product A to Product B. That is probably useful information and it may legitimately be used for **general marketing purposes** such as designing advertising messages or choosing distribution outlets.

However, even though you may know that a particular customer of yours (who took part in the research) is not yet a purchaser of Product A, and you now know that he fits the weight criteria, it is considered **unethical** to add that specific data (the customer's weight) to that specific customer's record, and less ethical still to bombard him with brochures about Product A as a result of information that was not given to you with that purpose in mind. To do so would contravene the MRS Code of Conduct and not be compliant with data protection laws.

It is only acceptable to enrich a customer database with marketing research information so long as **personal data** is represented in an **anonymous** form and is **partly aggregated**.

We can summarise that:

- Customer databases can contain a wide variety of information about the customer such as contact details, transaction history, personal details and preferences and so on. Information may come from a variety of sources besides transaction processing systems, including specialist geodemographic data and lifestyle information.

- Databases provide valuable information to assist with many marketing management tasks and decisions and can play a key part in customer relationship management because they permit mass customisation.

- Modern business databases are maintained on a central computer to enable sharing of data and avoid duplication. A typical relational database consists of a number of inter-related tables of records and fields.

- A key issue in setting up a database is data cleansing: ensuring that the information is correct, up-to-date, not duplicated and so on. Much can be done at the data entry stage, but where data is imported from other systems a good deal of preparatory work may be needed to ensure that it is in the correct format.

- The range of database applications include: focusing on prime prospects; evaluating new prospects; cross-selling related products; launching new products to potential prospects; identifying new distribution channels; building customer loyalty; converting occasional users to regular users; generating enquiries and follow-up sales; targeting niche markets.

- Building accurate and up-to-date profiles of customers enables the company to extend help to a company's target audience, to stimulate further demand, and to stay close to them. The company's own information can be enriched by collating it with geodemographic and lifestyle information from sources such as ACORN.

- Data warehousing involves extracting information from disparate organisational sources to build a coherent set of information available to be used across the organisation for management analysis and decision making. On-line analytical processing (OLAP) techniques allow the data to be viewed from many different perspectives.

- Data mining software examines the data in a database or data warehouse and discovers previously unknown relationships using complex statistical techniques. The hidden patterns and relationships the software identifies can be used to guide decision making and to predict future behaviour.

- Marketing managers must make a **distinction** between **information collected** in the **ordinary course of business** and **information collected via marketing research**. It is not acceptable to incorporate personal information derived from marketing research directly into a customer's record.

Learning objectives	Covered
1 Define customer databases	☑ Contains a variety of customer information
	☑ Manual or computerised source of data
	☑ Assists in decision making
2 Consider the benefits of customer databases	☑ Provide valuable information
	☑ Increased sales, market share, customer retention due to targeting
	☑ Improved decision making as a result if enhanced understanding
3 Link databases and CRM	☑ Facilitates customisation
	☑ Ability to deal with customers individually and personalise offerings
	☑ Calculation of customer lifetime value and identification of profitable customers
4 Consider the benefits of customer databases	☑ Provide valuable information
	☑ Increased sales, market share, customer retention due to targeting
	☑ Improved decision making as a result if enhanced understanding
5 Explain the process of setting up a database	☑ Components
	☑ User requirements and software evaluation
	☑ Data cleansing and validation
	☑ Database maintenance
6 Identify the uses of databases	☑ Database applications (direct mail, research, contacts, NPD)
	☑ Profiling customers (ACORN, MOSAIC, companies, lifestyle)
	☑ Data used to populate databases (behavioural, attributed, volunteered)
7 Explain data warehousing, data marts and data mining	☑ Complex and massive data storage in warehouses
	☑ Drill down functionalities
	☑ Data marts are smaller versions
	☑ Data mining looks for hidden patterns within data
8 Explore the relationship between databases and marketing research	☑ Distinguish information collected as part of business, for database and for research purposes
	☑ Ethical implications
	☑ Data protection issues (more detail in chapter 4)

1   Draw a diagram indicating the sources of information in a customer databases and the possible uses to which it can be put.

2   List five ways in which a database can help to improve a marketing manager's decision making.

3   A database is key to customer relationship management because it facilitates:
     M...................... C.......................... Fill in the gaps.

4   Which of the following is true?

     A   A relational database is one that includes information about the customer's family
     B   'Unclean' data is the fault of incompetent data entry staff
     C   Deduplication can usually be done automatically
     D   Computers are fast because they ignore things like spaces and punctuation in data

5   Give four examples of validation tests.

6   What kind of buying trends might be identified by an analysis of database information?

7   Give examples of the types of (externally-produced) profiling data that may enrich an organisation's customer database.

8   Data warehousing helps to avoid the problems caused by bad data entry. True or false? Explain your answer.

9   Data mining helps to uncover certain types of relationships summarised by the acronym CAF. What does CAF stand for?

10   Following a marketing research study your manager asks you to identify those respondents who are customers in your database and amend their profiles if they do not fit the standard ACORN profile for their post code. How should you respond?

1   You need to do this hands on.

2   Records are stored as rows as a convention, but it is much more practical than storing them in columns, because it is much easier (for humans) to **scroll down** through a list than to scroll **across** many columns.

3   EPOS and EFTPOS data is more likely to be reliable than many other sources of data and it is typically updated whenever a new transaction occurs. It could nevertheless be recorded in inconsistent formats, and the same customer could easily appear twice under two different card codes.

4   Again, you need to do this hands on.

5   Overkill is best avoided by organisations that are susceptible to fraud such as banks and credit card companies.

6   You may be quite surprised by the Acorn profile of your neighbours. Try to think about the reasons behind the profile. Next time you walk around your neighbourhood try to remember the Acorn profile to see if this sheds more light on the situation.

7   Data mining allows data to be used more productively through increased targeting and personalisation of the marketing mix. This assists with customer retention, which is crucially important in a highly competitive market.

1

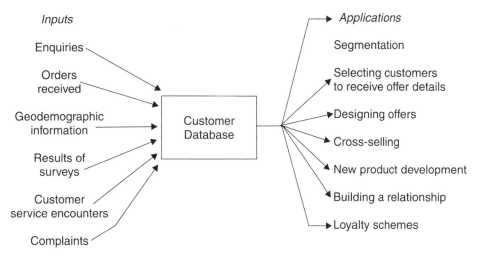

2   Here are the suggestions from earlier in the Text.

- Understanding customers and their preferences
- Managing customer service (helplines, complaints)
- Understanding the market (new products, channels etc)
- Understanding competitors (market share, prices)
- Managing sales operations
- Managing marketing campaigns
- Communicating with customers

3   Mass Customisation

4   C. Options A and D are quite untrue and option B is only one of many reasons.

5   Format checks

Range checks

Existence checks

Completeness checks

6
- Loyal repeat customers
- Backsliding customers
- Seasonal or local purchase patterns
- Demographic purchase patterns
- Purchase patterns in response to promotional campaigns

7   Examples include data about income levels, life stage and lifestyle data, age profiles, Internet browsing habits.

8   False. Data is not entered directly into a data warehouse, it is imported from other 'live' organisational sources as and when required.

9   Classification/Cluster, Association, Forecasting

10   You should point out to your manager that to do what he asks is considered unethical because the respondents did not give their information to the researchers for this purpose. It may be possible to make some changes in the database if you are very careful about aggregating personal data and keeping it anonymous.

References

Benjamin, K. (2008) '*Strategy: Data Cleansing – A fresh approach*' Marketing Direct, 5th March 2008.

Kotler, P. (1994) <u>Marketing Management: Analysis, planning, implementation and control</u>, Prentice Hall, New Jersey.

Tarren, B. (2007) ' *Dunnhumby wields Clubcard data for marketing mix optimisation tool*' Research, MRS, November 2007 edition, p. 11 London.

Wilson, A. (2006) <u>Marketing Research An Integrated Approach</u> 2nd Edition, Prentice Hall, Harlow.

Chapter 4

The market research industry

Topic list

1 The stages of the market research process
2 The nature and structure of the market research industry
3 Selecting a market research supplier
4 Ethical and social responsibilities

Introduction

The remainder of this book is more or less focused on **marketing research**. We refer to 'market research' in some of the section headings in this chapter, but that is just because the syllabus does this.

In this chapter we are taking a high level view, looking at the **overall process** and the **key players** in the marketing research market. Most organisations will employ an agency to carry out research because it is too expensive to maintain an in-house department, but the marketing department will still need someone familiar with marketing research to liaise with the agency or agencies that are actually doing the research.

We'll be looking at the matters that an organisation will take into account when **selecting an agency** to carry out its research.

Last, but by no means least there is the very important matter of the **responsibilities** that a researcher has towards respondents (which is likely to be governed by **data protection** legislation) and towards clients. Many of the issues are anticipated in the ICC/ESOMAR **code of conduct** for professional market researchers: the rules are reproduced in full at the end of the chapter. These issues have a bearing on the previous chapter, too, especially with regard to maintaining the **distinction** between **marketing research** and **direct marketing**.

Syllabus linked learning objectives

By the end of the chapter you will be able to:

Learning objectives	Syllabus link
1 Explain the stages of the market research process	3.2
2 Discuss the nature and structure of the market research industry	3.1
3 Identify different types of research agency	3.2
4 Explain the criteria for selecting a market research supplier	3.3
5 Discuss how to liaise with agencies	3.4
6 Evaluate the ethical and social responsibilities inherent in marketing research	3.6

1 The stages of the market research process

KEY CONCEPT

concept

Although you will see variations there is general agreement that the marketing research process involves the following stages:

- **Definition**: identify and define the opportunity or threat
- **Objectives**: determine precisely what you need to know to deal with the opportunity or threat
- **Design** the research and the methods to be used (exploratory, descriptive, causal)
- **Collect** the data
- **Analyse** the data
- **Report** on the findings

[handwritten annotation: are communication channels and opp + awo a threat if competitors do it better.]

If you read other books on marketing research you will find many slight variations on the suggested 'stages' of the market research process, partly depending on whether the book is written from the point of view of a client or a market research agency. There is fairly general agreement, however, that the process will entail the following stages, in this order (the process spells **DODCAR**, if you like mnemonics!).

Stage 1. **Definition**: identify and define the **opportunity or threat**

Stage 2. **Objectives**: determine precisely what you need to know to deal with the opportunity or threat

Stage 3. **Design** the research and the methods to be used

Stage 4. **Collect** the data

Stage 5. **Analyse** the data

Stage 6. **Report** on the findings

Where an organisation is using an agency or agencies to do the research it will send out a **research brief** at the end of Stage 2 and the various agencies that are asked to tender for the work will then submit **research proposals** (in outline, at least) covering Stage 3, explaining how they would do the work and why they should be chosen. Research proposals are discussed at more length in the next chapter.

The organisation will **select its preferred supplier(s)** based on the content and quality of their proposals (and on other factors such as cost, of course) and then Stage 3 will be done in detail.

How long the overall process takes really depends on the nature of the problem under investigation. Longitudinal studies for example can take several years to collect the data. The majority of research projects however are planned and completed within six months. Hague et al. (2004) summarised a general view of the typical duration of ad hoc research projects and the individuals who tend to be involved in the process, the table below is adapted from this summary.

What happens	Who is responsible	How long does it take
Idea generation – What is the problem to be investigated?	Organisations manager (client)	Days, a week, possibly a month
Internal debate / discussions- Further clarification of research problem	Client manager/ brand manager/ and internal market research manager (if there is one) and department / group heads or directors	A week or more
External debate and refinement of the research problem and research design	Client approaches agency to suggest a solution	One to two weeks
Data collection tool design and Information collection	Research agency	Four to twelve weeks

1.1 Stage 1: Identify and define the opportunity or threat

We've phrased this so that it reminds you of SWOT analysis, since the identification of a need for market research will usually arise from strategic and marketing planning processes and reviews.

(a) An **opportunity** is something that occurs in the organisation's environment that could be advantageous – a **change in the law**, say, or a **new technology** that could be exploited

(b) A **threat** is an environmental development that could create problems and stop the organisation achieving its objectives – a **new competitor**, perhaps, or an adverse change in **buying behaviour**.

In either case the organisation will **want to know more**. How can it best take advantage? What action is most likely to stave off or reverse the problem? The answers will depend on **how the market reacts** to different possible solutions, and the organisation can be much more sure about this if it conducts **research**.

Bear in mind that marketing research, however well organised, is not a substitute for decision making. It can help to reduce the risks, but it will not make the decision. Professional marketing depends partially on sound judgement and reliable information, but it also needs flair and creativity.

[handwritten note in left margin: Do we need to include what the identified opps or threat are in our proposals.]

1.2 Stage 2: Determine the objectives of the research

The objectives should set out the precise information needed, as clearly as possible: it is very wasteful of time and money to collect answers to questions that did not need to be asked. Ideally objectives should be SMART (specific, measurable, actionable, reasonable, timescaled). The objectives should relate only to the problem or opportunity.

Marketing research can sometimes be a waste of effort and resources.

(a) The research undertaken may be designed without reference to the decisions that will depend on, or be strongly influenced by, the results of the research.

(b) The research results may be ignored, misused, misunderstood, or misinterpreted. Sometimes this happens accidentally; more often it is deliberate because the results do not fit in with established beliefs.

(c) The research is poorly designed or carried out.

(d) The results of the research are themselves inconclusive, giving rise to different opinions about what the research signifies. *[handwritten: must not be inconclusive]*

[handwritten note in left margin: so need to know these for my essay]

With issues like this in mind Wilson (2006) suggests **early consultation and involvement** of all the parties that will be involved in putting into action the decisions taken as a result of the proposed research, for example by setting up a project team. This has the advantage that those closest to the project will probably have the best idea of what **knowledge** the organisation **already possesses**, and does not need to be researched. It also means that the questions that **need** to be answered are more likely to get asked.

Establishing clear research objectives is actually the key to a good piece of research. As such, these will be covered again in detail in Chapter 5.

[handwritten note in left margin: make reference to the project team in research]

ACTIVITY 1   application

Your company manufactures cruelty-free bath products for a number of supermarket chains. You have been given responsibility for finding out about the market for a new line of cruelty-free cosmetics. List the likely research objectives.

Other matters that would be considered at this stage would be the available **budget** and the **timescale** for the work, and perhaps there would be outline thoughts about the **methods** to be used (for instance the scale of the research and the segments of the market to be included). All of this information, together with the requirements for the final **report**, would be included in the **research brief** (see the next chapter) if the work was now to be put out to tender.

[handwritten note in left margin: Factors for the brief BUT make reference to them]

1.3 Stage 3: Design the research and the methods to be used

The **category** of research must first be decided upon: the methods used will depend on that. Research may be **exploratory**, **descriptive** or **causal**.

1.3.1 Exploratory research

As the name suggests, **exploratory** research tends to **break new ground**. For instance if your organisation has a **completely new idea** for a product or service which consumers have never been offered before then exploratory research will be most appropriate in the first instance.

(a)   Potential consumers may be totally uninterested, in which case exploratory research will quickly show that it is best to **abandon the idea** before any more money is spent on developing it.

(b)   Consumers **may not understand** how the offer could benefit them, in which case exploratory research would show that it may be worth simplifying the product and introducing it to them in a different way, with different promotional techniques and messages.

(c)   Consumers may not have responded because the **research methods used** were not appropriate, or because the wrong consumer group was chosen: exploratory research can help to define how more detailed research should be carried out.

Exploratory research may therefore be a **preliminary** to more detailed development of marketing ideas or a more detailed research project. It may even lead to abandonment of a product idea.

Research **methods** should involve as **little cost** and take as **little time** as possible. If use can be made of **existing research** by others then that is certainly desirable, as are methods that are not too labour and cost intensive such as **telephone** research or limited **Internet surveys**. (Research methods are covered in depth later in this book.)

1.3.2 Descriptive research

Descriptive research aims to describe what is happening now (a single snapshot) or what has happened over a limited period of time (several snapshots).

(a)   Now (a **'cross-sectional study'**): 'At present 45% of the target market are aware of our product whereas 95% are aware of Competitor A's product'.

(b)   Over time (a **'longitudinal study'**): 'During the period of the in-store promotion (February to April) awareness of our product rose from 45% to 73%'.

In other words descriptive research is useful for answering 'where are we now?' questions, and it can also be used to summarise how things have changed over a period in time. Published market research reports are examples of descriptive research: if you subscribe today you will find out 'where you were' when the report was last published, and if you wait a while for the next edition you will find out how you have progressed.

The main problem (for researchers) with longitudinal descriptive research is to ensure that their respondents are either the same people each time or, if that is not possible, that answers from very similar respondents are aggregated. Research **methods** are likely to include **telephone** research, with the consumer's agreement, and specially invited **panels** of respondents.

1.3.3 Causal research

Although descriptive research is very common and is much used it may not really tell us the **cause** of the event or behaviour it describes. To paraphrase Wilson, virtually all marketing research projects fall somewhere along a continuum between purely **descriptive** and purely **causal**.

For example, the descriptive result '*During the period of the in-store promotion (February to April) awareness of our product rose from 45% to 73%*' appears to suggest a reason for the change, but the only thing we know for certain is that two to three months have gone by. The change may be little or nothing to do with the in-store promotion. It may be due to a completely random factor such as temporary unavailability of a competitor's product, or uncontrolled and unmeasured actions taken by in-store staff, or to other promotional efforts such as TV ads.

The relationship between variables like this is not formally taken into account in descriptive research. **Causal** research attempts to identify and establish the relationship between all the variables, and determine whether one variable influences the value of others. **Experimental** research can be carried out, where one variable is deliberately changed to see the effect if any on other variables. The most obvious example is to see if lowering the price causes sales to rise.

Research **methods** might be similar to those for longitudinal descriptive research (panels of consumers for instance), but the information they are asked to provide will be more extensive and the time span may be longer. In particular the researcher will need to consider the **sampling** method and parameters (how many people and of what type), where the people can be found, and the means of obtaining information (**interviews**, **questionnaires** etc).

1.4 Stage 4: Collect the data

Data can be collected from either primary or secondary data sources. We will look at data collection in much more detail in Part D.

(a)   **Secondary data** is data collected for another purpose not specifically related to the proposed research, for instance all the **internal** information in the company's marketing information systems and databases, or information such as **published research** reports, **government** information, **newspapers** and trade journals.

(b)   **Primary data** is information **collected specifically for the study** under consideration. Primary data may be **quantitative** (statistics), **qualitative** (attitudes etc) or **observational** videos of people browsing in a store, for instance).

1.5 Stage 5: Analyse the data

This stage will involve getting the data into analysable form by entering it into a computer and using statistics (for quantitative data) and other means of analysis and summary (qualitative data) to find out what it reveals.

ASSIGNMENT TIP   concept

You are not required to analyse research data within this syllabus .

1.6 Stage 6: Report on the findings

The final report is likely to take the form of a PowerPoint type **presentation** given to an audience of interested parties and a detailed **written report** explaining and summarising the findings, with appendices of figures and tables. Reporting data is covered in Chapter 11 of this book.

2   The nature and structure of the market research industry

The UK market research industry was worth £1.353bn in 2007 according to the Market Research Society. ESOMAR's latest Global Market Research 2007 reported the total market for market research worldwide as US$24.6 billion. Europe accounted for 43 per cent of the total world market, and North America 36 per cent (MRS, 2008a).

The MRS publication 'Research' ran a piece in February 2008 dedicated to interviewing eight senior executives within the market research industry. When responding to questions about how the research industry is likely to develop and the challenges the industry will face in meeting clients needs, several themes emerged. The ability to provide faster, **more accurate 'insight'** as opposed to simple information was a key theme. The ability for research agencies to take on a **value added** solution focussed consultancy role rather than providing basic pieces of ad hoc information was regarded as highly important. The need to incorporate research with a **global perspective** whilst retaining local details and maintaining a consistent quality of research was also viewed as necessary. The **growth in online, digital and social networking research** was highlighted as a further key area where researchers should continue to develop expertise. (Doherty, 2008)

Market research suppliers differ according to whether they are in-house (within the organisation) or external suppliers. The diagram below which has been adapted from Malhotra (2004) depicts the industry structure.

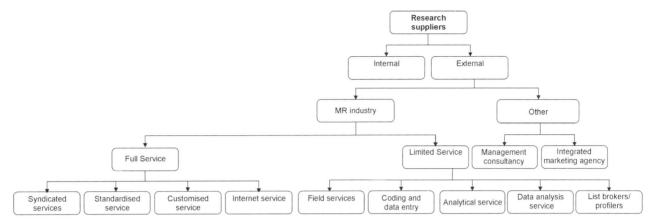

Market Research Suppliers

concept

Some larger organisations have their own marketing research (or 'customer insight') departments, but for most this would be too expensive.

2.1 Internal marketing research departments

Research may be carried out in-house or using **external specialists.** The decision of whether of plan and carry out research in-house, or use management consultants or a specialist research agency, depends on several factors.

External agencies offer several benefits:

- **Trained and experienced** staff, who can design appropriate programmes
- **Objectivity**, which may produce a clearer view of the questions to be asked
- **Security** and confidentiality: screened questioners, and respondent anonymity
- **Cost-effectiveness**, where the above are critical to the research's effectiveness

Do-it-yourself research often makes sense too:

- Where **data is readily available** to in-house staff
- Where in-house staff **understand** the nature of the problem and target audience
- Where the **budget is very limited**
- Where the **confidentiality** of the research is critical

If a consultancy is used, they will need to be provided with a detailed written brief

Need to keep these things in mind when writing my proposal.

- The **research problem** to which an answer is required
- The **intended use** of the data collected
- The **budgetary** constraints
- Any **background information** which will put the problem in context

Most organisations will have somebody who is responsible for marketing research, even if that simply means liaising with external agencies who actually carry out the work.

Larger organisations that have a regular need for marketing research information (particularly FMCG organisations) are likely to set up their own **marketing research department**.

MARKETING AT WORK

application

Catalyst, the left-wing think tank, established its own pool of freelance research assistants, reflecting the growing number of policy areas that it covers (such as housing, transport and regional policy). This will enable it to start work on projects when they arrive at short notice, assisting it with its purpose of promoting 'policies for the redistribution of wealth, power and opportunity'.

(www.research-live.com, accessed 18th March 2008)

2.2 Specialist agencies

KEY CONCEPT

concept

Agencies include **specialist agencies** of various kinds (field agencies, data analysis agencies and so on), syndicated research agencies, list brokers, profilers, full service agencies and independent consultants.

As the name implies a specialist agency specialises in a particular type of work.

(a) Some agencies specialise in particular **markets** or market **sectors** or **regions**

(b) Others specialise in a particular **research services** such as questionnaire design, or collection and analysis of qualitative information.

(c) **Field agencies** have specialised skills in **conducting** personal or telephone interviews and **administering** postal or e-mail surveys.

(d) **Data analysis agencies** can be employed to code up, read in or input data collected (in questionnaires, say, or perhaps recorded in personal interviews) and analyse it using state-of-the-art hardware (for instance highly accurate scanners) and software (for instance highly specialised statistical packages).

(e) There are numerous **independent consultants** who will undertake a variety of tasks, usually on a **smaller scale**. Such people are typically ex-employees of larger research organisations or have gained their expertise in related disciplines such as IT or retail.

It is a useful exercise to log onto the MRS's website and to look at the Research Buyers Guide. This will give you links to a wide range of research specialist agencies. Look at their websites and become familiar with the types of services they offer.

Is there any syndicated research available for my problem?

2.3 Syndicated research agencies

A syndicated service is one that is **not conducted for any specific client**. Regular research is conducted into areas that the agency knows for certain many organisations will be interested in (for instance newspaper and magazine readership) and is then sold to anyone willing to pay the price.

MARKETING AT WORK

application

Well-known examples of syndicated research agencies include **Datamonitor** (with products like MarketWatch: Drinks and MarketWatch: Food), and **Mintel** (www.mintel.co.uk) which has a huge number of regularly updated reports available on a subscription basis (eg *Agricultural Machinery*, *Nail Color and Care*, *Disposable Nappies and Baby Wipes*, and hundreds of others). See *http:reportsmintel.com*

2.4 List brokers

A list broker **creates or acquires lists** of potential consumers **for the purpose of selling them on** to companies who are interested. Lists may be created from publicly available sources like the telephone book, yellow pages or the electoral roll but they will usually be **organised** for convenience, presented in **formats** that can be easily incorporated into client systems, and **checked** for accuracy and up-to-date-ness. The client could possibly do this in-house, but it would be very **time-consuming**. 'Names' are typically sold by the thousand at 10p to 20p each – it would almost certainly be more **expensive** for the client to find and record the information without help.

Lists that have arisen as a result of some other exercise such as responses to mailshots or entry into a 'free' draw may also be **acquired** by list brokers. You have probably noticed that you are often asked whether you object to your details being given to **third parties** when you enter into correspondence with an organisation, or even just register on a website. Now you know that those third parties are likely to be list brokers!

2.5 Profilers

Profiling is something that we could then do with our info.

We encountered the best-known UK profiler, CACI (www.caci.co.uk) with products like ACORN, in the previous chapter. A profiler is able to take an organisation's database and **superimpose profiling information** (demographics, lifestyle and life stage information) on the basis of post codes. This allows the organisation's database to be segmented according to the criteria that are most appropriate to that organisation.

A profiler may also have access to other lists and be able to offer these to its clients, much like a list broker, except that the profiler has closer knowledge of the characteristics of the clients' existing customers and so the list may have more appropriate prospects.

2.6 Full service agencies

As the name implies a full service agency **offers all of the above services** and so will be able to conduct a research project from start to finish. Well-known international examples are **BMRB** (www.bmrb.co.uk), **Taylor Nelson Sofres** (www.tns-global.com) and **Ipsos** (www.ipsos.com).

In addition many full service **adverting agencies** offer marketing research services, as do firms of **management consultants** like McKinsey (www.mckinsey.com).

  ACTIVITY 2 application

An excellent way to get a flavour of the marketing research industry is to visit the websites mentioned above and click on 'Services' (or 'Solutions', or whatever) to see the range of work carried out by different types of organisation. Don't restrict your web survey to large multinational companies. See if you can find links to the websites of smaller organisations in your own country (try a directory such as *www.imriresearch.com*.) The MRS Researchers Buyers Guide will provide a number of agencies for you to look at. The Research Buyers Guide can be accessed via the MRS website. (We have previously highlighted this as a wider reading link but have duplicated it here as an activity because we feel it is essential for you to do!

2.7 Professional bodies

  KEY CONCEPT concept

The main professional bodies are the **Marketing Research Society** and **ESOMAR**.

Apart from the CIM, many of whose members are involved in marketing research in some capacity, most countries have an association of some sort for market researchers. The largest is the **Market Research Society** (www.marketresearch.org.uk) based in the UK, but with international membership.

Likewise the **World Association of Opinion and Marketing Research Professionals** (**ESOMAR**: the 'E' originally stood for European) (www.esomar.org) has members all over the world. MRS works closely with the ESOMAR in some respects: for instance later in this chapter we will look at the joint ESOMAR Code of Practice for research workers, to which the MRS subscribes.

3 Selecting a market research supplier

KEY CONCEPT

concept

Selecting an agency will involve considerations such as the agency's **previous experience** and **expertise** in the area of research, and the **geographical area** to be covered.

Very few organisations can shoulder the cost of a large full-time staff of marketing research workers, especially a 'field force' of researchers spread around the country, or around every country in which the organisation does business.

3.1 Choosing and using consultants

Choosing the right agency or consultant to work with is a key element in a successful working relationship. The external expert must become a trusted part of the team.

It is equally important that the market researcher has the specialist knowledge and research service capabilities needed by the organisation. In the UK you would expect a research organisation to be associated to the professional body, the Market Research Society, and for those working on the account to have relevant qualifications.

It helps if the agency has some knowledge of the market or business in which the company operates. Therefore, it may be worthwhile to develop a long-standing relationship with the research organisation, because their understanding of the company's business and the marketplace will develop over time.

3.2 External agencies versus in-house programmes

There are a number of advantages and disadvantages to each alternative.

(a) **Using an external agency**

　(i)　**Advantages**

　　　(1)　External agencies **specialising** in research will have the necessary expertise in marketing research techniques. This should allow them to develop a cost-effective research programme to a **tighter timescale**.

　　　(2)　Skills in **monitoring and interpreting data** will allow the programme to be reviewed and modified as required.

　　　(3)　Nationwide or global agencies will be able to offer much **broader geographical coverage**.

　　　(4)　An external agency can provide an **objective input** without the bias which often results from a dependence on internal resources.

　　　(5)　**Costs** can be determined from the outset, allowing better **budgetary control**.

　　　(6)　When conducting **confidential research** into sensitive area, there is less risk of information being 'leaked' to competitors.

    (ii)   **Disadvantage**

        Agency knowledge of the industry will be limited: a serious drawback if the agency needs a disproportionate amount of time to familiarise itself with the sector.

(b)   **In-house programme**

    (i)   **Advantages**

        (1)   **Costs can be absorbed** into existing departmental overheads.

        (2)   It can **broaden the experience** and skills of existing staff.

        (3)   It might promote a **team spirit** and encourage a 'results-oriented' approach.

    (ii)   **Disadvantages**

        (1)   There is a danger of **overstretching current resources** and adversely affecting other projects.

        (2)   There is a risk of developing an **inappropriate programme**, yielding insufficient or poor quality data with inadequate analysis and control.

        (3)   If additional **training or recruitment** is required this could prove expensive and time consuming.

        (4)   **Bias** could result from using staff with pre-conceived views.

        (5)   **Company politics** may influence the results.

        (6)   Considerable **computing resources** with appropriate software packages would be required to analyse the data.

        (7)   There may be a lack of **appropriate facilities**. For example, focus group research is often conducted off premises during evenings or weekends.

In view of the shortcomings of a purely in-house or external agency approach, a **combination** of the two might be more appropriate. For example, it might be deemed preferable to design the programme in-house but contract out certain aspects.

3.3 Tenders and beauty parades

The selection process will generally involve the organisation sending out its research brief to a number of agencies and inviting each to submit a research proposal (see the next chapter). It is common for the agencies to give an oral presentation of their case: this part of the procedure is known as a 'beauty parade'.

3.4 The final selection of an agency

The MRS (2008 b) suggest that the following questions are used when deciding between research agencies:

- Which company seems to have understood what you need?

- Which company has perhaps added to your thinking by coming up with ideas of their own?

- Does the proposed research design seem to match your expectations and, if not, are convincing alternatives presented and explained?

- Does the company have relevant experience, either in terms of methodology and/or the subject of your project?

- Assuming that they have understood your needs, do they seem to be offering value for money?

- Which company's work 'feels right'? From your contacts with the agency and from the documents it has produced for you, do you think you trust the organisation and can work with its staff?

3.5 Liaising with agencies

The MRS recommend that only a few (around 4) agencies are approached and asked to submit a proposal. This is because of the cost and time that it takes to put together research proposals. Keegan (2005) argued that many clients wasted the time of agencies because they did not act fairly when inviting agencies to pitch. She suggested that:

- Agencies should be advised if they are not the only ones who have been invited to pitch

- Clients should enable agencies the opportunity for a face to face meeting to ensure a proper briefing

- Researchers should be confident enough to question clients objectives and to refine them (covered in chapter 5 further) however if this turns into extensive consultancy work the agency should be compensated for their time.

Although it is not written solely from a research agency perspective the Best Practice Guidelines titled , 'Finding an Agency' has been produced by the five key trade and consultative bodies for the advertising, marketing and public relations industries: DMA, IPA, ISBA, MCCA and PRCA. You can access this document via any of their websites. The DMS's website is possibly the easiest to find the guide and so you may wish to try www.dma.org.uk/content/Pro-BestPractice.asp.

On a day to day basis there are a number of issues that can be agreed in order to help to ensure that working relationships remain healthy:

(a) Implement a Service Level Agreement which outlines the roles and responsibilities of the client and the agency, reporting procedures and expectations of both parties eg if the client would like a weekly update then this should be stipulated in the agreement, if the agency would like feedback on research design issues within a certain period.

(b) The use of periodic reviews of the research process and interim results in order to amend the research design, agree alternative courses of action or abort the project where necessary.

(c) Ensure that there is one key contact within both the agency and the client so that parties are not inundated by many individuals communicating different messages.

(d) If any part of the project is to be outsourced eg data collection, this should be clear at the research tender stage.

(e) Clarity over any changes in the research design as the project progresses should be formally agreed by both parties to avoid any surprises once the final research findings are presented (periodic reviews will avoid this issue).

4 Ethical and social responsibilities

Ethical issues relating to working relationships between clients and agencies because there is an inherent need for;

- **Goodwill** – on the part of the respondents volunteering information to the agency and client

- **Trust** – on the part of the client trusting the agency to conduct professionally and provide accurate information and the agency trusting the client to be open and provide sufficient background and supporting information

- **Professionalism** – on the part of both the agency and the client should be maintained at all times in order to maintain credibility.

- **Confidentiality** – investigating sensitive information about markets and competitive environments will require confidentiality agreements on the part of agencies. Agencies who disclose information to third parties without the prior consent of their clients risk losing valuable future business.

(Wilson, 2006)

 ASSESSMENT TIP

concept

Ethical topics arose in the December 2008 / March 2009 assignment – the ethics of marketing research and code of conduct issues.

Similar needs also exist for respondents because they expect that their information is kept confidential and that they will not become victims of Sugging (sales in the guise of research), Frugging (fund raising in the guise of research) or Data mugging (their details just being sold to populate a range of databases owned and used by unknown parties).

Marketing research aims to collect data about people. It could not take place at all if people were not willing to provide data, and that means that it is as much in the interests of the marketing research industry as it is of respondents for researchers to behave responsibly with the information collected.

4.1 Data protection

KEY CONCEPT

concept

Marketing researchers depend on the trust of their respondents. Most developed countries have **specific legislation** to **protect the privacy of individuals**. In the UK there is the Data Protection Act 1998 which establishes eight data protection principles.

Most developed countries have specific legislation to protect the **privacy of individuals**. Many people feel unhappy about their personal details being retained by commercial organisations. Here are some of the concerns that people have.

(a)   **Incorrect details** may be entered, causing anything from minor irritation to significant financial problems.

(b)   A list or database may be **sold** to other organisations, who then try to sell various goods and services to the people on it.

(c)   'Personalised' mailings may be inappropriate – they might be generated for people who have died, for instance.

4.1.1 The Data Protection Act 1998

Data protection legislation was introduced in the UK in the early 1980s to try to prevent some of these abuses. The latest version is the **Data Protection Act 1998**.

The Act is concerned with **'personal data'**, which is information about **living, identifiable individuals**. This can be as little as a name and address: it need not be particularly sensitive information. If it is sensitive (explained later) then extra care is needed.

The Act gives individuals (**data subjects**) certain rights and it requires those who record and use personal information (**data controllers**) to be open about their use of that information and to follow 'sound and proper practices' (the Data Protection Principles).

The Information Commissioner's Office has a website which explains the Data Protection Act, provides examples of legal outcomes from procedings and user-friendly fact sheets explaining the principles in different contexts. There are a couple of 'Good Practice Note' publications which relate to marketing and research topics. Go to www.ico.gov.uk for more information. ■

4.1.2 The eight data protection principles

Data must be:

- Fairly and lawfully processed
- Processed for limited purposes
- Adequate, relevant and not excessive
- Accurate
- Not kept longer than necessary
- Processed in accordance with individual's rights
- Secure
- Not transferred to countries that do not have adequate data protection laws

If your organisation holds personal information about living individuals on computer or has such information processed on computer by others (for example, a data analysis or database agency) your organisation probably needs to 'notify' under the Data Protection Act 1998.

'Notify' means that the organisation has to complete a form about the data it holds and how it is used and send it, with an annual registration fee, to the office of the Information Commissioner.

The Data Protection Act 1998 also covers some records held in **paper** form. These do not need to be notified to the Commissioner, but they should also be handled in accordance with the data protection principles. A set of **index cards** for a personnel system is a typical example of paper records that fall under the Data Protection Act 1998.

4.1.3 Fair processing for limited purposes

These two principles mean that when an organisation collects information from individuals it should be **honest and open** about why it wants the information and it should have a **legitimate reason** for processing the data. For instance organisations should explain:

- who they are
- what they intend to use the information for
- who, if anybody, they intend to give the personal data to.

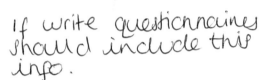
If write questionnaires should include this info.

4.1.4 Adequate, relevant and not excessive; accurate and no longer than necessary

Organisations should hold **neither too much nor too little** data about the individuals in their list. For instance, many companies collect date of birth or age range information from their customers, but in many cases all they actually need to know is that they are over eighteen.

Personal data should be **accurate and up-to-date** as far as possible. However, if an individual provides inaccurate information (for example lies about their age) the organisation would not normally be held to account for this.

There are only exceptional circumstances where personal data should be kept indefinitely. Data should be **removed when it is no longer required** for audit purposes or when a customer ceases to do business with you.

4.1.5 The rights of data subjects

Individuals have various rights including the following.

- The right to **be informed** of all the information held about them by an organisation
- The right to **prevent** the processing of their data for the purposes of direct marketing
- The right to **compensation** if they can show that they have been caused damage by any contravention of the Act
- The right to have any inaccurate data about them **removed** or corrected

need to include details on contact info for organisation so this is possible.

Organisations have obligations if they receive a **written request** from an individual asking to see what data it holds about them, or to obtain a copy of it, or to be given an explanation of what it is used for, or who it is given to. The organisation must deal with the request promptly, and in any case within 40 days. The organisation is entitled, if it wishes, to ask for a fee of not more than £10 in which case the 40 days does not begin until this is received.

4.1.6 Security

Organisations should make sure that they provide **adequate security** for the data, taking into account the nature of the data, and the possible harm to the individual that could arise if the data is disclosed or lost.

(a) Measures to ensure that **access** to computer records **by staff** is authorised (for instance a system of passwords).

(b) Measures to control **access** to records by **people other than staff**. For instance care should be taken over the siting of computers to prevent casual callers to the organisation's premises being able to read personal data on screen. Also there should be procedures to verify the identity of callers (especially telephone callers) seeking information about an individual.

(c) Measures to prevent of the **accidental loss or theft** of personal data, for example backups and fire precautions.

4.1.7 Overseas transfers

If an organisation wishes to transfer personal data to a country **outside the European Economic Area (EEA)** it will either need to ensure there is adequate protection (eg a Data Protection Act) for the data in the receiving country, or obtain the consent of the individual.

All countries in the EEA already have suitable protection.

4.1.8 Sensitive data

The Act defines eight categories of sensitive personal data. If an organisation holds personal data falling into these categories it is likely that it will **need the explicit consent** of the individual concerned. It will also need to ensure that its security is adequate for the protection of sensitive data.

Here are the eight categories.

- The racial or ethnic origin of data subjects
- Their political opinions
- Their religious beliefs or other beliefs of a similar nature
- Whether they are a member of a trade union
- Their physical or mental health or condition
- Their sexual life
- The commission or alleged commission by them of any offence
- Any details of court proceedings or sentences against them

4.1.9 Enforcement

If an organisation is breaching the principles of the Act, the Commissioner has various powers to force it to comply, including issuing an enforcement notice, and the power to enter and search their premises, and examine equipment and documents. It is an offence to obstruct the Commissioner, and there are also fines and criminal penalties for holding data without being registered; for failing to comply with an enforcement notice; and for unauthorised disclosure of personal data.

4.2 Professional codes of practice

 KEY CONCEPT  *State that research conducted is in line with this code.* concept

The ICC/ESOMAR have issued a **code of practice** for marketing research professionals. Broadly, this covers The Rights of Respondents, The Professional Responsibilities of Researchers, and Mutual Rights and Responsibilities of Researchers and Clients.

In addition to adhering to legislation marketing researchers should act in the interests of the marketing research profession, and to help them do so a number of codes of practice have been developed by the various professional bodies. These do **not have legal status**, but breaches may result in **disciplinary action** by the professional body, including barring the transgressor from membership of the body.

 The best known code is the ESOMAR code, the most important part of which is reproduced in full below with the permission of ESOMAR. The full document can be downloaded from the organisation's website: www.esomar.org. ∎

The MRS comply with the ESOMAR code but if you would like to specifically view the MRS code it is available in full from www.MRS.org.uk.

4.3 ICC/ESOMAR code of marketing and social research practice

General

B1 Marketing research must always be carried out objectively and in accordance with established scientific principles.

B2 Marketing research must always conform to the national and international legislation which applies in those countries involved in a given research project.

The Rights of Respondents

B3 Respondents' co-operation in a marketing research project is entirely voluntary at all stages. They must not be misled when being asked for co-operation.

B4 Respondents' anonymity must be strictly preserved. If the respondent on request from the Researcher has given permission for data to be passed on in a form which allows that respondent to be identified personally:

(a) the Respondent must first have been told to whom the information would be supplied and the purposes for which it will be used, and also

(b) Researcher must ensure that the information will not be used for any non-research purpose and that the recipient of the information has agreed to conform to the requirements of the Code.

B5 The Researcher must take all reasonable precautions to ensure that Respondents are in no way directly harmed or adversely affected as a result of their participation in a marketing research project.

B6 The Researcher must take special care when interviewing children and young people. The informed consent of the parent or responsible adult must first be obtained for interviews with children.

B7 Respondents must be told (normally at the beginning of the interview) if observation techniques or recording equipment are used, except where these are used in a public place. If a respondent so wishes, the record or relevant section of it must be destroyed or deleted. Respondents' anonymity must not be infringed by the use of such methods.

B8 Respondents must be enabled to check without difficulty the identity and bona fides of the Researcher.

The Professional Responsibilities of Researchers

B9 Researchers must not, whether knowingly or negligently, act in any way which could bring discredit on the marketing research profession or lead to a loss of public confidence in it.

B10 Researchers must not make false claims about their skills and experience or about those of their organisation.

B11 Researchers must not unjustifiably criticise or disparage other Researchers.

B12 Researchers must always strive to design research which is cost-efficient and of adequate quality, and then to carry this out to the specification agreed with the Client.

B13 Researchers must ensure the security of all research records in their possession.

B14 Researchers must not knowingly allow the dissemination of conclusions from a marketing research project which are not adequately supported by the data. They must always be prepared to make available the technical information necessary to assess the validity of any published findings.

B15 When acting in their capacity as Researchers the latter must not undertake any non-research activities, for example database marketing involving data about individuals which will be used for direct marketing and promotional activities. Any such non-research activities must always, in the way they are organised and carried out, be clearly differentiated from marketing research activities.

Mutual Rights and Responsibilities of Researchers and Clients

B16 These rights and responsibilities will normally be governed by a written Contract between the Researcher and the Client. The parties may amend the provisions of rules B19– B23 below if they have agreed this in writing beforehand; but the other requirements of this Code may not be altered in this way. Marketing research must also always be conducted according to the principles of fair competition, as generally understood and accepted.

B17 The Researcher must inform the Client if the work to be carried out for that Client is to be combined or syndicated in the same project with work for other Clients but must not disclose the identity of such clients without their permission.

B18   The Researcher must inform the Client as soon as possible in advance when any part of the work for that Client is to be subcontracted outside the Researcher's own organisation (including the use of any outside consultants). On request the Client must be told the identity of any such subcontractor.

B19   The Client does not have the right, without prior agreement between the parties involved, to exclusive use of the Researcher's services or those of his organisation, whether in whole or in part. In carrying out work for different clients, however, the Researcher must endeavour to avoid possible clashes of interest between the services provided to those clients.

B20   The following Records remain the property of the Client and must not be disclosed by the Researcher to any third party without the Client's permission:

(a) marketing research briefs, specifications and other information provided by the Client;

(b) research data and findings from a marketing research project (except in the case of syndicated or multi-client projects or services where the same data are available to more than one client).

The Client has, however, no right to know the names or addresses of Respondents unless the latter's explicit permission for this has first been obtained by the Researcher (this particular requirement cannot be altered under Rule B16).

B21   Unless it is specifically agreed to the contrary, the following Records remain the property of the Researcher:

(a) marketing research proposals and cost quotations (unless these have been paid for by the Client). They must not be disclosed by the Client to any third party, other than to a consultant working for the Client on that project (with the exception of any consultant working also for a competitor of the Researcher). In particular, they must not be used by the Client to influence research proposals or cost quotations from other Researchers.

(b) the contents of a report in the case of syndicated research and/or multi-client projects or services where the same data are available to more than one client and where it is clearly understood that the resulting reports are available for general purchase or subscription. The Client may not disclose the findings of such research to any third party (other than his own consultants and advisors for use in connection with his business) without the permission of the Researcher.

(c) all other research Records prepared by the Researcher (with the exception in the case of non-syndicated projects of the report to the Client, and also the research design and questionnaire where the costs of developing these are covered by the charges paid by the Client).

B22   The Researcher must conform to current agreed professional practice relating to the keeping of such records for an appropriate period of time after the end of the project. On request the Researcher must supply the Client with duplicate copies of such records provided that such duplicates do not breach anonymity and confidentiality requirements (Rule B4); that the request is made within the agreed time limit for keeping the Records; and that the Client pays the reasonable costs of providing the duplicates.

B23   The Researcher must not disclose the identity of the Client (provided there is no legal obligation to do so) or any confidential information about the latter's business, to any third party without the Client's permission.

B24   The Researcher must, on request, allow the Client to arrange for checks on the quality of fieldwork and data preparation provided that the Client pays any additional costs involved in this. Any such checks must conform to the requirements of Rule B4.

B25   The Researcher must provide the Client with all appropriate technical details of any research project carried out for that Client.

B26   When reporting on the results of a marketing research project the Researcher must make a clear distinction between the findings as such, the Researcher's interpretation of these and any recommendations based on them.

B27   Where any of the findings of a research project are published by the Client, the latter has a responsibility to ensure that these are not misleading. The Researcher must be consulted and agree in advance the form and content of publication, and must take action to correct any misleading statements about the research and its findings.

B28   Researchers must not allow their names to be used in connection with any research project as an assurance that the latter has been carried out in conformity with this Code unless they are confident that the project has in all respects met the Code's requirements.

B29   Researchers must ensure that Clients are aware of the existence of this Code and of the need to comply with its requirements.

- Although you will see variations there is general agreement that the marketing research process involves the following stages:

  - Definition: identify and define the opportunity or threat
  - Objectives: determine precisely what you need to know to deal with the opportunity or threat
  - Design the research and the methods to be used (exploratory, descriptive, causal)
  - Collect the data
  - Analyse the data
  - Report on the findings

- Some larger organisations have their own marketing research (or 'customer insight') departments, but for most this would be too expensive.

- Agencies include specialist agencies of various kinds (field agencies, data analysis agencies and so on), syndicated research agencies, list brokers, profilers, full service agencies and independent consultants.

- The main professional bodies are the Marketing Research Society and ESOMAR.

- Selecting an agency will involve considerations such as the agency's previous experience and expertise in the area of research, the geographical area to be covered.

- Marketing researchers depend on the trust of their respondents. Most developed countries have specific legislation to protect the privacy of individuals. In the UK there is the Data Protection Act 1998 which establishes eight data protection principles.

- The ICC/ESOMAR have issued a code of practice for marketing research professionals. Broadly, this covers The Rights of Respondents, The Professional Responsibilities of Researchers, and Mutual Rights and Responsibilities of Researchers and Clients.

Learning objectives	Covered
1 Explain the stages of the market research process	☑ Definition
	☑ Objectives
	☑ Design
	☑ Collect
	☑ Analyse
	☑ Report
2 Discuss the nature and structure of the market research industry	☑ In house vs agency
	☑ Agency type
	☑ MRS / ESOMAR
3 Identify different types of research agency	☑ MR industry vs consultancies
	☑ Full service vs specialist
4 Explain the criteria for selecting a market research supplier	☑ External vs in-house
	☑ Proposals, tender beauty parades
	☑ Final selection questions
5 Discuss how to liaise with agencies	☑ Service level agreements
	☑ Working procedures
6 Evaluate the ethical and social responsibilities inherent in marketing research	☑ Client-agency relationships
	☑ Data protection act
	☑ ESOMAR code of conduct

1 What does DODCAR stand for?

2 The most elaborate kind of research is Causal/Descriptive/Exploratory. Delete as appropriate.

3 What is syndicated research?

4 Full service agencies do not have specialist research skills. True or false? Explain your answer.

5 What are five disadvantages of in-house market research departments?

6 List the eight data protection principles.

7 The ICC/ESOMAR code of conduct sets out six rights of respondents. Summarise them.

8 Which of the following is a requirement of the ICC/ESOMAR code?

    A   The Client has the right to exclusive use of the Researcher's services
    B   Researchers must not make false claims about their skills and experience
    C   The Researcher must make a clear distinction between the findings and any recommendations based on them
    D   The Researcher may refuse to allow the Client to check the quality of fieldwork

1   We've not given you enough information to enable you to be too precise. You would have much more information in real life of course.

To collect information about the market for a new line of cruelty-free cosmetics (lipsticks, eyeshadow and so on) with a view to drawing up and implementing a marketing plan.

(a)   The size of market, value, number of items sold, number of customers

(b)   The leading companies and their respective market share

(c)   The breakdown of market by type of cosmetic (lipstick, eyeshadow etc)

(d)   Current consumer trends in buying cruelty-free cosmetics (price, colour and so on)

(e)   Consumer preferences in terms of packaging/presentation

(f)   The importance to consumers of having a choice of colours within the range

(g)   The influence on consumers of advertising and promotion that emphasises the cruelty-free nature of products.

Remember that objectives need to be SMART.

Research objectives	Discover re Action Programme above:
Specific	Size of market for *cruelty-free* cosmetics not cosmetics in general
Measurable	Respective market share in percentage terms of leading players
Actionable	Price range within which consumers will buy
Reasonable	A defined number of preferred colours
Timescaled	Information within 3 months so product can be marketed for Christmas

2   This is a hands-on exercise.

1   Definition, Objectives, Design, Collect, Analyse, Report. In other words the marketing research process.

2   Causal

3   Syndicated research is research undertaken on a regular basis, but not for any specific client. It is of sufficient interest to be saleable to many clients.

4   False, as a rule.

5   **Five from**

(1)   There is a danger of **overstretching current resources** and adversely affecting other projects.

(2)   There is a risk of developing an **inappropriate programme**, yielding insufficient or poor quality data with inadequate analysis and control.

(3)   If additional **training or recruitment** is required this could prove expensive and time consuming.

(4)   **Bias** could result from using staff with pre-conceived views.

(5)   **Company politics** may influence the results.

(6)   Considerable **computing resources** with appropriate software packages would be required to analyse the data.

6   Data must be:

- Fairly and lawfully processed
- Processed for limited purposes
- Adequate, relevant and not excessive
- Accurate
- Not kept longer than necessary
- Processed in accordance with individual's rights
- Secure
- Not transferred to countries that do not have adequate data protection laws

7
- Respondents' co-operation in a marketing research project is entirely voluntary
- Respondents' anonymity must be strictly preserved
- The Researcher must try to ensure that Respondents are not adversely affected as a result of taking part in research
- The Researcher must take special care when interviewing children and young people
- Respondents must be told if observation techniques or recording equipment are used
- Respondents must be enabled to check the identity and bona fides of the Researcher.

8   B and C are correct. (All the options are paraphrased to some extent.)

Doherty, C. (2008) '*Eight Leaders on Research*' Research, MRS, February 2008 Edition, p.28, London.

Hague, P. et al. (2004) *Market Research in Practice: A guide to the basics*, Kogan Page, London.

Keegan, S. (2005) '*Price of Pitching*' , discussion paper, Association of Qualitative Research, Cambs.

Malhotra, N. (2004) *Marketing Research: an applied orientation*, Pearson.

MRS (2008)a '*Media Information*' Available online from 'http://www.mrs.org.uk/media/qanda.htm [accessed 18.4.08]

MRS (2008)b '*A Newcomers Guide to Market and Social Research*' Available online from: http://www.mrs.org.uk/mrindustry/downloads/newcomers.pdf [Accessed 12.3.08].

Wilson, A. (2006) *Marketing Research An Integrated Approach*, 2nd Edition, Prentice Hall, Harlow.

Chapter 5

Information requirements, research projects, briefs and proposals

Topic list

Introduction

The bulk of this chapter sets marketing research in the context of typical **marketing decisions** and the sort of **information** that may be required to make them. For the most part we have used the familiar **4Ps** framework, since this will hopefully help you to relate marketing research to your studies for other marketing papers.

It is useful that you understand the differences between research contexts so you can apply a research design to your own situation within your assignment.

Two topics that are highly likely to feature in your assignment are: the structure and contents of a **research brief** and a **research proposal**. You probably won't actually be able to write a decent proposal as yet, at least not in any depth, because you need to read more about marketing research methodologies, and evaluation and reporting techniques. But once you have read the remainder of the book this chapter is a key place to return to with your assignment work in mind.

ACTIVITY 1

application

Since you know quite a lot about the 4Ps already, see if you can list the type of research information that might be sought under each of them.

Syllabus linked learning objectives

By the end of the chapter you will be able to:

Learning objectives	Syllabus link
1 Identify the purpose and components of a research brief	3.5
2 Explain the contents and purpose of a research proposal	3.5
3 Discuss the importance of clear research objectives	3.5
4 Identify different types of market research projects	3.5

1 The research brief

KEY CONCEPT

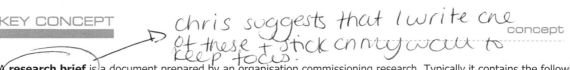

chris suggests that I write one of these + stick on my wall to keep focus.

concept

A **research brief** is a document prepared by an organisation commissioning research. Typically it contains the following sections: Background, Rationale, Budget, Timescale, Objectives, Methods and Reports. The budget would typically not be revealed to agencies.

The key to good research information, whether collected by an in-house section or an external agency, lies in the quality of the research brief. A research brief is **prepared by the organisation commissioning the research**.

Hague et al (2004) suggest using a series of questions as a framework in order to make sure a thorough brief is written. These are:

1   Why do this research?- what action will be taken when the research is completed?

2   What has caused this problem or led to this opportunity?

3   What is known about the area of research already? – is there any research that the organisation already has conducted or known secondary sources?

4   Who are the target groups for the research?

5   What specific information is needed from the research (eg market size, trends, buying behaviour, customers needs, segmentation)?

6   What is the proposed budget?

7   Are there any initial ideas for the research method?

8   Are there any reporting requirements?

9   When are the findings required?

(Hague, 2004)

ASSIGNMENT TIP

concept

Your assignment will assume that a brief has already been prepared by someone else within your organisation. It is however still important that you appreciate what is included.

The research brief will normally include the following sections.

(a)   **Background**. This covers relevant information about the company, its products and services, its market place.

(b)   **Rationale**. How the need for information arose and what the users intend to do with the information when they have it (what decisions will be taken).

(c)   **Budget**. In general the benefits of collecting information should be greater than the costs of collecting it, but benefits in particular are not always easy to quantify. In any case the budget may be limited by other organisational factors such as availability of cash or a head office allocation of, say, £5,000 per annum for marketing research purposes. Clearly this will affect the scale and type of information search that can be carried out. This item will probably not be revealed to external suppliers however: see below.

(d)   **Timescale**. Quite obviously, if the decisions have to be made by May then the information needs to be collected and analysed before then. Once again this will have an impact on the scale and type of information search that can be carried out.

(e) **Objectives**. The precise information needed, set out as clearly as possible. For instance 'To determine customer response to a price reduction of £250 in terms of repeat purchasing, word-of-mouth recommendations and willingness to purchase our other products and services'. The objectives should relate **only** to the rationale: it might be 'nice to know' what type of car customers drive, but if this will make no difference to the decisions that will be taken once the information has been collected, there is no need to know about customers' cars in the first place.

(f) **Methods**. This need only be an outline, setting out, for instance, the scale of the search, the mix of quantitative and qualitative information needed, the segments of the market to be included.

(g) **Reports**. How the final information should be presented. Considerations here might include style of reports, degree of summarisation, use of charts and other graphics, format for quantitative information (eg in Excel spreadsheets, for ease of further analysis).

According to Wilson (2006) 'The **budget** available is rarely included within the brief' and that is most probably true of briefs that are **sent out to marketing research suppliers**, who will hopefully return research proposals that meet the organisation's needs, not just as much research as they are prepared to do for the price. However, the organisation obviously needs to have a clear idea of how much it is willing to spend on research. Hague (2004) for example argues that many comprehensive plans are sent back to the drawing board because they are too expensive when agencies have no budget boundaries.

2 Research proposals

concept

Research proposals are prepared and submitted to the client by agencies who receive the brief. Typical contents are as follows: Background, Objectives, Approach and Method, Reports, Timing, Fees and expenses, Personal CVs, Relevant experience, Contractual details.

Research proposals are **prepared by research agencies** who have been sent the brief and asked to put in a bid to do the job.

In structure a research proposal is similar to the research brief, but it will be much more detailed in certain parts.

(a) **Background** and **rationale**. This sets out the agency's understanding of the client company, its products and services and its market place, an understanding of why the research is required and what decisions need to be made. (If they've misunderstood the situation it will be clear to the client at the outset!)

(b) **Objectives**. These will probably be much the same as those in the brief, although the agency's understanding of research techniques may have helped to define them more precisely still. We will look at these in more detail in the next section of this chapter.

(c) **Approach and Method**. How the agency proposes to carry out the research, what methods will be used, where the sample will be taken from.

(d) **Reports**. How the final information will be presented and whether interim reports will be made. Reporting is covered in Chapter 11.

(e) **Timing**: how long the research will take and how it will be broken down into separate stages if appropriate.

(f) **Fees and expenses**: this is self-explanatory

(g) **Personal CVs** of the main agency personnel who will be involved in the project.

(h) **Relevant experience/references:** the agency will wish to assure the client that it is capable of carrying out the research, so it will include information about similar projects undertaken in the past, and possibly reference details (previous clients who are willing to testify to the competency of the agency).

(i)   **Contractual details** will set out the agency's terms of trade and clarify matters about ownership of the data collected. See the relevant parts of the ESOMAR code of practice in the previous chapter for an indication of likely contents of this section.

2.1 The Research proposal in more detail

To help you better understand the research proposal, we will use a hypothetical case of a small chain of health spas who require research. Look for this example in Marketing at Work.

 ASSIGNMENT TIP   *format and presentation*

One of the key elements of your assignment will be to prepare a research proposal. You should therefore be fully prepared and ensure that you are highly familiar with the elements. You will need to come back to this part of the text on several occasions as you learn more about the process of research.

2.1.1 Background

(handwritten margin note: to brief background to clarify factors in which actor operates)

The background is an important section because here as a supplier of research the agency needs to demonstrate to the client that they have understood the company and their markets. Often agencies will conduct a some secondary research into the market to demonstrate that they are aware of the broader issues and have taken the time to research their potential client.

 ASSIGNMENT TIP   *format and presentation*

Within your assignment you need to take on the role of the research agency proposing a piece of research but for the organisation you work for or one that you are familiar with. It is essential that you write a comprehensive background because it is only from this that the examiner marking your work will be able to appreciate the nature of your organisation.

Make sure that you include:

(handwritten margin note: include)

The nature of the organisation – size, a brief historical background and any status within a group of companies

Products and services offered – market, competitors, threats, any specific issues of importance

Details of a specific division or department requesting the research – specific product area, NPD and marketing etc

The research rationale – the key issues to be addressed and the importance of the research to the client in line with the decisions that need to be made

 MARKETING AT WORK   *application*

A Background for our Spa Example.

Refresh is a small chain of day spas with six spas currently located in Bath, Covent Garden (London), Henley on Thames, Cheltenham, Cambridge and Oxford. The first spa opened in Bath in 1996 and then Covent Garden in 2004. The company then acquired an existing chain (Detox Day Spa) six months ago. The company is now undergoing a re-branding exercise to bring the remaining sites under the Refresh brand with equivalent facilities and treatments available in each of the locations.

The spas are 'day only' with no overnight facilities. The main USP is that they are dedicated day spas rather than simply offering treatments within a branded hotel as is the case with many of their competitors. In addition, other dedicated spas who offer a similar approach are traditional 'health farms' where customers are encouraged to book into overnight stay packages.

Currently there are no membership options to join the spas with the focus being on full or half day 'top to toe' packages. Prices differ according to the day of the week with peak periods being Friday, Saturday and Sunday. Monday to Thursday 20% discounts are offered and additional offers are made periodically such as 'bring a friend for free' and specialised talks organised with celebrity health and beauty advisors.

Refresh has been positioned to appeal to women between the ages of 25- 60 who are interested in their health and beauty regimes but who are looking for relaxation opportunities.

Detox, (the acquired branches) had been a members only spa with a brand positioning which focussed on diet and fitness. Over the last four years, Detox lost 30% of their membership base and currently existing members are aware that Detox will change to the Refresh brand in the long term.

The research will help the Detox marketing team make decisions about:

- Whether membership options should be offered by Refresh
- The new positioning strategy across the chain
- The facilities and treatments that should be offered

2.1.2 Objectives

Setting research objectives is one of the most critical stages in the entire research programme. Research which is based on flawed objectives often merely leads to a finding that more research is required in order to address an underlying problem or issue.

ASSIGNMENT TIP

concept

In his comments on the December 2008 / March 2009 sitting, the examiner noted that stronger candidates had clear research objectives and detailed information targets.

[handwritten margin note: ensure that objectives are clear and detailed.]

Drayton Bird, an established direct marketing expert, has criticised market research as creating a 'blind alley' because he believes that a large proportion of research is fundamentally flawed because researchers fail to address the right questions (Young, 2008). By asking the wrong question Bird was not simply referring to questions within a survey but the fundamental objectives of the research. For example a company may commission research to find out whether customers would buy a new product. The issue that the company should have really investigated is whether customers would replace what they already buy with the new product. In other words, do they like the new product enough to change their behaviour.

[handwritten margin note: good way of thinking about research objectives]

Objectives are usually refined through a series of discussions between the research agency and the client. Rarely are the objectives that the client included in their brief the final objectives used to direct the research design (Dillon et al, 1994).

Malhotra (2004) observed that frequently objectives are too broad (not providing sufficient direction) or too narrow (precludes consideration of other courses of action).

(a) Overly broad objectives could be stated as: (1) developing a marketing strategy – this project could be endless (2) improving the competitive position of the firm – from which basis? (3) improving the company image – amongst whom, any ideas how?

(b) Too narrow objectives could be stated as: (1) decrease the price of the brand to match competitors price cut – is this really the central issues? (2) to specify whether blue or green should be used for new product packaging – are other colours also appropriate? (3) to outline why customers will buy this product – could it also be that they won't and so wouldn't it be better to take Drayton Bird's view and ask what would lead them to switch.

In order to ensure that your objectives are clear, and neither too broad or narrow it is good practice to use **research questions** (Dillon et al, 1994; Malhotra, 2004) which follow directly from the objective. The research objectives should flow directly from the overall research aim or rationale, research questions then flow from the objectives.

Research questions should not be confused with fieldwork questions which are used within surveys and interviews. Research questions are not normally phrased in a way so that you could use them directly with respondents.

Research questions are questions that the objective will address stated in very specific terms. They should not be confused with fieldwork questions.

The diagram below outlines the relationship between the different levels of defining the research problem. Please note that to be able to show the relationship more clearly, only the research questions and fieldwork questions for objective 1 are shown. In reality, the diagram would look like a pyramid with one aim at the top which then cascades down to several objectives each of which have several research questions. Each research question will then have several fieldwork questions which may or may not be used within the same data collection tool eg survey, focus group etc.

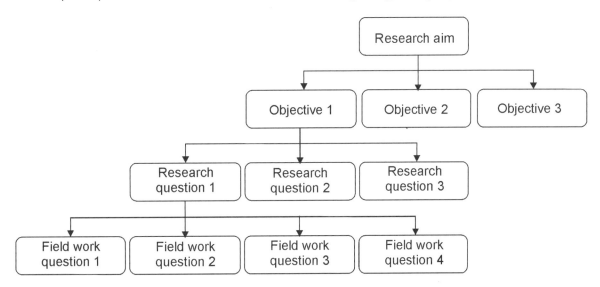

MARKETING AT WORK

application

Aims, objectives and research questions for our Spa Example.

Aim – To assist with decision making relating to the rebranding of Detox.

Objective 1 – To identify whether Refresh should offer membership packages.

Research questions following objective 1

(a)   Would the introduction of membership adversely affect the ethos and atmosphere of the day spa?
(b)   Who would be likely to join as members?
(c)   Should the membership packages remain similar to those offered by Detox?
(d)   What would be the effect of removing memberships from existing Detox members?

Objective 2 – To evaluate alternative positioning strategies

(a)   What is the perception of Refresh amongst existing customers?
(b)   How do Detox members perceive Refresh?
(c)   What positioning would attract new customers into the spa?
(d)   Should Refresh be positioned as a spa exclusively for women?
(e)   Should the diet and fitness image of Detox be blended with the relaxation image of Refresh?
(f)   What would be the impact on Refresh if the existing positioning was modified?

Objective 3 – To suggest appropriate treatment and product mixes

(a)   Should 'top to toe' days and half days remain the core focus?
(b)   What do customers and potential customers like and dislike about the current treatment range?
(c)   What treatments do competitors offer?
(d)   What new treatments are likely to be available in the future?
(e)   What treatments are most popular amongst spa goers?
(f)   What treatments would both Refresh and Detox customers expect – are their requirements different?

Objective 4 – To review the facilities that should be incorporated

(a)   What aspects of Refresh's facilities are liked and which improvements do customers think could be made?
(b)   What facilities do competitors offer?
(c)   What state of the art facilities will be available in the near future?
(d)   What is the relative importance of different facilities to customers and potential customers?
(e)   Is it important for all sites to have the same facilities?

2.1.3 Approach and method

The approach and method is the most comprehensive section of the proposal and it is here that the research outlines their overall research design. There are many alternative ways to conduct research and often there isn't one best approach (Dillon et al, 1994). The researcher at this stage should evaluate alternative courses of action and decide upon the most suitable. Decisions will be based upon:

how to choose which research methods use.

(a)   The **value of the information** gained by using a particular approach
(b)   The **cost and time** implications
(c)   **Practical issues** eg the ability to easily gather respondent views, ease of data collection
(d)   Requirements of the **research objectives** and **research questions**

The next chapter will cover this in more detail, it is important that whatever research methods are used, the objectives of the research are fully covered.

Several issues need to be included in this section of the proposal including:

Points to cover on research methods

(a)   **Phases of research** eg will data collection be split into a number of phases which will help in refining later phase data collection tools (Malhotra, 2004). For example phase one may involve secondary research, phase two a qualitative focus group before a final phase three using a quantitative online survey.

(b)   **A justification** outlining why this is an appropriate research design

(c)   The **overall sampling plan** eg who will be selected to participate in the various research phases, how will they be selected, how many will need to be approached to participate, what can be done to encourage them to respond.

(d)   The **data collection** fieldwork methods eg focus groups, questionnaires, online panel etc

(e)   Any **limitations** of the proposed approach

2.1.4 Reports

Typically a very brief research report, cross tabulated data (for quantitative studies), verbatim comments (for qualitative studies) and a research presentation are used.

It is important to clarify the reporting requirements because these can have a deep financial impact on the agency. There will be a huge difference for example in the cost of the overall project if an in-depth report is required because of the time needed to write it. Likewise 800 printed copies of a research presentation for use in a large internal training session will place very different financial demands on the overall cost of the research.

MARKETING AT WORK $\Rightarrow$ *how can I make the reporting style different?* .... application

Agencies are increasingly using their reporting style as a differentiating devise to attract potential clients. Using actors to act out typical verbatim responses unearthed during qualitative focus groups, using exhibitions as a means of presenting research and the use of online presentations have been used recently by more creative agencies.

2.1.5 Timing

Within this section the researcher will break down all timings within the overall project. Timings are usually broken down into weekly or sometime daily time periods. Tables or Gantt charts are the most common methods of presenting timings. The researcher should be very specific here and also include time scales for clients to review data collection tools or provide supporting information.

$\rightarrow$ which is the easiest to decipher?

2.1.6 Fees and expenses

Fees should be broken down as much as possible so that the client can see exactly how much the entire project will cost but also have the flexibility to pick out elements of the research design to cover at a later date if budgets do not allow the entire project to be completed.

Typically fees are broken down into:

Need to include realistic prices

- Individual research methods eg survey, focus group
- Expenses to be incurred eg incentives for respondents, materials as research prompts, any significant travel
- Use of third party eg focus group viewing facilities, database purchase

 ESOMAR publish a guide to average research prices which you may use to help you with your assignment. It may also be worth contacting a few agencies, telling them that you are studying for this qualification and ask for ballpark rates for a range of research methods. For example focus groups are likely to cost in the region of £1,000 - £2,000 each depending on the context and complexity of the research. ▪

2.1.7 Personal CV's / experience and references / contract details

These sections are fairly self explanatory and so we do not need to elaborate much here, however, you should not underestimate their importance. Remember the research proposal is effectively a 'sales pitch' and therefore flagging up the agencies credentials and experience is essential. Clients also like to know a little more about the team who will be addressing their problem and so clarity here helps agency-client relationships enormously. Including references helps to build the credibility of the agency.

It is important that agencies identify who the main day to day contact will be with.

ASSIGNMENT TIP format and presentation

Within your assignment you are expected to include these sections. Clearly they will be hypothetical , however in order to present your work professionally you will need to include them.

2.2 Selecting the agency

Most firms retain an agency after a careful selection process. It is useful to have a list of selection criteria.

- **Size.** Is the agency's size/status comparable to the client organisation?
- **Service levels**. Can the agency source all the client's needs?
- **Experience**. Do they have suitable experience, both as an agency and the individual staff?

- **Confidentiality**. What if they undertake research projects for competitors?
- **Location/logistics**. Are they nearby / easily contactable?
- **Administrative arrangements**. Are they to the client's satisfaction?

3 Examples of Research Projects

So that you can put your own research requirements into context for your assignment, it will be useful to spend some time now familiarising yourself with some typical market research projects.

 MARKETING AT WORK application

Following a review of the Market Research Society's magazine titled 'Research' for 2007 and to April 2008 for agency business wins, we can see some examples of typical research projects.

Type of research	Client and (Agency)	Aim of research and details
Online forum	RAC (Virtual Surveys)	An online forum with Virtual Surveys to monitor the mood of UK motorists. Virtual Surveys moderate the site and provide insight about queries and complaints.
Client panel	The London Paper (Skopos)	5000 member panel of online and paper based readers to gather opinions on everyday events and public interest stories.
Audience measurement	US Broadcaster Scripps Network (TNS)	Data from digital TV set top boxes from 300,000 LA subscribers.
Longitudinal brand tracking	Saab (ORC International)	£500,000 contract to track and benchmark against competitors brand awareness, brand appeal and purchase consideration.
E-commerce visitor activity tracking	Borders (Omniture)	Web analytic software to see how consumers interact with the sites features eg. the site has a 'Magic Shelf' which is a virtual representation of an in-store display.
Web survey	The Sunday Times (Maven and FDS)	A web based survey to find the Best Green Companies.
Continuous sales tracking	US convenience retailers (Nielsen)	Weekly sales data from 7400 US convenience stores available for consumer goods manufacturers to purchase.
Website measurement	P&O Ferries (Speed-Track)	Gathering and analysing real-time data about customers experiences of the website.
Brand and communications tracking	Weetabix (HPI Research)	The research will keep tabs on the health of the company's stable of brands, as well as tracking all its TV, radio and other advertising to see how it performs against competitors in improving awareness and recall among consumers. Brands included in the research are Weetabix, Alpen and Ready Brek.
Customer satisfaction	Greens Health and Fitness (ORC International)	A membership satisfaction programme across its chain of 15 UK leisure clubs. Members will be asked to rate their experience of their club, and results will feed in to an online portal which club managers can access to see how they score and where they fall down in the service stakes.

Type of research	Client and (Agency)	Aim of research and details
Social lifestyle study	The Newspaper Society (Millward Brown)	Qualitative and quantitative study of lifestyles within the UK. NS marketing director Robert Ray said the work would provide a 'real benchmark of life in the UK and how this impacts on people's sense of community and their relationship with news and information sources'.
Stakeholder research	Unite (TNS)	Student accommodation provider Unite has commissioned TNS to carry out an integrated study of employee commitment within the organisation. It is part of a three-pronged approach by Unite to better understand its key stakeholders: customers, employees and external stakeholders.

3.1 Market research

KEY CONCEPT

concept

Marketing research typically embraces six major areas: market research; product research; sales research; price research; distribution research; and advertising/communications research.

Market research is one aspect of marketing research. Market research – that is, research into **markets** – is concerned with quantifying information to provide a forecast of sales and to assess potential sales. Market research is therefore based on the use of **mathematical and statistical techniques** to reduce uncertainty.

3.1.1 Market forecasts and sales forecasts

Market forecasts and sales forecasts complement each other. They should not be undertaken separately. The market forecast should be carried out first of all and should cover a longer period of time.

(a) **Market forecast**. This is a forecast for the market as a whole. It is mainly involved in the assessment of environmental factors, outside the organisation's control, which will affect the demand for its products/services. Often it consists of three components.

   (i) **The economic review** (national economy, government policy, covering forecasts on investment, population, gross national product)

   (ii) **Specific market research** (to obtain data about specific markets and forecasts concerning total market demand)

   (iii) **Evaluation of total market demand for the firm's and similar products** (covering profitability, market potential)

(b) **Sales forecasts**. These are estimates of sales of a product in a future period at a given price and using a stated method(s) of sales promotion which will cost a given amount of money.

Unlike the market forecast, a sales forecast concerns the firm's activity directly. It takes into account such aspects as sales to certain categories of customer, sales promotion activities, the extent of competition, product life cycle, performance of major products. Sales forecasts are expressed in volume, value and profit.

3.1.2 Research into potential sales

Market research tries to **quantify** information to provide sales forecasts and assess potential sales.

Sales potential is an estimate of the part of the market which is within the possible reach of a product. The potential will vary according to the price of the product and the amount of money spent on sales promotion, and market research should attempt to quantify these variations. Sales potential also depends on:

- How essential the product is to consumers
- Whether it is a durable commodity whose purchase is postponable
- The overall size of the possible market
- Competition

Whether sales potential is worth exploiting will depend on the cost of sales promotion and selling which must be incurred to realise the potential. Consider a company which has done market research which indicates that the sales potential of product X is as follows.

	Sales value	Contribution earned before selling costs deducted	Cost of selling
either	£100,000	£40,000	£10,000
or	£110,000	£44,000	£15,000

In this example, it would not be worth spending an extra £5,000 on selling in order to realise an extra sales potential of £10,000, because the net effect would be a loss of £(5,000 − 4,000) = £1,000.

Sales potential will influence the decisions by a company on how much of each product to make. The market situation is dynamic, and market research should reveal changing situations. A company might decide that maximum profits will be earned by concentrating all its production and sales promotion efforts on one segment of a market. Action by competitors might then adversely affect sales and market research might reveal that another market segment has become relatively more profitable. The company might therefore decide to divert some production capacity and sales promotion spending to the new segment in order to revive its profits.

3.1.3 Other aspects of market research

Market research, to be comprehensive, must show an awareness of the various environmental influences which may affect supply and demand for a product.

Market research also involves investigation of the following.

- The expansion or decline of demand within a particular **market segment**
- The expansion or decline of demand within a particular **geographical area**
- The **timing of demand** (Is there a cyclical or seasonal pattern of demand?)

3.1.4 Concentration ratios

One way of expressing concentration ratios is to assess the percentage of the market that is held by the top firms. For example, an industry might have the following concentration ratios.

	% of market
Top three firms	60
Top five firms	68
Top ten firms	85

3.2 Product research

KEY CONCEPT

concept

Product research seeks to achieve a **marketing orientation** to the organisation's research-and-development focus.

Product research is concerned with the product itself, whether new, improved or already on the market, and customer reactions to it.

This aspect of marketing research attempts to make product **research and development** customer orientated.

New product ideas may come from anywhere – from research and development personnel, marketing and sales personnel, competitors, customers, outside scientific or technological discoveries, individual employees or executives. Research and development is carried out by company scientists, engineers or designers; much wasted effort can be saved for them, however, if new ideas are first tested in the market, in other words if product research is carried out.

3.2.1 The process of product research

New ideas are first screened by a range of specialists (market researchers, designers, research and development staff) and are rejected if they have any of the following characteristics.

- They have a low profit potential or insufficient market potential.
- They have a high cost and involve high risk.
- They do not conform to company objectives.
- They cannot be produced and distributed with the available resources.

Ideas which survive the screening process should be product tested and possibly test marketed. Test marketing in selected areas will give a better indication of how well the product will sell if produced for a wider market, but it also gives competitors an early warning of what is happening.

Product research also includes the need to keep the product range of a company's goods under review for the following reasons.

(a) **Variety reduction** may be desirable to reduce production costs, or when there are insufficient sales of certain items in the product range to justify continued production. In practice, there is often strong resistance, both from within a company and from customers, to the elimination of products from the market.

(b) **Product diversification** increases a product range by introducing new items, and a wide range of products can often improve a company's market image.

(c) **Segmentation** is a policy which aims at securing a new class of customer for an existing range of products, perhaps by making some adjustments to the products to appeal to the new segments.

Product research also involves finding **new uses for existing products**, and this could be considered a means of extending a product range. The uses for plastics and nylon, for example, have been extended rapidly in the past as a result of effective research.

3.2.2 Product life cycle research

KEY CONCEPT

concept

The **product life cycle** is a useful model for marketing planning and control, although there are difficulties in predicting the precise shape of the PLC curve for any given product/service.

The product life cycle

The profitability and sales of a product can be expected to change over time. The **product life cycle** (PLC) is an attempt to recognise distinct stages in a product's sales history. Although you will have encountered the PLC before, a brief recap is provided below.

Marketing managers distinguish between the following.

(a) **Product class**: this is a broad category of product, such as cars, washing machines, newspapers, also referred to as the generic product.

(b) **Product form**: within a product class there are different forms that the product can take, for example five-door hatchback cars or two-seater sports cars; twin tub or front loading automatic washing machines; national daily newspapers or weekly local papers.

(c) The particular **brand or make** of the product form (for example Ford Escort, Vauxhall Astra; **Financial Times**, **Daily Mail** and **Sun**).

The product life cycle applies in differing degrees to each of the three cases. A product-class may have a long maturity stage, and a particular make or brand might have an erratic life cycle. Product forms however tend to conform to the 'classic' life cycle pattern, commonly described by a curve as follows. You will be familiar with each of the stages.

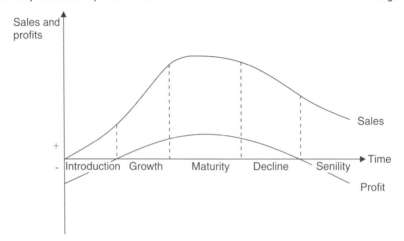

The relevance of the product life cycle to planning and control

A company selling a range of products must try to look into the longer term, beyond the immediate budget period, and estimate how much each of its products is likely to contribute towards sales revenue and profitability. It is therefore necessary to make an assessment of the following.

(a) The stage of its life cycle that any product has reached

(b) For how much longer the product will be able to contribute significantly to profits and sales, allowing for price changes, other marketing strategies, cost control and product modifications

Another aspect of product life cycle analysis is new product development, and strategic planners must consider the following.

(a) How urgent is the need to innovate, and how much will have to be spent on R & D to develop new products in time?

(b) New products cost money to introduce. Not only are there R & D costs, but there is also capital expenditure on plant and equipment, and probably heavy expenditure on advertising and sales promotion. A new product will use up substantial amounts of cash in its early life, and it will not be until its growth phase is well under way, or even the maturity phase reached, that a product will pay back the initial outlays of capital and marketing expenditure.

It is essential that firms plan their portfolio of products to ensure that new products are generating positive cash flow before existing 'earners' enter the decline stage. In this situation the company is likely to experience cash flow problems:

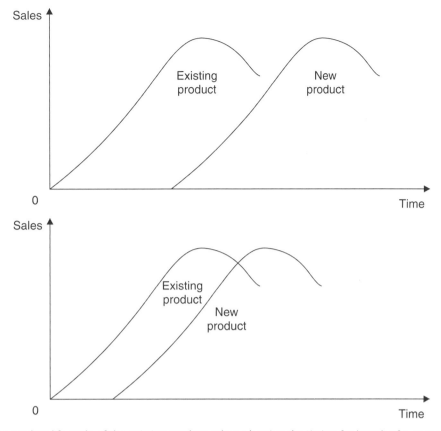

By considering the product life cycle of the existing product, when planning the timing for launch of a new product, cash flow problems can be avoided.

It is perhaps easy enough to accept that products have a life cycle, but it is not so easy to sort out how far through its life a product is, and what its expected future life might be. Information about the stage a product has reached in its life cycle may be an important indication of how long its market will continue and how soon new product developments must be introduced to replace it.

(a)   There ought to be a **regular review** of existing products, as a part of marketing management responsibilities.

(b)   Information should be obtained about the likely future of each product and sources of such information might be as follows.

- An analysis of past sales and profit trends
- The history of other products
- Market research
- If possible, an analysis of competitors

The future of each product should be estimated in terms of both sales revenue and profits.

Once the assessments have been made, decisions must be taken about what to do with each product. The choices are as follows.

(a)   To **continue selling** the product, with no foreseeable intention yet of stopping production

(b)   To initiate action to **prolong a product's life**, perhaps by product modification, advertising more, by trying to cut costs or raise prices, by improving distribution, or packaging or sales promotion methods, or by putting in more direct selling effort

(c)   To plan to **stop producing the product** and either to replace it with new ones in the same line or to diversify into new product-market areas

3.2.3 Category management

KEY CONCEPT

concept

Effective category management requires analysis of accurate data from consumers, EPOS and market research.

Category management has been defined as 'the distributor/supplier process of managing categories as strategic business units, producing enhanced business results by focusing on delivering consumer value' (Joint Industry Project on Efficient Consumer Response).

Category management is a comparatively new theme in retailing and emphasises decision making based upon analysis of consumer data, EPOS data and market research data. The aim of the new discipline is to reduce costs and inventories while improving the consumer's choice.

A category is defined as a distinct, manageable group of products or services that customers perceive to be related and/or substitutable in meeting a consumer need. Thus tinned vegetables (tomatoes, baked beans, sweetcorn) might form a category, or frozen desserts or household paper products. The retailer manages each category as a **strategic business unit**.

Each category is managed according to its own particular strategy. Typical strategies might include traffic building (increasing the number of customers passing through the category shelfspace), profit contribution or cash penetration. Category management is therefore intensely data-driven, and needs accurate data at store level. For example, a store might want to rank profit or volume sales of a particular product and compare that with national or regional figures. The scanned data from the store can be combined with market sales data and consumer information to identify where, for example, sales are below what would be expected. The category or product may become the focus for enhanced promotion to boost sales, or re-pricing to improve its contribution margin.

3.2.4 Product testing

KEY CONCEPT

concept

Product testing is 'the evaluation and development of the products themselves from a marketing point of view'.

The following circumstances should be taken into account when establishing the most appropriate product test design.

(a) **Management information required**. For example, is information required on the best shape/colour mix, or on whether it is worth investing more time and money in the product, or which is the best of a group of similar products.

(b) **The market in which the product will be sold**. If the market consists of children, for example, their inability to perform certain tasks must be taken into account. Industrial and consumer markets obviously differ and a highly-branded market means that the product will need to be well branded.

(c) **The type of product being tested**. The following product characteristics are likely to affect the design of product tests.

- How new the product is to users (a new product cannot be compared to another)
- How easily the product can be assessed by users
- How much information consumers gather before selecting a product

(d) **The availability of time and finance**.

(e) **The need for standardisation of the procedures across a wide range of products**. Standardised tests mean that researchers gain more experience of the procedures, the procedure can be refined and results of different tests are more likely to be comparable.

The essential differences between product tests centre around the following.

(a) **Sample size** (cost and data reliability must be weighed up)

(b) **The type of people used as testers** (current users of the brand, current users in the product field, users in the product field plus potential users or a general cross section of the population?)

(c) **The type of test given to the testers**

    (i) **Monadic**. Each person is given just one product (either a new product or a line extension) to evaluate.

    (ii) **Comparative**. Each person is given two or more products to compare on the same occasion. Such tests are typically used for new product formulation.

    (iii) **Sequential**. Each person tries one product, waits a specific time period, tries a second and then gives an opinion.

    (iv) **Conjoint**. Such tests focus on product features rather than identifying the best product.

    Other choices face the researcher in terms of what testers are asked to do.

- Whether the products should be branded or blind
- Whether competitors' brands should be included among the products tested
- Which order the products should be presented in comparative tests
- Whether the test should be on the spot or in use (at home)
- Which attributes are to be tested
- The time given to testers

(d) The **analysis techniques** used on the collected data will vary.

3.2.5 Attitude measurement

[handwritten: → comes under product management research currently]

 KEY CONCEPT  concept

An **attitude** is a predisposition to act in a particular way. A knowledge of attitudes may therefore enable predictions about likely behaviour patterns. A significant proportion of marketing research is aimed at finding out about consumer attitudes.

A favourable pre-disposition towards a product may lead to a purchase. However, such causal relationships are very seldom this direct.

There are three components to 'attitude'.

[handwritten margin note: Attitudes are multidimensional researcher to check this!!! W canny search design effect this? to look at other projects that have investigated attitudes.]

(a) A **cognitive component** which is what the individual knows or believes about an object or act

(b) An **affective component** which is what the individual feels emotionally about an object or act

(c) A **conative component** which is how the individual is disposed to behave towards an object or act

Attitude is multi-dimensional and any attempt to measure attitudes needs to recognise this. For example, a number of different attitudes could affect a particular buying decision. 'I like the coat, it's red' but 'red reminds me of blood and danger' and 'it's not a bad price, I can afford it' but 'my parents would never have spent so much on a coat' and yet 'it does feel good on' and 'the shop assistant said it looks good on' but 'it has a real fur collar and an animal has been killed to make this coat' and yet 'animal skins have been a source of clothing for thousands of years' but 'I'm a vegetarian' and so on. Eventually, a decision to buy or not to buy may be made on the basis of the buyer's various attitudes and which attitudes are the most powerful, but these attitudes may also be balanced by social pressures *[handwritten: could this have an influence in my research?]*

It is therefore important that attitudes are incorporated into marketing research. Two scaling techniques which attempt to measure attitude are **Likert scales** and **semantic differential scales**.

Buyer motivation

It is in an organisation's interests to know the **reasons or motives** behind people's behaviour. The reasons why people seek a product or product category, and how they go about obtaining it, are of vital importance to the marketer.

[handwritten: Need to investigate this also so how could a) change opinion and b) develop method further]

Patronage motives (price, service, location, honesty, product variety) influence where a person purchases products on a regular basis.

To analyse the major motives that influence consumers to buy or not buy their products, markets conduct motivation research using **in-depth interviews**, **focus groups** and **projective techniques**.

3.3 Price research

 KEY CONCEPT

concept

Price sensitivity is influenced by five major factors, including the extent to which customers use the '**just price**' concept, the **nature of the purchase** involved, and **perceptions of price versus** 'value'.

3.3.1 Reasons for conducting price research

Reasons for conducting price research are as follows.

(i)   Where a firm is aware of competitive pricing and offers, it can use the data as a **reference point** for its own pricing.

(ii)   Once the firm has established the market prices, it can, through market research, calculate the **price elasticity of demand** and hence derive anticipated sales volume based on proposed price levels.

(iii)   Given the market price, the firm can benchmark its level of **product / service quality**

(iv)   Pricing research can help identify more profitable customers and market segments as well as compare costs with a view to **maximising profitability**.

3.3.2 Price sensitivity

Price sensitivity will vary amongst purchasers. Those who can pass on the cost of purchases will be least sensitive and will respond more to other elements of the marketing mix.

(a)   Provided that it fits the corporate budget, the business traveller will be more concerned about the level of service and quality of food when looking for an hotel than price. In contrast, a family on holiday are likely to be very price sensitive when choosing an overnight stay.

(b)   In industrial marketing the purchasing manager is likely to be more price sensitive than the engineer who might be the actual user of new equipment that is being sourced. The engineer and purchasing manager are using different criteria in making the choice. The engineer places product characteristics as first priority, the purchasing manager is more price oriented.

Price decisions are often seen as highly sensitive and as such may involve top management more clearly than other marketing decisions. Price has a very obvious and direct relationship with profit. Ethical considerations, such as whether or not to exploit short-term shortages through higher prices, are a further factor.

3.3.3 Finding out about price sensitivity

Research on price sensitivity of customers has demonstrated the following.

(a)   Customers have a concept of a '**just price**' – a feel for what is about the right price to pay for a commodity.

(b)   Unless a regular purchase is involved, customers search for price information before buying, becoming price aware when wanting to buy but forgetting soon afterwards.

(c)   Customers will buy at what they consider to be a bargain price without full regard for need and actual price.

Bell Telephones in the US were concerned about the lack of sales of extension telephones. When, as part of a market research survey, customers were asked to name the actual price of an extension telephone, most overestimated it. By keeping the existing price but running an advertising campaign featuring it, Bell were able to increase sales as customers became aware of the lower than anticipated price.

3.3.4 Finding out about price perception

Price perception is important as it determines ways customers react to prices. The economist's downward sloping demand curve may not in fact hold, at least in the short term. For example, customers may react to a price increase by buying for one or more of a number of reasons.

- They expect further price increases to follow. (They are 'stocking up'.)
- They assume the quality has increased.
- The brand takes on a 'snob appeal' because of the high price.

3.3.5 Factors affecting pricing decisions

Several factors complicate the pricing decisions which an organisation has to make.

Intermediaries' objectives

If an organisation distributes products or services to the market through independent intermediaries, the objectives of these intermediaries have an effect on the pricing decision. Thus conflict over price can arise between suppliers and intermediaries which may be difficult to resolve.

Competitors' actions and reactions

An organisation, in setting prices, sends out signals to **rivals**. These rivals are likely to react in some way. In some industries (such as petrol retailing) pricing moves in unison; in others, price changes by one supplier may initiate a price war, with each supplier undercutting the others.

Suppliers

If an organisation's **suppliers** notice that the prices for an organisation's products are rising, they may seek a rise in the price for their supplies to the organisation.

Inflation

In periods of inflation the organisation's prices may need to change in order to reflect increases in the prices of supplies, labour, rent and so on. Such changes may be needed to keep relative (real) prices unchanged (this is the process of prices being adjusted for the rate of inflation).

Quality connotations

In the absence of other information, customers tend to judge quality by price. Thus a price change may send signals to customers concerning the quality of the product. A rise may be taken to indicate improvements, a reduction may signal reduced quality.

New product pricing

Most pricing decisions for existing products relate to price changes. Such changes have a reference point from which to move (the existing price). But when a new product is introduced for the first time there may be no such reference points; pricing decisions are most difficult to make in such circumstances. It may be possible to seek alternative reference points, such as the price in another market where the new product has already been launched, or the price set by a competitor.

Income effects

In times of rising incomes, price may become a less important marketing variable than, for instance, product quality or convenience of access. When income levels are falling and/or unemployment levels rising, price will become a much more important marketing variable.

MARKETING AT WORK

application

Accenture, the global consulting firm, has developed a tool called 'Personalised Pricing Tool' to enable firms to set prices that will boost prices and increase customer satisfaction.

It does this by helping the retailer to understand the purchasing behaviour of individual customers, providing clues about future buying decisions.

As a customer enters a store, he or she receives coupons from a kiosk, using a loyalty card. These coupons are tailored to their product preferences and price sensitivities.

(*www.accenture.com*)

Multiple products

Most organisations market not just one product but a range of products. These products are commonly interrelated, perhaps being **complements** or **substitutes**. Take, for example, the use of **loss leaders**: a very low price for one product is intended to make consumers buy other products in the range which carry higher profit margins: razors are sold at very low prices whilst blades for them are sold at a higher profit margin. Loss leaders also attract customers into retail stores where they will usually buy normally priced products as well as the loss leaders. This is the rationale behind the leading supermarkets' own-label and price-conscious ranges.

3.4 Distribution research

KEY CONCEPT

concept

Distribution research addresses such issues as **timeliness** of distribution channels, the distribution **options** available (and whether traditions can be challenged) and the **profitability** of various distribution methods.

Place as an element in the marketing mix is largely concerned with the selection of distribution channels and with the physical distribution of goods.

In selecting an **appropriate marketing channel** for a product, a firm has the following options.

(a) **Selling direct to the customer**. Consumer goods can be sold direct with mail order catalogues, telephone selling, door-to-door selling of consumer goods, or selling 'off the page' with magazine advertisements. Industrial goods are commonly sold direct by sales representatives, visiting industrial buyers.

(b) **Selling through agents or recognised distributors**, who specialise in the firm's products. For example, a chain of garden centres might act as specialist stockists and distributors for the products of just one garden shed manufacturer.

(c) **Selling through wholesalers** or to retailers who stock and sell the goods and brands of several rival manufacturers.

Some organisations might use channels of distribution for their goods which are unprofitable to use, and which should either be abandoned in favour of more profitable channels, or made profitable by giving some attention to cutting costs or increasing minimum order sizes.

As well as **cost and profitability analyses**, distribution research can embrace the following.

(a) To what extent is the distribution channel **actually working**? In other words, how effective is the distributor at delivering products to customers?

(b) To what extent is the distributor favouring its own brand or competitors' products over your own, in terms of shelf space and positioning and in-store promotions?

This latter point is important as own-brand products are becoming increasingly competitive with branded goods. Supermarket chains promote their own brand extensively.

Normal **market research techniques** can be used to assess the effectiveness of distribution channels. Questions in market research questionnaires can ask how easy it is for customers to obtain products and information, and where they are obtained. An example might be a newspaper readership questionnaire, which will ask where the customer acquires the newspaper (eg delivered at home, or bought on way to work).

3.5 Marketing communications research

 KEY CONCEPT  concept

Advertising is normally measured against four specific criteria: **impact**, **persuasion**, **message delivery** and **liking**.

Advertising may be judged to have been effective if it has met the objectives or tasks previously set for it. The following table gives some examples.

Advertising task/objectives	Example of measure of effect
Support increase in sales For example a local plumber's advert in a regional newspaper	Orders; levels of enquiries
Inform consumers For example an Amnesty International advert about political prisoners	Donations Number of new members clipping appeal coupon
Remind For example a Yellow Pages television commercial	Awareness levels
Create/reinforce image For example Halifax's 'people' commercials	Awareness levels Image created
Change attitude For example British Nuclear Fuel Ltd's Sellafield open door poster campaign	Attitude

Although there may well be a number of short-term effects resulting fairly soon after an advertising campaign has appeared, a brand will probably reap positive long-term effects from advertising effort stretching over a number of years. All advertising, whatever the objectives for any individual campaign, will contribute to the overall perception of that brand by the consumer.

3.5.1 Creative development research

This is research carried out early in the advertising process, using **qualitative techniques** to guide and help develop the advertising for a product or service. It can be used to help feed into initial creative ideas or, alternatively, to check whether a rough idea is understood by consumers. Storyboards, outline scripts or rough layouts of mocked up adverts may be shown to groups of consumers to monitor their response.

3.5.2 Pre-testing

Advertising pre-testing is research for **predictive** purposes. Advertisements are tested quantitatively, at a much more highly finished stage than in creative development research, against set criteria. Recently, quantitative pre testing has seen a resurgence in popularity. As advertising budgets are made to work harder, advertisers have felt the need to build in more checks to ensure that their advertising is on target.

Quantitative testing can be administered via **hall or studio tests**. Specialist research agencies can cater for all kinds of media executions. Respondents are shown clusters of TV commercials either on their own or within television programmes; print executions are shown in folders amongst other adverts; poster executions may be shown in a simulated road drive scene via 35mm slides.

Advertisements are measured against specific criteria such as those listed below.

(a)   **Impact**. Does the advert stand out against others?

(b)   **Persuasion**. Does the advert create favourable predisposition towards the brand?

(c)   **Message delivery**. Does the advert deliver the message in terms of understanding and credibility?

(d)   **Liking**. This attribute is deemed to mean not only that the advert is enjoyable and interesting, but is also personally meaningful to the consumer, relevant and believable. Thus, an RSPCA advert depicting a maltreated animal might not be likeable in the conventional sense, but may be rated highly by a respondent on this attribute because it draws attention to an issue which is important to the consumer.

The specialist research agencies that carry out this form of research have developed a set of normal values or scores, which act as **benchmarks** against which to measure quantitative results.

3.5.3 Tracking studies

Advertising effects may be measured over time via tracking studies which monitor **pre– and post-advertising variables**. Clients will normally buy into a series of **omnibus surveys** to monitor criteria such as:

•   Brand/product awareness (unprompted *versus* prompted recall)
•   Attitudinal change
•   Imagery associations

Panel research is another form of tracking study. For instance, Taylor Nelson's Superpanel monitors changes in grocery shopping behaviour of 8,500 households. The research company have placed portable bar code scanners in homes and families undertake to use the device to record purchases made. The data is collated every week and gives diagnostic information. For instance, if the panel buy less of a particular brand, it is possible to identify what brand they have switched to instead.

With tracking studies, it is important to try to examine **all possible reasons** for any changes in audience behaviour. An increase in level of sales as tracked over time by panel-based research may be ascribed in part to the effect of the advertising. However, sales increases are equally likely to have come about due to changes in price levels, seasonality, competitive activity or a change in product quality levels.

3.5.4 Communications research

[handwritten: → I think consumer comes into this section ???]

Advertising research as described above is but one aspect of communications research. As a marketing manager you will be concerned with the following aspects of your decision making.

(a)   **Economy** – The need to minimise the cost of inputs   *[handwritten: business concerns]*
(b)   **Efficiency** – The process of maximising the productivity of inputs
(c)   **Effectiveness** – The extent to which the output generated meets the objectives set for the organisation.
[handwritten: but both of them rely on this – likely to be effective if customer wants the type of contract.]
You will therefore be continuously assessing the effectiveness as well as the relative costs of each element of the promotional mix using research methods.

(a)   **Sales research**

•   What are the selling costs for different customers?
•   How can we improve sales presentations so as to obtain more orders?
•   Should we have fewer personal visits and more telephone calls?
•   Is personal selling more effective than direct marketing?

[handwritten left margin: Also need to consider what the contract is going to be. → sales → service → follow up → the preferred method will be different depending on what it is.]

(b) **Sales promotion research**

- What extra sales resulted from the extra costs for these promotions?

- What level of retention of extra sales was there post promotion?

- What proportion of the budget should go on consumer incentives as opposed to dealer incentives or salesforce incentives?

(c) **PR/publicity research**

- How effective is PR relative to other forms of promotion?
- How can changes in image and attitudes be measured?
- How much notice do potential customers take of editorials?

To summarise this important chapter,

- A research brief is a document prepared by an organisation commissioning research. Typically it contains the following sections: Background, Rationale, Budget, Timescale, Objectives, Methods and Reports. The budget would typically not be revealed to agencies.

- Research proposals are prepared and submitted to the client by agencies who receive the brief. Typical contents are as follows: Background, Objectives, Approach and Method, Reports, Timing, Fees and expenses, Personal CVs, Relevant experience, Contractual details.

- Setting and refining objectives is key to effective research.

- Marketing research typically embraces six major areas: market research; product research; sales research; price research; distribution research; and advertising/communications research.

- Market research tries to quantify information to provide sales forecasts and assess potential sales.

- Product research seeks to achieve a marketing orientation to the organisation's research-and-development focus.

- Price sensitivity is influenced by the extent to which customers use the 'just price' concept, the nature of the purchase involved, and perceptions of price versus 'value'.

- Distribution research addresses such issues as timeliness of distribution channels, the distribution options available (and whether traditions can be challenged) and the profitability of various distribution methods.

- Advertising is normally measured against four specific criteria: impact, persuasion, message delivery and liking.

- Research agencies have made use of considerable technology advances.

Learning objectives	Covered
1 Identify the purpose and components of a research brief	☑ An invitation to an agency to pitch for business
	☑ Provides the rationale for the research
	☑ Contains: Background, Rationale, Budget, Timescale, objectives, Methods, Reports
2 Explain the contents and purpose of a research proposal	☑ An agencies 'pitch' for research work
	☑ Response to a brief and clarifies objectives
	☑ Contains: Background, Objectives, Approach and Method, Reports, Timing, Fees and expenses, Personal CV's Relevant experience, Contractual details
3 Discuss the importance of clear research objectives	☑ Is the key to a successful research project
	☑ Should be SMART if possible
	☑ All aspects of the research design should be traced back to the research objectives
	☑ Research questions should be identified- these are questions that the research will answer and are NOT fieldwork questions
4 Identify different types of market research projects	☑ Market research – sales, segments, demand
	☑ Product research-R&D, PLC, category management, product testing, attitude measurement
	☑ Price research- sensitivity, perception, pricing decisions
	☑ Distribution research- timeliness, cost, profitability
	☑ Marketing communications research- Creative, testing, tracking, communications mix

1 Why should an agency tell a client about the client's background in a research proposal?

2 What are three common components of a market forecast?

3 Why might a new product idea be rejected?

4 Why does product research include the need to keep the product range of a company's goods under review?

5 What is category management?

6 What circumstances should be taken into account when establishing the most appropriate product test design?

7 What is meant by the term 'attitude'?

8 Why conduct price research?

9 List five possible objectives or aims associated with advertising.

10 What are the four criteria used to assess the effectiveness of advertising?

1 *Type*   *Application*

Product research (Product)   Likely acceptance of new products
Analysis of substitute products
Comparison of competition products
Test marketing
Product extension
Brand name generation and testing
Product testing of existing products
Packaging design studies

Price research (Price)   Competitor prices (analysis)
Cost analysis
Profit analysis
Market potential
Sales potential
Sales forecast (volume)
Customer perception of price
Effect of price change on demand
(elasticity of demand)
Discounting
Credit terms

Distribution research (Place)   Planning channel decisions
Design and location of distribution centres
In-house versus outsource logistics
Export/international studies
Channel coverage studies

Advertising and communications   Brand preferences
research (Promotion)   Brand attitude
Product satisfaction
Brand awareness studies
Segmentation studies
Buying intentions
Monitor and evaluate buyer behaviour
Buying habit/pattern studies

1   To set out the agency's understanding in order to avoid costly mistakes.

2   Economic review; specific market research; evaluation of total market demand.

3   Low profit or insufficient market potential; high cost or low risk; do not conform to company's objectives; cannot be produced and distributed within the available resources.

4   Variety reduction (cost control); product diversification opportunities; segmentation; (appeal to new types of customer).

5   Decision making based upon analysis of market data, EPOS data and market research data.

6   Management information required; market in which they are sold; type of product being tested; available time and finance; need for standardisation.

7   A pre-disposition to act in a certain way.

8   To establish an organisation's position in relation to its competitors; price elasticity of demand; for benchmarking; to identify more profitable target markets and customers.

9   Support increase in sales; inform consumers; remind; create/reinforce image; change attitudes.

10   Impact; persuasion; message delivery; liking.

References

Dillon, W., Madden, T. & Firtle, N. (1994) *Marketing Research in a Marketing Environment*, 3rd Edition, Irwin, Illinois.

Hague, P. *et al*. (2004) *Market Research in Practice: A guide to the basics*, Kogan Page, London.

Malhotra, N. (2004) *Marketing Research: an applied orientation* Pearson, New Jersey.

Wilson, A. (2006) *Marketing Research An Integrated Approach*, 2nd Edition, Prentice Hall, Harlow.

Young (2008) 'Direct Speech' Research, MRS, February 2008 Edition, p 32, London.

Chapter 6

An overview of research methods

Topic list

Introduction

To be able to put together a research proposal which will fulfil the rationale of a research brief and meet the project objectives, **a clear programme of research should be designed**. This chapter summarises the various approaches to research that can be taken. In the last chapter we looked at the components of a research proposal and in this chapter we highlight the issues to include within the **approach and methods section**.

Ideally if you want to find out about something you **ask everybody involved** or look at every single example. Clearly that is **not practical** if you are researching a market with many thousands or millions of customers: it would cost too much and take too long.

Alternatively, you could examine a **'representative sample'** in other words a few of those individuals. The key issue however is how do you get a sample that is representative?

This chapter tells you about a variety of approaches to sampling. We also look at possible flaws and limitations associated with samples and research designs generally.

Syllabus linked learning objectives

By the end of the chapter you will be able to:

Learning objectives	Syllabus link
1 Describe how to design a programme of research	3.5, Introduction to syllabus section 4
2 Distinguish qualitative and quantitative research methods	3.5, Introduction to syllabus section 4
3 Explain why samples are used within marketing research	4.7
4 Identify the sampling process	4.7
5 Discuss the difference between probability and non-probability samples	4.7
6 Distinguish between convenience, judgement and quota methods to select a sample	4.7
7 Identify problems associated with sample data	2.1, 2.4

1 The overall research design

Let's begin by reviewing what we already know about marketing research.

 KEY CONCEPT concept

Marketing research is made up of market research, product research, price research, sales promotion research and distribution research.

Strictly speaking **marketing** research is any kind of information gathering and analysis that aids the **marketing process** as a whole (a study of competitors' strengths and weaknesses) while **market** research is research into the characteristics of a **market** (France as opposed to India, or people aged under 30 as opposed to people aged over 65).

 KEY CONCEPT concept

Marketing research. 'The collection, analysis and communication of information undertaken to assist decision making in marketing.' (Alan Wilson, 2006). Market-**ing** research includes market research, price research and so on (see below).

Market research. Sometimes used synonymously with marketing research; strictly speaking, however, it refers to the acquisition of primary data about customers and customer attitudes.

In brief, the marketing research process has the following stages.

- Define the problem and research **objectives**
- Develop the research **plan**
- Collect and process **data**
- **Analyse and interpret** information
- **Report** on the findings

To give you an idea of the **scope** of marketing research, the various components are summarised below, under the acronym 'MPPSD':

Research type	Application	
Market research	Forecasting demand (new and existing products)	Market trends
	Sales forecast by segment	Industry trends
	Analysis of market shares	Acquisition/diversification studies
Product research	Likely acceptance of new products	Product extension
	Analysis of substitute products	Brand name generation and testing
	Comparison of competitors products	Product testing of existing products
	Test marketing	Packaging design studies
Price research	Competitor prices (analysis)	Sales forecast (volume)
	Cost analysis	Customer perception of price
	Profit analysis	Effect of price change on demand
	Market potential	(elasticity of demand)
	Sales potential	Discounting
		Credit terms

Research type	Application	
Sales promotion research	Analysing the effect of campaigns	Copy research
	Monitoring/analysing advertising media choice	Public image studies
	Evaluation of sales force performance	Competitor advertising studies
	To decide on appropriate sales territories and make decisions as to how to cover the area	Studies of premiums, coupons, promotions
Distribution research	Planning channel decisions	Export/international studies
	Design and location of distribution centres	Channel coverage studies
	In-house versus outsourced logistics	

The following diagram summarises the marketing research process. We looked at this also in Chapter 4.

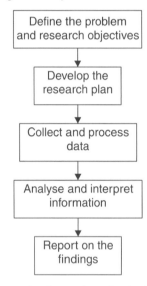

In putting together the research plan, decisions need to be made under the following headings.

Data sources	Primary data (data the organisation collects itself for the purpose)
	Secondary data (collected by someone else for another purpose which may provide useful information)
Type of data required	Continuous/ad hoc Quantitative (numbers) Qualitative (important insights)
Research methods	Observation Focus groups Survey Experiment
Research tools	Interviews (semi-structured, structured, unstructured; open v closed questions) Questionnaires Mechanical tools (video, audio)
Sampling plan (if required)	Sampling unit Sample size Sample procedure
Contact methods	Telephone Mail Face to face

1.1 Research approach

Within research we distinguish between qualitative (contextual insight) and quantitative data. Both qualitative and quantitative data is collected using different fieldwork methods.

 KEY CONCEPT concept

Qualitative research generates contextually rich data. It is generally unstructured and only a small number of carefully selected individuals are used to produce non-quantifiable insights.

Quantitative research is highly structured research conducted using a large sample of respondents to provide quantifiable insights.

The specific research methods are covered in the next few chapters of this text but they are shown in the diagram on the following page.

To ensure that all research objectives are met, it is good practice to use a table as shown below (based on the spa example we have used previously) to help you to keep a 'bigger picture' of the overall research program in mind.

Objective	Research Question	Sample	Data collection	Fieldwork question
1. To measure levels of satisfaction amongst existing customers	1.1 Satisfaction with service levels?	Detox members and Refresh day customers	Kiosk based online survey	Q4 Using the following scale of 1-10
	1.2 Satisfaction with the overall offering?	Detox members and Refresh day customers	Kiosk based online survey	Q4 Using the following scale of 1-10
	1.3 Compared to view of competitors?	Detox members and Refresh day customers	Focus group	Topic- other spas

 ASSIGNMENT TIP evaluation

Create a table like the one above when you are designing your research for your assignment. Examiners frequently complain that students fail to fully address the research objectives either within their approach and methods or within the specific data collection tools used. This table will provide an audit trail so that you can ensure that every question within a questionnaire or a topic within a discussion guide can be traced back to the research objectives.

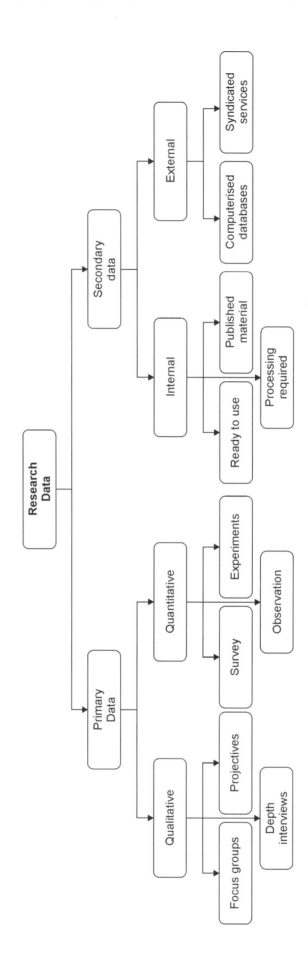

2 Sampling

Sampling is a key topic in marketing research. Various sampling methods are examined in this chapter.

A **population** in statistics simply means the set of individuals, items, or data from which a statistical sample is taken. For example you might send a questionnaire to a sample of 100 people who are aged 30 to 40: the population is ALL people aged 30 to 40.

Sampling is one of the most important tools of marketing research because in most practical situations a population will be far too large to carry out a complete survey.

The key to sampling is to remember the practical issues, and it's purpose. Once you have decided who you need to invite to participate in research they should be referred to as the **'population of interest'**.

A familiar example of sampling is a poll taken to try to predict the results of an election. It is not practical to ask everyone of voting age how they are going to vote week after week: it would take too long and cost too much. So a sample of voters is taken, and the results from the sample are used to estimate the voting intentions of everyone eligible to vote.

Occasionally a population (set of items) is small enough that **all of it can be examined**: for example, the examination results of one class of students. When the population is examined, the survey is called a **census**. This type of survey is quite rare, however, and usually the researcher has to choose some sort of sample.

A sample is often preferable to researchers who do not have the resources, or the need, to conduct a census. There is often a lot of wastage in conducting a census. Let's think about a practical everyday scenario to demonstrate the benefits of a sample. Imagine you are cooking a pot of pasta. To test whether it was cooked you wouldn't eat the whole pot full and then decide if it was ready because it is likely that you could tell just by testing a small amount. The chances are that if you test a fair proportion of the pasta then you will know if it is cooked or not. This however presupposes that each of the pieces of pasta were sufficiently alike in their characteristics – don't, for example, try cooking fusil and expecting it to cook at the same rate as a whole sheet of lasagne in the same pan. The same is true of people, if there are characteristics which are sufficiently alike within a specific group (population of interest), then it is possible to assume they may have similar beliefs and attitudes, therefore, you will only need to include a proportion of these within your research.

You may think that using a sample is very much a **compromise**, but you should consider the following points.

(a)   It can be shown mathematically that once a certain sample size has been reached, **very little extra accuracy** is gained by examining more items.

(b)   It is possible to **ask more questions** with a sample.

(c)   The **higher cost** of a census may **exceed the value** of results.

(d)   **Things are always changing**. Even if you took a census it could be out of date by the time you completed it.

2.1 The sampling process

When designing your sample, you will need to address just five key questions :

1.   **Who** do we need to research? – (population of interest)
2.   **Where** do we find them?
3.   How should we **select** individual respondents?- in other words what sampling technique should be used?
4.   **How many** respondents do we need?- this will determine should sample size.
5.   Will research respondent views be **representative** of the views of everybody else in that situation?

The diagram below outlines the sampling process

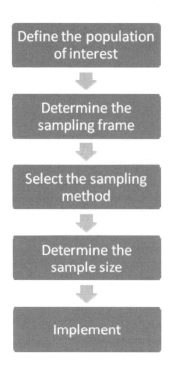

Adapted from Malhotra (2004)

2.1.1 Population of interest

Once you know who should be included within your sample, you should refer to this as you population of interest.

KEY CONCEPT

concept

A **population of interest** refers to the group that the researcher would like to respond within the investigation.

It is essential to correctly define the population of interest eg if the researcher wishes to elicit responses from dedicated gym goers then they should clearly define what constitutes 'dedicated' and plan to only include those individuals in the research.

2.1.2 Sampling frames

The next stage is the development of a sampling frame.

KEY CONCEPT

concept

A **sampling frame** refers to the group that the researcher would like to respond within the investigation.

Sampling frames are lists or set of directions for identifying the population of interest.

The term sampling frame originates from science. You may remember your science classes at school when you were given a rectangular frame (similar to an empty picture frame) and were then asked to throw it randomly on the ground. Typical experiments then included counting the number of bugs or plants that you found within that sampling frame.

In market research terms, the picture frame equivalent is usually something tangible from where you can select respondents, such as a database, a directory or instructions about a specific location to visit or stand.

MARKETING AT WORK

You may have been approached by a survey interviewer whilst walking in a shopping centre. The researcher will have been given specific instructions in terms of the time and location from where they should approach shoppers. The directions they would have been given is the sampling frame.

2.1.3 Select the sampling method

The technique you use to select your sample is broadly grouped into one of two types, either a probability sample, which is taken at random, or a non-probability sample, where respondents are selected on characteristics rather than by pure chance.

KEY CONCEPT

concept

When **probability samples** are taken, every individual within the population of interest has an **equal chance** of being selected to participate in the research

When **non-probability samples** are taken the respondents are **not selected by chance** but as a result of planning by the researcher

Factors affecting sampling approach	Non -Probability sampling	Probability sampling
Nature of research	Exploratory	Conclusive
Research flaws likely to be due to sampling or non-sampling errors	Non-sampling errors are larger	Sampling errors are larger
Similarity in population characteristics	Homogenous (similar)	Heterogeneous (different)
Statistical analyses	Not as statistically sound	Statistically sound
Operational issues	Convenient, cost effective, fast	Expensive, time consuming

Adapted from Malhotra (2004)

The diagram below shows the most common types of sample selection methods.

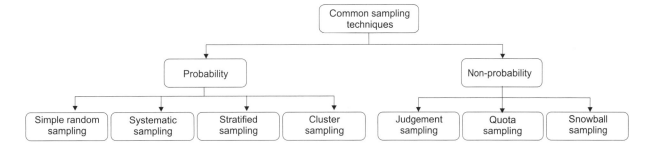

ASSIGNMENT TIP

concept

Within your syllabus the senior examiner has specified that you will only be expected to know the difference between probability and non-probability samples. You will also be able to explain and outline when you could use convenience, judgement and quota sampling methods.

ACTIVITY 1

evaluation

Why is a telephone directory an unsuitable sampling frame?

2.2 Probability random sampling

To ensure that the sample selected is **free from bias**, random sampling must be used. Inferences about the population being sampled can then be made validly.

KEY CONCEPT

concept

A **simple random sample** is a sample selected in such a way that every item in the population has an equal chance of being included.

For example, if you wanted to take a random sample of library books, it would **not be good enough to pick them off the shelves, even if you picked them at random**. This is because the **books which were out on loan** would stand no chance of being chosen. You would either have to make sure that all the books were on the shelves before taking your sample, or find some other way of sampling (for example, using the library index cards).

A random sample is **not necessarily a perfect sample**. For example, you might pick what you believe to be a completely random selection of library books, and find that every one of them is a detective thriller. It is a remote possibility, but it could happen. The only way to eliminate the possibility altogether is to take 100% survey (a census) of the books, which, unless it is a tiny library, is impractical.

ACTIVITY 2

evaluation

You want to take a random sample of people who live in a particular area. Why would the electoral register not be a satisfactory sampling frame?

In many situations it might be **too expensive** to obtain a random sample, in which case quasi-random sampling is necessary, or else it may not be possible to draw up a sampling frame.

KEY CONCEPTS

concept

Systematic sampling: sampling units are chosen from the sampling frame at a uniform rate (eg every tenth item from a chosen start point in a directory of names

Stratified sampling: the population is divided into mutually exclusive groups (eg income) and a random sample is taken from each group

Cluster sampling: clusters are chosen using a range of measures – geography, income, age – and individuals within the clusters are chosen at random

2.3 Non-probability sampling

Non-random sampling is used **when a sampling frame cannot be established**.

2.3.1 Judgemental sampling

Judgemental sampling involves selecting respondents because they possess particular characteristics which the researcher believes are **representative of the population of interest** as a whole. 'Typical' residents for example may be selected from a selection of streets that a researcher believes are representative of an entire neighbourhood.

Snowball sampling is sometimes considered to be a form of judgemental sampling (Dillon et al, 1996) because this method involves the respondent suggesting other individuals for selection because they are similar to themselves. Snowball sampling is used when respondents are hard to find and tends to be only relevant for small samples in qualitative studies.

2.3.2 Convenience sampling

Convenience sampling refers to samples that are selected because the **population of interest are easy to access** by the researcher. Convenience samples are sometimes considered to be biased and unprofessional (Wilson, 2006) however if the easiest to access respondents are reasonably similar to the population of interest then it can be a justifiable method on a cost and resource basis.

Many online surveys use convenience sampling because it is difficult to establish common patterns between users of websites (Wilson, 2006).

2.3.3 Quota sampling

In quota sampling randomness is forfeited in the interests of **cheapness and administrative simplicity**. Investigators are told to interview all the people they meet up to a certain quota. A large degree of bias could be introduced accidentally. For example, an interviewer in a shopping centre may fill his quota by only meeting people who can go shopping during the week. In practice, this problem can be **partly overcome by subdividing the quota** into different types of people, for example on the basis of age, gender and income, to ensure that the sample mirrors the structure or stratification of the population. The interviewer is then told to interview, for example, 30 males between the ages of 30 and 40 from social class B. The actual choice of the individuals to be interviewed, within the limits of the **quota controls**, is left to the field worker.

 ACTIVITY 3    application

The number of marketers and their sex in each type of work in a particular country are as follows.

	Female	Male	Total
Lecturers	100	100	200
Commercial companies	400	300	700
Public sector	100	200	300
Marketing research and agencies	500	300	800
			2,000

What would an investigator's quota be, assuming that a sample of 200 is required?

3 The size of a sample

As well as deciding on the appropriateness of a particular sampling method for a given situation, the size of the sample actually selected must also be given consideration.

Although, in certain circumstances, statistical processes can be used to calculate sample sizes, as we'll see in a moment there is **no universal law** for determining the size of the sample. Researchers may simply rely on their **experience** from other studies similar to the project in hand. Two general considerations should, however, be borne in mind.

(a) The larger the size of the sample, the more accurate the results.

(b) There reaches a point after which there is little to be gained from increasing the size of the sample.

Despite these principles other, more administration-type factors, play a role in determining sample size.

(a) **Money** and **time** available.

(b)   **Degree of precision required**. A survey may have the aim of discovering residents' reaction to a road widening scheme and hence a fairly small sample, producing imprecise results, would be acceptable. An enquiry into the safety of a new drug would, on the other hand, require an extremely large sample so that the information gained was as precise as possible.

(c)   **Number of subsamples required.** If a complicated sampling method such as stratified sampling is to be used, the overall sample size will need to be large so as to ensure adequate representation of each subgroup (in this case, each stratum).

(d)   **Blind guess** (although this is not really acceptable in most circumstances).

(e)   **Industry standards** or rules of thumb; certain industries assume particular benchmark sample sizes eg 200-300 for a product test (Dillion et al, 1994).

If you type into an internet search engine a term like 'sample size calculator', you will find that there are a number of websites where you can download, for free, a calculator to help you work out statistically your sample size.

MARKETING AT WORK

application

'Sugging' or sales under the guises of research, is the term used to refer to telemarketers posing as researchers in order to make sales. Research in Canada showed that 40% or Canadians received these calls. The Canadian Marketing Research and Intelligence Association conducted the research as part of a Vox Pop campaign to educate the public about the benefits of research and their rights as respondents. (Research, 2008).

4   Problems with sample data and research designs

KEY CONCEPT

concept

There are many **potential problems** with sample data including **bias**, **unrepresentative data**, and **insufficient data**, perhaps because of non-response.

There are several faults or weaknesses which might occur in the design or collection of sample data. These are as follows.

(a)   **Bias**. In choosing a sample, unless the method used to select the sample is the random sampling method, or a quasi-random sampling method, there will be a likelihood that some 'units' (individuals or households etc) will have a poor, or even zero chance of being selected for the sample. Where this occurs, samples are said to be biased. A biased sample may occur in the following situations.

   (i)   The sampling frame is out of date, and excludes a number of individuals or 'units' new to the population.

   (ii)   Some individuals selected for the sample decline to respond. If a questionnaire is sent to 1,000 households, but only 600 reply, the failure of the other 400 to reply will make the sample of 600 replies inevitably biased.

   (iii)   A questionnaire contains leading questions, or a personal interviewer tries to get respondents to answer questions in a particular way.

(b)   **Insufficient data**. The sample may be too small to be reliable as a source of information about an entire population.

(c)   **Unrepresentative data**. Data collected might be unrepresentative of normal conditions. For example, if an employee is asked to teach a trainee how to do a particular job, data concerning the employee's output and productivity during the time he is acting as trainer will not be representative of his normal output and productivity.

(d) **Omission of an important factor**. Data might be incomplete because an important item has been omitted in the design of the 'questions'.

(e) **Carelessness**. Data might be provided without any due care and attention. An investigator might also be careless in the way he gathers data.

(f) **Confusion of cause and effect (or association)**. It may be tempting to assume that if two variables appear to be related, one variable is the cause of the other. Variables may be associated but it is not necessarily true that one causes the other.

(g) Where questions call for something **more than simple 'one-word' replies**, there may be difficulty in interpreting the results correctly. This is especially true of 'depth interviews' which try to determine the reasons for human behaviour.

One method of checking the accuracy of replies is to insert control questions in the questionnaire, so that the reply to one question should be compatible with the reply to another. If they are not, the value of the interviewee's responses are dubious, and may be ignored. On the other hand, the information that the interviewee is genuinely confused about something, and so offers contradictory answers, may be valuable information itself, or it may reflect the way the questions are structured.

4.1 Non-sampling error

A non-sampling error is an error that results solely from the manner in which the observations are made, and leads to inaccurate conclusions being drawn from the group being studied. In other words, there is a problem with the way the data is collected. It can occur whether a total population or a sample is being used. The simplest example of a non-sampling error is inaccurate measurements due to poor procedures or data input errors. Unintended errors may result from any of the following.

- The manner in which the response is elicited – no two interviewers are alike, and questions may be worded poorly

- The suitability of the persons surveyed – some may give deliberately inaccurate answers

- The purpose of the study – if the respondent knows what it is, it may affect the responses given

- The personal biases of the interviewer or survey writer – questionnaires must be designed to draw out useful responses

- Non-response – either through refusal or non-availability

4.2 Non-response

Non-response (of a sample member) cannot be avoided. It can, however, (apart from in mail surveys) be kept at a reasonable level. Experience has shown that the non-response part of a survey often differs considerably from the rest. The types of non-response are as follows.

(a) **Units outside the population**. Where the field investigation shows that units no longer exist (eg demolished houses), these units should be considered as outside the population and should be subtracted from the sample size before calculating the non-response rate.

(b) **Unsuitable for interview**. This is where people who should be interviewed are too infirm or too unfamiliar with the language to be interviewed.

(c) **Movers**. People who have changed address since the list was drawn up cannot be interviewed.

(d) **Refusals**. Some people refuse to co-operate.

(e) **Away from home**. People might be away from home for longer than the field work period and call-back might not be possible.

(f) **Out at time of call**.

These sort of problems occur chiefly in **random** sample surveys. Some of the above do not apply when interviewing is done in factories, colleges or offices. In quota sampling (c), (e) and (f) do not appear. Although the interviewer may miss some people for these reasons, he or she simply continues until he or she fills the quota.

Social change can influence the level of non-response. Rising crime means that householders may be afraid to answer the door to strangers and there are other employment opportunities for 'doorstep interviewers'. Response rates are therefore slipping as more people either refuse to be or cannot be interviewed.

MARKETING AT WORK

application

The director general of the Market Research Society, the industry's professional body, says falling response levels are not just a UK phenomenon. He is concerned that the quality of research will begin to be affected, for the lower response rates are, the greater the departure from ideal cross-sections of opinion, and the less accurate findings are likely to be.

Another problem is that of **'data fatigue'**, as the public becomes tired of filling in questionnaires and more cynical about the real motives of 'market researchers' because of 'sugging' (selling under the guise of research) and 'frugging' (fundraising under the guise of research).

4.3 How to deal with non-response

Taking **substitutes** (such as the next house along) is no answer because the substitutes may differ from the non-respondents. Instead the interviewer can try to increase the response rate.

(a)   Little can be done about **people not suitable** for interview.

(b)   **People who have moved** are a special category. It is usually not practical to track them down. It is acceptable to select an individual from the new household against some rigorously defined procedure.

(c)   To minimise **'refusals'**, keep questionnaires as brief as possible, use financial incentives, and highly skilled interviewers. Refusal rates tend to be low (3-5 per cent).

(d)   People **'away from home'** may be contacted later, if this is possible.

(e)   People **'out at time of call'** is a common problem. The researcher should plan the calling time sensibly (for example, as most breadwinnners are out at work in the day-time, call in the evening). Try to establish a good time to call back – or arrange an appointment.

The CIM's supplimentary reading list for this unit has a number of texts which are very reader freindly.

Bradley, N. (2007) Marketing research: tools and techniques. Oxford, Oxford University Press.

This text is has an excellent Marker Researchers Toolkit section at the bakc. Within this toolkit are revews and checklists for selecting primary research, sampling options and five reflective research questions outlined. It is worth using if you like texts which use lots of images.

Chisnall, P. (2004) Marketing research. 7th edition. Maidenhead, McGraw Hill.

Chapters 2 and 3 cover the overview of marketing research methods and sampling. They are clearly written and provide some good practical issues to consider. This is a good text to use to help you to choose between methods for a particular research design.

Proctor, T. (2005) Essentials of marketing research. 4th edition. Harlow, Prentice Hall.

This text has some excellent case studies on sampling.

Each of these texts covers the content that we move onto for the remainder of this study text clearly and allthough they include a little more detail than you are required to (especially in regard to

sampling methods) if you supplement your reading using these texts you will be demonstrating evidence of 'wider reading' to the CIM.

Overall when we look at research design we can summarise that:

- Marketing research is made up of market research, product research, price research, sales promotion research and distribution research.

- In brief, the marketing research process has the following stages.

  - Define the problem and research objectives
  - Develop the research plan
  - Collect and process data
  - Analyse and interpret information
  - Report on the findings

- Sampling is a key topic in marketing research. Various sampling methods were examined in this chapter.

- A sample can be selected using random sampling, quasi-random sampling (systematic, stratified and multistage sampling) or non-random sampling (quota and cluster sampling). Ensure that you know the characteristics, advantages and disadvantages of each sampling method.

- There are many potential problems with sample data including bias, unrepresentative data, and insufficient data, perhaps because of non-response.

- Non-sampling errors occur as a result of the way the data is collected or inaccurate responses being given or recorded.

Learning objectives	Covered
1 Describe how to design a programme of research	☑ Research objectives
	☑ Research questions
	☑ Fieldwork questions
	☑ Approach and method
2 Distinguish qualitative and quantitative research methods	☑ Qualitative research (contextually rich)
	☑ Quantitative research (numbers)
3 Explain why samples are used within marketing research	☑ Practical and cost implications of sample vs census
	☑ Ability to find a 'representative' sample
4 Identify the sampling process	☑ Population of interest
	☑ Sampling frames
	☑ Sample method
	☑ Sample size
	☑ Implement
5 Discuss the difference between probability and non-probability samples	☑ Probability – equal chance of selection
	☑ Non-probability – not selected randomly
6 Distinguish between convenience, judgement and quota methods to select a sample	☑ Convenience – easy to reach, cost effective
	☑ Judgement- researcher requirements, criteria
	☑ Quota – proportionate
7 Identify problems associated with sample data	☑ Sampling error – bias, insufficient data, unrepresentative data
	☑ Non-sampling error- related to the process of the data collection

Learning objective review

1   What does MPPSD stand for?

2   Draw a diagram summarising the marketing research process.

3   What factors make sampling worthwhile rather than a compromise?

4   What is a simple random sample?

5   What is a sampling frame?

6   List three administrative factors which may affect the size of a sample.

7   List five faults or weaknesses that may occur in the collection of sample data.

---

1   Not everyone has a telephone and not all of those who do have a telephone are listed.

2   (a)   Those under 18 are not included on the register since they are not entitled to vote.

         (b)   Mobile individuals such as students are frequently not registered where they actually live.

         (c)   The register is not up to date and so those who have recently moved to the area are omitted and those who have recently left the area are still included.

3   The investigator needs to interview $200/2,000 \times 100\% = 10\%$ of the population.

Using quota sampling, the investigator would interview the first 10 ($100 \times 10\%$) male marketing lecturers that he met, and the first 40 ($400 \times 10\%$) female marketers in commercial companies.

	Female	Male	Total
Lecturers	10	10	20
Commercial companies	40	30	70
Other commercial	10	20	30
Marketing research and agencies	50	30	80
			200

---

1   Market, Product, Price, Sales promotion, Distribution

2

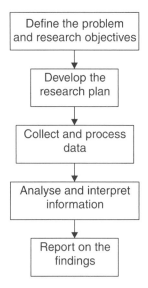

Define the problem and research objectives

Develop the research plan

Collect and process data

Analyse and interpret information

Report on the findings

3   Very little extra accuracy is achieved by larger sample if done effectively; it gives the opportunity to ask more questions; higher cost of more respondents may reduce value of results; could be out-of-date by the time of completion.

4   A sample selected in such a way that every item in the population has an equal chance of being included.

5   A numbered list of all the items in the population.

6   Money/time; degree of precision required; number of sub-samples required.

7   Bias; insufficient data; unrepresentative data; omission of an important factor; carelessness; confusion of cause and effect; ambiguity.

References

Bradley, N. (2007) *Marketing research: tools and techniques*, Oxford University Press, Oxford.

Chisnall, P. (2004) *Marketing research*, 7th Edition, McGraw Hill, Maidenhead.

Dillon, W., Madden, T. & Firtle, N. (1994) *Marketing Research in a Marketing Environment*, 3rd Edition, Irwin, Illinois.

Hague, P. et al. (2004) *Market Research in Practice: A guide to the basics*, Kogan Page, London.

Malhotra, N. (2004) *Marketing Research: an applied orientation* Pearson, New Jersey.

Proctor, T. (2005) *Essentials of marketing research*, 4th Edition, Prentice Hall, Harlow.

Research (2007) '*MR challenged on 'cold calls*' Research, MRS, November 2007 Edition, London.

Tarren, B. (2008) '*Pollster Gallup adds cell-only homes to general population sample*' Research, MRS, February 2008 Edition, p. 6 London.

Wilson, A. (2006) *Marketing Research An Integrated Approach*, 2nd Edition, Prentice Hall, Harlow.

Chapter 7
Secondary data

Topic list

Introduction

KEY CONCEPT

Secondary data is data that already exists in some form. Collection of secondary data is known as 'desk research'. Originally this was to distinguish it from research that involves getting out and about in the world, talking to people and watching them. In fact a great deal of research can now be **done from your desk** in a literal sense, using your desktop computer and the Internet.

Secondary data is data (including internal data) not created specifically for the purpose at hand but used and analysed to provide marketing information where primary data is not (yet) available or not sufficient.

Desk research is the term used to describe a proactive search for existing data, usually as an initial, exploratory research task.

It may seem odd that we deal with 'secondary' data **before we look at primary data**, but it would very silly to embark on substantial amounts of **primary** research without seeing what secondary data already exists. **Checking what is known already** is also likely to give insights into how and what to investigate further.

Syllabus linked learning objectives

By the end of the chapter you will be able to:

Learning objectives	Syllabus link
1 Define secondary data	4.1
2 Evaluate the benefits and limitations of secondary data	4.1
3 Identify sources of secondary information	4.1

Typical desk research activities

Desk research typically involves **knowing where and how to look for** existing information. That is not necessarily as easy as it sounds, but there are clear principles. Here are some typical activities.

(a) Accessing the **organisation's own information systems** records and databases. As we've seen, internal information gathered by other departments for a different purpose to the research in hand would include:

    (i) Production data about quantities produced, materials and labour used etc

    (ii) Data about inventory/stock

    (iii) Data from the sales system about sales volumes, analysed by sales area, salesman, quantity, profitability, distribution outlet, customer etc

    (iv) Data about marketing itself – promotion and brand data, current marketing plans, previous marketing audits.

(b) Tapping into the **Internet** and subscription-based **on-line databases**.

(c) Making use of **library sources**, such as journals, periodicals, recent academic books etc.

(d) **Buying in data and reports** prepared externally, either as secondary data likely to be of interest to many users or as primary data collected for another organisation but then syndicated.

ACTIVITY 1

Can you think of any limitations to desk research?

---

1 Secondary data

KEY CONCEPT

The **collection of secondary data** is often referred to as **desk research**, since it does not involve the collection of raw data from the market direct. Desk research includes using library sources, the organisation's information system, databases and internal reports.

As consumers ourselves (as well as marketers) we are continually using secondary data for our own purchasing decisions. If a movie is recommended by a friend you may well go and see it, too, even though your friend did not see it for your benefit. Secondary data is **data neither collected by, nor specifically for, the user**, and is often collected under conditions not known by the user.

Secondary data **cannot replace the experience itself** nor the more rigorous enquiries we might decide to make ourselves. If you know that your friend usually likes the same sort of movies as you there is a good chance that you will like your friend's latest recommendation. But the movie may contain violent scenes that you cannot stomach, or you may hate musicals because they are unreal, or whatever. Likewise you might see a dress or suit that is recommended in a fashion magazine: you would still go out and look at the garment 'in the flesh', feel it, try it on and so forth, before you decided to buy it.

ACTIVITY 2

How true do you think it is that people want to look at their purchases in the flesh before buying? Consider a variety of different purchases, such as clothes, food, electrical goods and cars.

1.1 The use of secondary data

Secondary information is now **available** in every form and on a **huge scale**. The problem is how to decide what information is required. The use of secondary data will generally come **early** in the process of **marketing research**. In some cases, secondary data may be sufficient in itself, but not always.

Secondary data:

- Can provide a backdrop to primary research
- Can act as a substitute for field research
- Can be used as a technique in itself

1.1.1 Backdrop to primary research

In **unfamiliar territory**, it is natural that the marketer will carry out some **basic research** in the area, using journals, existing market reports, the press and any contacts with relevant knowledge. Such investigations will aid the marketer by providing guidance on a number of areas.

- Possible data sources
- Methods of data collection (relevant populations, sampling methods)
- The general state of the market (demand, competition and the like)

1.1.2 Substitute for primary research

The often substantial **cost** of primary research **might be avoided** if existing secondary data is sufficient. This data might not be perfect for the needs of the business, though and to judge whether it *is* enough, or whether primary research ought to be undertaken, a cost-benefit analysis should be implemented weighing up the advantages of each method.

There are some situations in which secondary data is bound to be **insufficient**. For instance if your brand new version of an existing product is hugely superior to your competitors' versions because of your unique use of new technology, you have changed the entire market. Primary research will be a necessity to find out the impact of your product.

1.1.3 A technique in itself

Some types of information **can only be acquired** by examining secondary data, in particular **trends over time**. Historical data cannot realistically be replaced by a one-off study and an organisation's internal data would only give a limited picture (Dillon, 1994).

Research: 1st February 2002

There are many varied secondary sources and it can be quite complex to classify them in specific ways. The diagram that follows shows a basic overview.

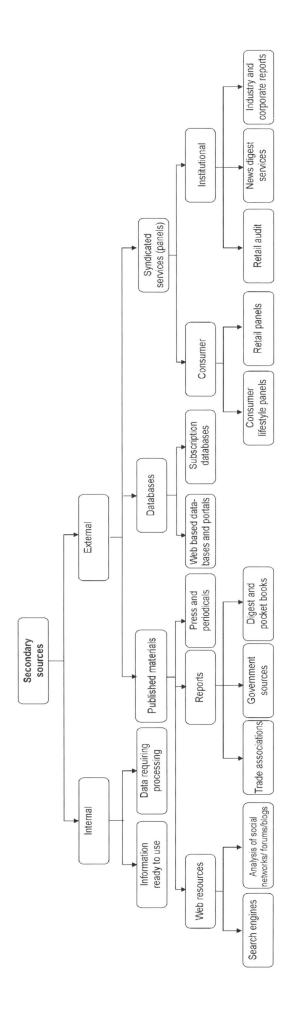

2 The Internet

KEY CONCEPT

The **Internet** is the richest secondary source of information of all, on practically any subject you can think of. Not all of it is good information, however, and although in theory it is easy to search the Internet, in practice it often takes longer to find exactly what you want than another method would have taken. Knowing which search tool to use and how to use it is a key skill for a researcher.

There are a number of ways to access information on the Internet.

*   Go directly to a site, if you have the address
*   Browse or surf
*   Explore a subject directory or portal
*   Conduct a search using a search engine
*   Explore information stored in live databases on the Web, known as the 'invisible web or the 'deep web'

The distinctions between directories, search engines and so on are becoming increasingly blurred, as each type of search tool picks up and adopts ideas from its competitors.

2.1 Going directly to an Internet address (URLs)

You may know the precise address of an Internet site that you wish to visit. TV and radio programs and advertisements frequently give you a web address to visit to find more information. You will also see addresses in newspapers, magazines and books. You may be sent a link in an e-mail.

Typically the format is something like 'www.bbc.co.uk'. This is also known as a **Uniform Resource Locator** or **URL** for short.

All you need to do is type the URL into the Address box of your browser.

ACTIVITY 3

Up-to-date versions of Microsoft Internet Explorer and Netscape Navigator can sometimes find the precise site you are looking for if you just type a guess directly in the address box.

Try this with four or five well-known organisations and see what results you get. Can you see any drawbacks to this method of finding sites?

2.2 Browsing or surfing

Random browsing of pages on the Web is another haphazard way of collecting information, although it can be very interesting if you are not pressed for time.

For instance you may visit a particular news site regularly and find that an article contains links to other pages, either within that site or on an external site that contain more information about the topic. To see this in action find an article of interest to you at www.bbc.co.uk and follow up some of the external links.

2.3 Directories and portals

A directory is a service that offers links to web pages organized into subject categories. Directory services supposedly contain links only to pages that have been evaluated by human beings, using various selection criteria, though the selectivity varies among services.

The best known example of a directory is Yahoo! (www.yahoo.com), although Yahoo! does not evaluate sites as carefully as some other directories and it is aimed more at the leisure interests of home computer users than at the serious academic or business researcher.

Most directories also include some kind of search facility, which either searches the directory only or (confusingly) searches the web in general, perhaps using another type of search tool. Yahoo searches, for instance, are powered by the Google search engine (described below), so Yahoo is actually a mixture between a directory and a search engine.

The best subject directories include notes about sites written by independent reviewers, describing and evaluating site content. For instance you would probably find a site such as the Social Science Information Gateway (SOSIG) (www.sosig.ac.uk) far more informative about useful business-related sites than Yahoo.

A **portal** is similar to a directory (and the terms are often used interchangeably) but many portals are much narrower in scope, restricting their links to specific subjects. Examples include www.thisislondon.co.uk and www.fool.com (for investors) or, more generally, the home pages of most of the leading ISPs.

Yet another term you may see used is **vortal** (vertical industry portal) which is a portal providing information and resources for a particular industry. Examples include www.accountingweb.co.uk and www.privatehealth.co.uk amongst thousands of others.

Typical services offered by portal or vortal sites include a directory of related websites, a facility to search for other sites, news, and community services such as discussion boards and suppliers directories.

2.4 Search engines

Search engines such as AltaVista or Google retrieve links to, and brief descriptions of, websites containing a word or phrase entered by the user. The descriptions are derived from the webpage itself: there is no human judgement involved other than the judgement of the original author of the page.

Search engines are fairly indiscriminate. Some of the results they give may come from reputable sources and provide you with valuable up to date information, but others may be out of date, inaccurate or incomplete.

With a **'first generation'** search engine such as the original **AltaVista** (www.altavista.com) the results of a search are usually presented in 'term ranked' order. This means that a document appears higher in the list of results if your search terms occur very frequently in the document, or in the document title, or near the beginning of the document, or close together in the document.

Many, if not all, first generation search engines have transformed themselves into portals and/or have some 'second-generation' features, because basic term-ranked searching is indiscriminate and gives far too many results.

 MARKETING AT WORK application

'Second generation' search engines such as **Google** (www.google.com) order search results by links or popularity, by concept, by keyword, or by type of site. These search engines generally give better quality results because there is at least some human element in determining what is relevant.

For example, one of the ways that **Google** ranks pages is according to the number of other pages that link to it. The more web authors there are who have decided that it is worth including a link to a page the more likely it is that the page is useful and relevant to the topic you are searching for.

Ixquick (www.ixquick.com) is a **metasearch engine**, which means that it uses multiple other search engines simultaneously and returns the results in a single list with duplicate files removed.

Ixquick only returns the top ten results from the source search services, so in theory you can harness the collective judgement of many search tools about the relevancy and usefulness of sites on a topic all in a single search.

By default the sources Ixquilt uses are country specific. In other words it checks where you are dialling in from and then uses search tools that mainly return results from that country. You can of course override this, if you wish to look at sites from other countries.

2.5 Internet databases (the 'deep web')

Many websites consist of pages that are generated 'dynamically' using content stored in a database. In other words the contents that you see are only assembled – and put into a web page that your browser can read – on request. The page does not actually exist in the form of a saved file and therefore it can't be found by a search engine or listed in a directory.

Typical sites that use databases will be those that have often-changing data such as airline information sites, and news-related sites with up to the minute current stories and archived stories and articles going back several years.

Such content is called the 'invisible' web or the 'deep' web and estimates suggest that there is now at least 500 times more material in this form than there is on the conventional web. The reason is because it is more efficient to store data in this way. Most web pages consist of standard elements like logos and navigation menus and tables defining layout, so it is more efficient to create a single template for all the elements that do not change and simply 'plug' the required information into a space in the template.

Clearly you cannot afford to ignore such a large source of information, but how do you find it? The only way you can do so is to search the database itself. This is not as complicated as it sounds: from the point of view of the user you either just click on what appears to be an ordinary link or you type a few words in the 'Search' box on the site itself.

For example if you were using www.dictionary.com and wanted to find definitions for the term 'dynamic' you would simply type 'dynamic' into the search box and click on the 'Look it up' button. This takes you to the URL dictionary.reference.com/search?q=dynamic: the part of the URL after the question mark is actually an instruction to extract relevant material from the site's database about the term 'dynamic' and present it in a web page.

2.6 Refining a search

Many people – especially new users – find searching the web extremely frustrating because they cannot find what they are looking for quickly enough. In this section we describe some of the things you can do to make your searches more productive.

2.6.1 Use your initial search proactively

If you are researching a new topic the chances are that you will not be very familiar with the concepts and terminology of that subject.

In this case, when you do an initial search spend a few moments skim reading the first few results pages. They probably won't tell you what you want to know, but they may well include words and phrases that you could add to your search terms to give more useful results, or words and phrases that you could exclude from your search (we'll explain how to do this in a moment).

Some search engines display words such as More Like This or Similar pages next to each entry. For instance if you searched for 'management tips' you would find that one of the first few results was to do with time management. If time management happened to be your specific interest you could get a new list of sites specifically on that subject simply by clicking on the Similar Pages or More Like This link.

2.6.2 Restrict the search area

Some search engines have options to restrict the number of sites searched, for instance to UK sites only, or to English language sites only. Even if that option is not available you will generally find that if you simply add UK to your search term the results will be closer to the ones you need.

2.6.3 Advanced search techniques

On many (though not all) sites the search facility allows you to use **symbols** and/or what are known as **Boolean operators** to help refine what should and should not be searched for. These so-called 'advanced' searching techniques are extremely useful.

Different search engines have slightly different rules for formulating queries, so it is always a good idea to **read the help files** at the site before you start a search.

(a)   **Plus signs (+)** If you put a plus sign (+) directly in front of a word (with no space) this tells the search engine that the word **must** be present in all the pages that are found. So if you type **+management +tips**, you will only get pages that contain both words (though not necessarily together or in the order you specify).

(b)   **Minus signs (−)** As you might expect, the − sign works in the opposite way to +. If you put a minus sign directly in front of a word the search engine will **ignore** any documents that contain that word. So, if you type **+management +tips −racing** you will avoid pages that have tips on the horses! However intuitive you are at using the minus sign you are still likely to get links that you are not interested in. You probably would not think of typing, say, **+management +tips −pest,** for example, because the idea of pest management in gardening would probably not occur to you when you were thinking about managing your workteam.

(c)   **Quotation marks (')** To find **only** pages that contain the phrase **management tips,** with the words together in that order, you enclose them in double quotation marks: **'management tips'**. This is very useful so long as your phrase is only two or three words long or if you know exactly how the phrase should be worded (because it is a famous quotation, say).

(d)   **OR** There is a good chance that some of the pages relevant to your search will use alternative words to the ones you first think of. If you can guess what the alternatives might be you can use OR to make the search engine look for pages that contain at least one of them: for instance **management +tips OR hints OR advice**.

ACTIVITY 4   application

Try all of these techniques in a search engine such as Google and observe the different results that you get. You can either use our example 'management tips' or some other phrase of your own, if you prefer.

3   Published secondary data

KEY CONCEPT   concept

Many useful reports and statistics are published by government and non-government sources.

By published we mean **published in any form** – on the web, in book form, on CD. Much published data is now available in several forms.

3.1 Directories

Directories can make a good starting point for research. The information provided is usually on industries and markets, manufacturers (size, location), products, sales and profits. Examples of business directories include the following (although there are many others).

(a)   *Kompass Register (Kompass)*

        (www.kompass.co.uk)

(b)   *Who owns Whom (Dun and Bradstreet)*

        (www.dnb.com)

(c)   *Key British Enterprises (Dun and Bradstreet)*

        (www.dnb.com/UK) ▌

3.2 Computerised databases

These include the following.

- ACORN (consumption indices by class of neighbourhood) (www.caci.co.uk)
- Marketing Surveys Index (CIM) (www.cim.co.uk)
- MRS Yearbook (Market Research Agencies and their specialisms) (www.mrs.org.uk)
- TGI and other syndicated omnibus surveys (www.tgisurveys.com)
- Kompass Online (www.kompass.co.uk)
- Financial Times Company Information (www.ft.com) and many other newspapers
- Hoppenstedt Austria/Germany/Netherlands (www.hoppenstedt.de)
- Jordanwatch (www.jordans.co.uk)
- Reuters (www.reuters.com)
- LexisNexis (www.lexisnexis.com)

Such databases are generally **subscription-based**. Subscriptions are not cheap, but it is usually much less expensive than collecting the information oneself. A trained operator should be used to begin with, to avoid expensive waste of the resources.

3.3 Associations

There are associations in almost every field of business and leisure activity. All these bodies collect and publish data for their members which can be of great interest to other users. Examples of such bodies include the Road Haulage Association (RHA), the British Association of Ski Instructors and … you name it, there will almost certainly be an association for it.

The Trade Association Forum Website which can be found at www.taforum.org *has an online database of UK trade associations and links to their websites. This can provde a host of valuable secondary information.* ▌

3.4 Government agencies

There is a wealth of published statistics which can be used in marketing research. There are two prime sources – government and non-government.

Governments are a major source of economic information and information about industry and population trends. To find material from the UK on the web the best place to start is www.statistics.gov.uk. Other countries have similar government sites.

Official statistics are also published by other government bodies such as the European Union, the United Nations and local authorities.

3.4.1 Non-government sources of information

There are numerous other sources.

(a) Companies and other organisations specialising in the provision of economic and financial data (eg the Financial Times Business Information Service, the Data Research Institute, LexisNexis, Reuters, the Extel Group).

(b) Directories and yearbooks, such as Kompass or Kelly's Directory (online as www.kellysearch.com)

(c) Professional institutions (eg Chartered Institute of Marketing, Industrial Marketing Research Association, Institute of Management, Institute of Practitioners in Advertising)

(d) Specialist libraries, such as the City Business Library in London, collect published information from a wide variety of sources

(e) Trade associations, trade unions and Chambers of Commerce

(f) Trade journals

(g) Commercial organisations such as banks and TV networks

(h) Market research agencies

3.5 Environmental scanning

 KEY CONCEPT

concept

Environmental scanning is an informal process resulting in the possession of market intelligence. Sources include newspapers, journals and attending conferences.

Environmental scanning means **keeping your eyes and ears open to** what is going on generally in **the market place**, especially with respect to competitors, and more widely in the technological, social, economic and political environment. Much of the data will be qualitative but could be systematically logged and backed up by quantitative data if possible.

The result of environmental scanning is market intelligence. Excellent sources are as follows.

(a) Business and financial newspapers, especially the *Financial Times* and the *Wall Street Journal*

(b) General business magazines, such as the *Economist*, *Business Week* and *The Marketer* (published by the Chartered Institute of Marketing (CIM) and sent to CIM students)

(c) Trade journals, such as *Research*, for marketing research or *The Grocer* for retailers or a huge host of others for all sorts of businesses

(d) Academic journals, such as *Harvard Business Review*

(e) Attending conferences, exhibitions, courses and trade fairs

(f) Making use of salesforce feedback

(g) Developing and making use of a network of personal contacts in the trade

(h) Watching competitors (extremely important)

With regard to watching competitors, a **competitor intelligence system** needs to be set up to cope with a vast amount of data from:

- Financial statements
- Common customers and suppliers
- Inspection of a competitor's products
- The competitor's former employees
- Job advertisements

In other words there is a combination of published data and 'field data', which need to be compiled (eg clipping services on- or offline, standard monthly reports on competitors' activities), catalogued, and analysed (summarised, ranked by reliability, extrapolated data from financial reports).

The object of what is usually an informal but constant process is to ensure that the organisation is not caught by surprise by developments which could have and should have been picked up. The organisation needs to be able to adapt to changing circumstances.

3.6 Other published sources

This group includes all other publications. The following is just a tiny selection to indicate the type of data available.

(a)   Some **digests** and **pocket books**

- Lifestyle Pocket Book (annual by the Advertising Association) (www.adassoc.org.uk)
- Retail Pocket Book (annual by Nielsen) (www.acnielsen.com)
- A to Z of UK Marketing Data (Euromonitor) (www.euromonitor.com)
- UK in figures (annual, free from Office for National Statistics) (www.ons.gov.uk)

(b)   Some important **periodicals** (often available in the public libraries)

- *Economist* (general) (www.economist.com)
- *Campaign* (advertising) (www.campaignlive.com)
- World Advertising Research Center (www.warc.com), publishers of ADMAP (advertising)
- Mintel (consumer market reports) (www.mintel.com)
- BRAD (all media selling advertising space in the UK including TV, radio, newspapers and magazines) (www.intellagencia.com)

3.7 Web 2.0

Web 2.0 refers to the new generation of tools and services that allow **private individuals to publish** and collaborate in ways previously available only to corporations with serious budgets, or to dedicated enthusiasts and semi-professional web builders (Cooke & Buckley, 2008).

Blogs, online forums and social networks are increasingly being used as a means of gathering insights into consumers and organisations because they are viewed in the course of their natural behaviours. It also means that there is a wealth of new information available. The availability of this technology is also being used extensively by research agencies who specialise in research panels because of the ability to maintain fast contact with respondents who have agreed to remain on panels are frequent participants. Panels are discussed in the next section and certainly are a key growth area for researchers.

Many consumers particularly are increasingly choosing to join a wide range of research panels.

4   Panels and indexes

 KEY CONCEPT

 concept

Data and reports can be **bought in** from **marketing research organisations**. Often these are the result of continuous research using consumer and retail panels.

The sources of secondary data we have looked at so far have generally been **free** because they are **in the public domain**. Inexpensiveness is an advantage which can be offset by the fact that the information is unspecific and needs considerable analysis before being useable.

A middle step between adapting secondary data and commissioning primary research is the **purchase of data collected by market research companies** or business publishing houses. The data tend to be expensive but less costly than primary research.

There are a great many commercial sources of secondary data, and a number of guides to these sources are available.

- *The Source Book*, Key Note Publications
- *Guide to Official Statistics*, HMSO
- *Published Data of European Markets*, Industrial Aids Ltd
- *Compendium of Marketing Information Sources*, Euromonitor
- *Market-Search*, British Overseas Trade Board

Commonly used sources of data on particular industries and markets are:

- Key Note Publications
- *Retail Business*, Economist Intelligence Unit
- Mintel publications
- *Market Research GB*, Euromonitor

4.1 Consumer panels

A form of continuous research which results in secondary data is that generated by **consumer panels**. These constitute a representative sample of individuals and households whose buying activity in a defined area is monitored either continuously (every day, with results aggregated) or at regular intervals, **over a period of time**. There are panels set up to monitor purchases of groceries, consumer durables, cars, baby products and many others.

Most consumer panels consisting of a **representative cross-section of consumers** who have agreed to give information about their attitudes or buying habits (through personal visits or postal questionnaires) at regular intervals of time. Consumer panels with personal visits are called **home audit panels**.

There are some problems with such panels:

(a) It is **difficult** to select a panel which is a **representative** sample. The panel must be representative of:

    (i) All the customers in the target market.
    (ii) The decision making units who will make the purchase decision (eg male as well as female partners).

(b) Panel members **tend to become sophisticated** in interviewing techniques and responses and so the panel becomes 'corrupt'.

(c) It is **difficult to maintain a stable personnel**; turnover of members may be high and this will affect results as new members are enlisted.

Consumer panels generate a vast amount of data which need to be sorted if they are to be digestible. Analyses available include:

(a) **Standard trend analysis**, showing how the market and its major brands have fared since the last analysis, grossed up to reflect the entire population or a particular region.

(b) **Special analyses** depending on industrial preferences. Common ones are:

    (i) Source of purchase analysis
    (ii) Frequency of purchase analysis
    (iii) **Demographic analysis** (in terms of household age, number of children, ACORN classification)
    (iv) Tracking of individuals, to show their degree of brand loyalty, how and when they change brands.

 MARKETING AT WORK   application

You Gov is a panel based research agency which encourages members of the public to join their panel and pays between 50p and £1 for each completed survey. You Gov publishes reports within a number of categories such as consumer, political, financial and economic, social, Europe and Iraq. Reports are then available to purchase.

It would we worthwhile looking at the You Gov website at www.yougov.com.

4.2 Retail panels

Trade audits are carried out among panels of wholesalers and retailers, and the term 'retail audits' refers to panels of retailers only. A research firm sends 'auditors' to selected outlets at regular intervals to count stock and deliveries, thus enabling an estimate of throughput to be made. Sometimes it is possible to do a universal audit of all retail outlets. EPOS makes the process easier (Wilson, 2006)

The audits provide details of the following.

(a) Retail sales for selected products and brands, sales by different types of retail outlet, market shares and brand shares.

(b) Retail stocks of products and brands (enabling a firm subscribing to the audit to compare stocks of its own goods with those of competitors).

(c) Selling prices in retail outlets, including information about discounts.

4.2.1 The Nielsen Retail Index

Nielsen was the first market research organisation to establish continuous retail tracking operations in the UK. The Nielsen Index refers to a **range of continuous sales and distribution measurements**, embracing ten separate product fields.

- Grocery
- Health and beauty
- Confectionery
- Home improvements
- Cash and carry outlets

- Sportswear
- Liquor
- Toys
- Tobacco
- Electrical

These indexes together measure a large number of sales and distribution variables for over 600 different product categories and over 120,000 brands and associated brand variants.

Data are collected from the **major multiples** (like Tesco and Sainsbury) through their EPOS systems. For other types of shop where EPOS data are not available, a monthly audit of stocks is undertaken and, using data from deliveries, the level of what sales must have been since the last audit is determined.

Increasingly, **Nielsen clients receive their data electronically** on databases, Nielsen having developed a range of data management and analysis software. A Nielsen service called Inf*Act Workstation offers a powerful yet flexible personal, computer-based decision support system.

4.3 Taylor Nelson Sofres Superpanel

The Superpanel (www.tnsofres.com/superpanel) consists of 8,500 households, covering the **purchases of some 28,000 individuals** aged between 5 and 79, who are resident in **domestic households** across Great Britain.

Data collection is through **personal data terminals** equipped with a laser light pen. The terminal is designed to resemble a digital phone and is kept in a modem linked to the domestic power supply and the telephone socket. Data capture is via overnight polling (which means that AGB's central computer dials each panel number in turn and accesses the data stored in the modem).

All that is required from informants is that when they unpack their shopping, they pass the laser light pen over the barcode for each item, and also enter standardised data about the date, shop(s) visited and prices paid. The process incorporates procedures for entering details of products either without barcodes or which have a bar-code that is difficult to read.

Recruitment to the AGB Superpanel uses a multi-stage procedure. A large sample of households are screened to identify those in each sampling point eligible for the service and with known demographics. For this purpose, AGB uses personal home interviews, some 200,000 annually, within 270 parliamentary constituencies (about half the total number).

The households with the relevant target demographics are then selected and the 'housewife' (who may be male or female) for each household is contacted by phone. If the initial contact proves positive, the household as a whole is briefed and the equipment installed.

4.4 Taylor Nelson Sofres Omnimas

Omnimas (www.tnsofres.com/consumeromnibus/omnimas) is one of the largest single **random omnibus surveys** in the world, with some **2,100 adults being interviewed face-to-face** every week.

A random sampling approach is employed, using the **electoral registers** from 233 parliamentary constituencies selected in proportion to size within each of the ten standard regions of the UK.

Each interviewer has a minimum of 13 interviews to do a week. Because the only quota set is that the interviewer should obtain either six men and seven women, or vice versa, there is a control on sex, but everything else depends on the randomness of the sample.

The Omnimas questionnaire is divided into three sections.

(a)   A **continuous section**, including questions asked on every survey and inserted on behalf of a particular client.

(b)   An **ad-hoc section** of questions included on a one-off basis.

(c)   A **classification section** that includes all the demographic questions.

Given an average completion time of 25 minutes per respondent and the 20-30 seconds needed to administer an average question, the total number of Omnimas questions will not be more than about 60-70. Most questions are fixed-choice, with a predetermined number of possible responses, but some clients require open-ended questions and the Omnimas approach allows for a few of these to be included.

4.5 Target Group Index (TGI)

TGI is owned by BMRB (www.bmrb.co.uk) but has its own website (www.tgisurveys.com). The purpose of TGI (www.tgisurveys.com) is to increase the efficiency of marketing operations by identifying and describing **target groups** of consumers and their **exposure to the media** (newspapers, magazines, television and radio) and the extent to which they see or hear other media.

In design, TGI is a regular interval survey and is also 'single source', in that it covers both **product usage data** and **media exposure data**.

Respondents are questioned on a number of areas; **purchase behaviour and media use are cross-tabulated** to enable more accurate media audience targeting.

*   Their use of 400 different products covering 3,500 brands
*   Their readership of over 170 magazines and newspapers
*   Cinema attendance
*   ITV television watching
*   Listening patterns for commercial radio stations
*   Their lifestyles, based on nearly 200 attitude questions

The major **product fields** covered are foods, household goods, medicaments, toiletries and cosmetics, drink, confectionery, tobacco, motoring, clothing, leisure, holidays, financial services and consumer durables. It is worth noting that respondents are only asked about the use, ownership and consumption of the products identified, not about purchases made or prices paid.

The **lifestyle questions** are in the form of Likert-type attitude statements with which people are asked to agree or disagree on a five-point scale from 'definitely agree' to 'definitely disagree'. These attitude statements cover the main areas of food, drink, shopping, diet/health, personal appearance, DIY, holidays, finance, travel, media, motivation/self-perception, plus questions on some specific products and attitudes to sponsorship.

Each questionnaire runs to more than 90 pages and can take four hours to complete. However, the document is totally pre-coded and adapted for optical mark reading, with respondents being able to indicate their replies by pencil strokes. There are three versions of the questionnaire, for men, for housewives, and for other women.

TGI results supply enormous amounts of information, both within categories and cross-tabulated against other relevant categories. There are about 25,000 responses per annum.

(a)   **Total numbers of product users** for each demographic category.

(b)   **Percentages of product users** in each demographic category.

(c)   Information on **heavy/medium/light** and **non-users** for each product or product category.

(d)   For **brands and product fields** with more than one million claimed users, consumption can be **cross-tabulated** against a range of **demographic variables** including sex, age, social class, area, number of children, and media usage.

(e)   Brand usage tables, listing the following.

- **Solus users** – users of the product group who use the brand exclusively.
- **Most-often users** – those who prefer it, but use another brand as well.
- **Minor users** – those who do not discriminate between brands.

TGI appears in 34 volumes, published annually in July and August, but subscribers have **on-line access** to datasets for which they have subscribed, and they can analyse the data on their own PCs.

5 Benefits, risks and dangers of reliance on secondary data

 KEY CONCEPT concept

Secondary sources of data are of **limited use** because of the **scope for compounding errors** arising from why and how the data were collected in the first place, who collected them and how long ago.

When considering the quality of the secondary data it is a good idea to consider the following characteristics of it:

(a)   The **producers** of the data (they may have an axe to grind; trade associations may not include data which runs counter to the interest of its members).

(b)   The **reason for the data** being collected in the first place.

(c)   The **collection method** (random samples with a poor response rate are particularly questionable).

(d)   How **old** the data is (government statistics and information based on them are often relatively dated, though information technology has speeded up the process).

(e)   **How parameters were defined**. For instance, the definition of family used by some researchers could be different to that used by others.

(Malhotra, 2004; Dillon et al, 1994)

5.1 Advantages and disadvantages of secondary data

 KEY CONCEPT concept

Secondary data can be **immensely cost-effective**, but have to be **used with care**.

The **advantages** arising from the use of secondary data include the following.

(a)   Secondary data may solve the problem without the need for any primary research: **time and money is thereby saved**.

(b)   Cost savings can be substantial because secondary data sources are a great deal **cheaper** than those for primary research.

(c) Secondary data, while not necessarily fulfilling all the needs of the business, can be of great use by:

    (i)   **Setting the parameters**, defining a hypothesis, highlighting variables, in other words, helping to focus on the central problem.

    (ii)   **Providing guidance**, by showing past methods of research, for primary data collection.

    (iii)   **Helping to assimilate the primary research** with past research, highlighting trends and the like.

    (iv)   **Defining sampling parameter**, (target populations, variables).

There are, of course, plenty of **disadvantages** to the use of secondary data.

(a)   **Relevance**. The data may not be relevant to the research objectives in terms of the data content itself, classifications used or units of measurement.

(b)   **Cost**. Although secondary data is usually cheaper than primary data, some specialist reports can cost large amounts of money. A cost-benefit analysis will determine whether such secondary data should be used or whether primary research would be more economical.

(c)   **Availability**. Secondary data may not exist in the specific product or market area.

(d)   **Bias**. The secondary data may be biased, depending on who originally carried it out and for what purpose. Attempts should be made to obtain the most original source of the data, to assess it for such bias.

(e)   **Accuracy**. The accuracy of the data should be questioned. Here is a possible checklist.

- Was the sample representative?
- Was the questionnaire or other measurement instrument(s) properly constructed?
- Were possible biases in response or in non-response corrected and accounted for?
- Was the data properly analysed using appropriate statistical techniques?
- Was a sufficiently large sample used?
- Does the report include the raw data?
- To what degree were the field-workers supervised?

In addition, was any raw data omitted from the final report, and why?

(f)   **Sufficiency**. Even after fulfilling all the above criteria, the secondary data may be insufficient and primary research would therefore be necessary.

The golden rule when using secondary data is **use only meaningful data**. It is obviously sensible to begin with internal sources and a firm with a good management information system should be able to provide a great deal of data. External information should be consulted in order of ease and speed of access: directories, catalogues and indexes before books, abstracts and periodicals. A good librarian should be a great help (Hague, 2004)

Bradley (2007) has a very good section on evaluating secondary research (from page 106)

Chisnall (2004) has a very useful appendix of secondary research sources on page 509 – which are still mostly up to date.

Proctor (2005) provides a useful case study about how Montres d'Occasion have used secondary research (page 95). ■

Overall, secondary research can be summarised as:

- The collection of secondary data is often referred to as desk research, since it does not involve the collection of raw data from the market direct. Desk research includes using library sources, the organisation's information system, databases and internal reports.

- The Internet is the richest secondary source of information of all, on practically any subject you can think of. Not all of it is good information, however, and although in theory it is easy to search the Internet, in practice it often takes longer to find exactly what you want than another method would have taken. Knowing which search tool to use and how to use it is a key skill for a researcher.

- Many useful reports and statistics are published by government and non-government sources.

- Environmental scanning is an informal process resulting in the possession of market intelligence. Sources include newspapers, journals and attending conferences.

- Data and reports can be bought in from marketing research organisations. Often these are the result of continuous research using consumer and retail panels.

- Secondary sources of data are of limited use because of the scope for compounding errors arising from why and how the data were collected in the first place, who collected them and how long ago.

- Secondary data can be immensely cost-effective, but have to be used with care.

Learning objectives	Covered
1 Define secondary data	☑ Data that exists already
	☑ Sometimes called desk research
2 Evaluate the benefits and limitations of secondary data	☑ Provides backdrop to primary research
	☑ Can be a substitute for primary research
	☑ May not directly address the research objectives
	☑ Needs carefully evaluating
3 Identify sources of secondary information	☑ Diagram of secondary research
	☑ Published sources
	☑ Internal sources
	☑ Free of charge verses subscribed or paid for
	☑ Growth in panel sources of secondary data

1   Secondary data is external data. True or false? Explain your answer.

2   Secondary data can perform three roles: what are they?

3   Why might a directory be a better source of useful information than a general purpose search engine?

4   Why might this search produced unexpected results?

secondary data

Google Search   I'm Feeling Lucky

5   What are three difficulties with consumer panels?

6   BARCAS is a possible mnemonic for some of the limitations of secondary data. What does it stand for?

1   The limitations of desk research are as follows.

(a)   The data gathered is by definition not specific to the matter under analysis. It was gathered and prepared for another purpose and so is unlikely to be ideal.

(b)   Because it was gathered for another purpose, the data are likely to require a fair amount of adaptation and analysis before they can be used.

(c)   The data gathered are historical and may be some time out of date.

2   It is worthwhile having a discussion with colleagues about this because people vary considerably in their views. For example the writer of this book would not dream of buying a car online, but would happily buy any of the other items mentioned in the question. You may feel quite differently.

3   This approach is too haphazard, as you have probably discovered, having tried this activity. The main drawback is that you usually need to guess the second part of the address (.com, .co.uk, .org, .net): it may take several goes before you get it right, in which case it would have been quicker to use a proper search tool.

4   This is a 'hands-on' exercise.

1   False. Secondary data may be any information not created specifically for the research task including internal data such as sales transaction data.

2   It can provide a backdrop to primary research; it can act as a substitute for field research; and it can be used as a technique in itself.

3   Good directories are compiled by human experts who can review the quality and usefulness of links, whereas a general purpose search engine is fairly indiscriminate about the quality of the pages it turns up in a search.

4   The results will be (probably millions of) pages that contain the words secondary and data, but not necessarily the phrase 'secondary data'. The phrase should be enclosed in inverted commas.

5   It is difficult to select a panel which is a representative sample; panel members tend to become sophisticated in interviewing techniques and responses and so the panel becomes 'corrupt'; and it is difficult to maintain a stable personnel.

6   Bias, Availability, Relevance, Cost, Accuracy, Sufficiency. Make sure you could expand upon each of these terms.

References

Bradley, N. (2007) *Marketing research: tools and techniques*, Oxford University Press, Oxford.

Chisnall, P. (2004) *Marketing research,* 7th Edition, McGraw Hill, Maidenhead.

Cooke, N. & Buckley, N. (2008) '*Web 2.0, social networks and the future of market research*' International Journal of Market Research, Vol 50 Issue 2.

Dillon, W., Madden, T. & Firtle, N. (1994) *Marketing Research in a Marketing Environment*, 3rd Edition, Irwin, Illinois.

Hague, P. *et al.* (2004) *Market Research in Practice: A guide to the basics*, Kogan Page, London.

Malhotra, N. (2004) *Marketing Research: an applied orientation* Pearson, New Jersey.

Proctor, T. (2005) *Essentials of marketing research* 4th Edition, Harlow, Prentice Hall.

Research (2002) '*Grapevine – youth research*' Research, MRS, February 2002 edition, London.

Wilson, A. (2006) *Marketing Research An Integrated Approach* 2nd Edition, Prentice Hall, Harlow.

Chapter 8
Collecting qualitative data

Topic list

Introduction

Qualitative research is a process which aims to collect primary data. Its main methods are the open-ended interview, whether this be a **depth interview** (one-to-one) or a **group discussion** (focus group), and **projective techniques**. The form of the data collected is narrative, rather than isolated statements reducible to numbers. The main purpose is to **understand** consumer behaviour and perceptions rather than to measure them.

Qualitative research is 'research which is undertaken using an unstructured research approach with a small number of carefully selected individuals to produce non-quantifiable insights into behaviour, motivation and attitudes.' (Wilson, 2006).

We'll begin this chapter by considering when it might be **appropriate** to conduct qualitative research. Then we go on to consider each of the main methods before considering how qualitative research can be analysed.

Consensus Global is a company specialising in speaking to 'decision makers' and 'opinion leaders'. This aids researchers in organising interviews or focus groups with people who are usually very difficult to reach.

(*www.research-live.com*)

Syllabus linked learning objectives

By the end of the chapter you will be able to:

Learning objectives	Syllabus link
1 Identify and evaluate the techniques for collecting qualitative data	4.3
2 Review in depth interviews	4.3
3 Explain projective techniques	4.3
4 Describe the use of focus groups	4.3
5 Explain how to analyse qualitative data	4.3

1 Using qualitative research

KEY CONCEPT

concept

Qualitative research is particularly useful for new product research, marketing communications development and preliminary (exploratory) research prior to a more detailed, probably quantitative study.

1.1 New products or services

New products and services (and also proposed improvements to existing products and services) have the disadvantage that there is **no existing data** to measure and perhaps **nothing more tangible than an idea** to present to people.

Qualitative research can help at the initial stages of development to help the company decide whether or not to continue with development at all, and later on, once there is a prototype of some kind, to find out what **further development** is necessary – what **other benefits** customers would like to see that could be included.

It may also help the company to decide **what part of the market** to target: the idea may be very warmly received by some groups but generate no interest whatever amongst others.

1.2 Advertising and promotion

Qualitative research is fairly widely used in the **development** of marketing communications messages to assess how consumers feel about a product or service and what sort of message they are most likely to respond to.

Qualitative methods can also be used to **pre-test** marketing communications messages to make sure the message is understood and that no unintended messages are conveyed.

1.3 Other exploratory research

For existing products and services qualitative research may be used to find the answers to a variety of questions about customer attitudes and perceptions, segmentation and buying behaviour, often as a **preliminary** to help define the direction of **more detailed research**. For instance if ultimately you want statistical data about the decision-making process amongst different buyer segments you need to know what the different decision-making processes are in the first place, so you know what to measure.

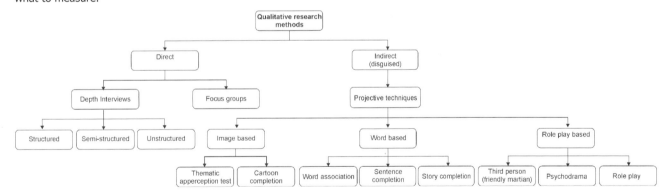

2 Interviews

KEY CONCEPT

concept

The main method of qualitative research is the **interview**.

The key to qualitative research is to allow the respondents to say what they feel and think in response to flexible, 'prompting' questioning, rather than to give their responses to set questions and often set answers in a questionnaire.

2.1 Unstructured interviews

Neither interviewer or respondent is bound by the structure of a questionnaire in an unstructured interview. Interviewers may have a checklist of topics to cover in questioning, but they are free to word such questions as they wish. The order in which questions are covered may also be varied. This will allow the respondent to control the data flow and for the interviewer to explore more thoroughly particular views of the respondent and why they are held. Unstructured interviews are a very useful way of capturing data which is qualitative in nature. Such interviews may also provide the researcher with relevant questions which could be put to a wider audience of respondents using structured or semi-structured interview techniques, especially if quantitative data is required. (Chisnell, 2004)

2.2 Depth interviews

Motivational research often uses the psychoanalytic method of **depth interviews**. The pattern of questioning should assist the respondent to explore deeper levels of thought. Motives and explanations of behaviour often lie well **below the surface**. It is a **time-consuming** and **expensive** process. Taped interviews and analysis of transcripts are often used. A single individual or a small team may conduct depth interviewing. Depth interviews may have fewer than ten respondents although 20 seems to be a universally accepted rule of thumb. (Dillon, 1996)

The **strengths of depth interviews** include the following.

(a)   **Longitudinal information** (such as information on decision-making processes) can be gathered from one respondent at a time, thereby aiding clarity of interpretation and analysis.

(b)   Intimate and **personal material** can be more easily accessed and discussed.

(c)   Respondents are **less likely to confine themselves** simply to reiterating socially acceptable attitudes.

There are, however, **disadvantages** of depth interviews.

(a)   They are **time consuming** to conduct and to analyse. If each interview lasts between one and two hours, a maximum of three or four per day is often all that is possible. There is also a knock on effect with regards to the time taken to analyse findings. Every hour of an in depth interview can lead to around 30 pages of typed A4 paper!

(b)   They are more **costly** than group discussions (due to time and travel expenses).

(c)   There is a temptation to begin treating depth interviews as if they were simply another form of questionnaire survey, thinking in terms of quantitative questions like 'how many' rather than qualitative issues like 'how', 'why' or 'what'.

In a depth interview the key line of communication is between the interviewer and the respondent. They have an **open-ended conversation**, not constrained by a formal questionnaire, and the qualitative data are captured as narrative by means of an audio or video tape.

 ACTIVITY 1

application

Which do you think is preferable: audio or video tape?

The factors to consider when planning a depth interview are as follows.

(a)   **Who should the respondent be?**

(i)   The kind of person depends on the subject being discussed. It may be a consumer interview for discussion of consumer goods or an executive interview for discussing industrial buying.

(ii)   The number of people undergoing depth interviews in the course of the research should be considered in the light of the time they take. 10-15 is usually more than enough.

(iii)   Respondents for consumer interviews are pre-recruited and asked to agree to the interview.

(b)   **What type of interview?** Although depth interviews are usually one-to-one, there may be more than one respondent and there may also be an informant, there to give information about tangible things (eg how big the organisation's purchase budget is) but not about his own attitudes.

(c)   **How long should it be?** Genuine depth interviews interpret the meanings and implications of what is said and can therefore take some time. By contrast, a mini-depth interview may take only 15 minutes, because it can focus on one, predefined topic like a pack design.

(d)   **How structured should it be?** It can be totally open-ended, ranging over whatever topics come up, or it can be semi-structured with an interview guide and perhaps the use of show material.

(e)   **What material should be used?** The type of material that is commonly used includes mock-ups or prototypes, storyboards or concept boards, narrative tapes and animatics, a form of cartoon.

(f)   **Where should the interview take place?** Usually at home or in the workplace.

3 Projective techniques

KEY CONCEPT

concept

Projective techniques attempt to draw out attitudes, opinions and motives by a variety of methods.

Many interview techniques rely on the assumption that you need only to ask people and they will tell you what you want to know. This is not always the case. People may respond differently to how they would act. People may tell you what they think you want to hear or give a different answer because their true answer may reflect badly on them or because they consider it too personal.

Alternatively, people may find difficulty in articulating their motives which lie buried deep within the sub-conscious mind. So as to overcome problems associated with articulating complex or sub-conscious motives, researchers have borrowed techniques developed by psychologists in their studies of mentally disturbed people who have difficulty explaining why they do things.

These techniques are referred to as **projective techniques**. Attitudes, opinions and motives are drawn out from the individual in response to given stimuli.

A number of techniques might be employed.

(a)   **Third person**, or 'friendly Martian' as it is sometimes called, is designed to get the respondent talking about issues which do not interest them. The researcher asks the respondent to describe what someone else might do (a friendly Martian). For example, if someone wanted to buy a house, what do they need to do? Can you describe the steps they would need to take?

(b)   **Word association** is based on an assumption that if a question is answered quickly, it is spontaneous and sub-conscious thoughts are therefore revealed. The person's conscious mind does not have time to think up an alternative response.

(c)   **Sentence completion** is a useful way to get people to respond quickly so that underlying attitudes and opinions are revealed.

- Men who watch football are ....?
- Women wear red to ....?
- People who Morris dance are ....?

(d)   In **thematic apperception tests** (TAT tests), people are shown a picture and asked to describe what is happening in the picture. They may be asked what happened just before or just after the picture. It is hoped that the descriptions reveal information about deeply held attitudes, beliefs, motives and opinions stored in the sub-conscious mind.

(e)   **Story completion** allows the respondent to say what they think happens next and why.

(f)   **Cartoon completion** is often used in competitions. There are usually speech balloons which need to be completed. A comment may be present in one and another left blank for the respondent to fill in.

(g)   **Psychodrama** consists of fantasy situations. Respondents are often asked to imagine themselves as a product and describe their feelings about being used. Sometimes respondents are asked to imagine themselves as a brand and to describe particular attributes.

 MARKETING AT WORK

 application

Household goods maker Reckitt Benckiser uses face to face interviewing for its brand tracking. The company believes that this allows it far more flexibility with the stimulus material that it can use to test brand responses.

 Although generally Malhotra's (2004) text is more detailed than you need at Professional Certificate level, he does cover projective techniques more clearly than many other texts. ∎

3.1 Problems and the value of projective research methods

There are a few problems associated with projective techniques.

(a)   Hard evidence of their validity is lacking. Highly exotic motives can be imputed to quite ordinary buying decisions. (One study concluded that women preferred spray to pellets when it came to killing cockroaches because being able to spray the cockroaches directly and watch them die was an expression of hostility towards, and control over, men!)

(b)   As with other forms of intensive qualitative research, the samples of the population can only be very small, and it may not be possible to generalise findings to the market as a whole.

(c)   Analysis of projective test findings – as with depth interviews – is highly **subjective** and prone to bias. Different analysts can produce different explanations for a single set of test results.

(d)   Many of the tests were not developed for the study of marketing or consumer behaviour, and **may not therefore be considered scientifically valid** as methods of enquiry in those areas.

(e)   There are **ethical problems** with 'invasion' of an individual's subconscious mind in conditions where he is often not made aware that he is exposing himself to such probing. (On the other hand, one of the flaws in projective testing is that subjects may be all too well aware of the nature of the test. The identification of sexual images in inkblots has become a standard joke.)

The major drawback with projective techniques is that answers given by respondents require considerable and **skilled analysis and interpretation**. The techniques are most valuable in providing **insights** rather than **answers** to specific research questions.

However, motivational research is still in use. Emotion and subconscious motivation is still believed to be vitally important in consumer choice, and qualitative techniques can give marketers a deeper insight into those areas than conventional, quantitative marketing research.

Since motivational research often **reveals hidden motives** for product/brand purchase and usage, its main value lies in the following.

(a)   Developing **new promotional messages** which will appeal to deep, often unrecognised, needs and associations

(b)   Allowing the **testing of brand names**, symbols and advertising copy, to check for positive, negative and/or irrelevant associations and interpretations

(c)   Providing **hypotheses which can be tested** on larger, more representative samples of the population, using more structured quantitative techniques (questionnaires, surveys).

ASSIGNMENT TIP

concept

There is debate within the marketing literature about whether projective techniques are a qualitative or quantitative research tool as they are used in both research designs. For instance they can be used successfully within quantitative questionnaires (Bradley, 2006, Dillon et al, 1996). Wilson (2006) on the other hand directly states that projective techniques are used in group discussions and depth interviews. The CIM's view with regards to the assignment appears to be that projective techniques are best used within depth interviews and focus group scenarios. It is highly likely that your assignment will include the design of a group discussion using appropriate projective techniques.

4 Focus groups

These are useful in providing the researcher with qualitative data.

KEY CONCEPT

concept

Focus groups usually consist of 8 to 10 respondents and an interviewer taking the role of group moderator. The group moderator introduces topics for discussion and intervenes as necessary to encourage respondents or to direct discussions if they threaten to wander too far off the point. The moderator will also need to control any powerful personalities and prevent them from dominating the group.

The researcher must be careful not to generalise too much from such small scale qualitative research. Group discussion is very dependent on the skill of the group moderator. It is inexpensive to conduct, it can be done quickly and it can provide useful, timely, qualitative data.

Focus groups are often used at the early stage of research to get a feel for the subject matter under discussion and to create possibilities for more structured research. Four to eight groups may be assembled and each group interviewed for one, two or three hours.

When planning qualitative research using focus groups, a number of factors need to be considered.

(a)   **Type of group**. A standard group is of 7-9 respondents, but other types may also be used.

(b)   **Membership**. Who takes part in the discussion depends on who the researcher wants to talk to (users or non-users, for instance) and whether they all need to be similar (homogenous).

(c)   **Number of groups**. Having more than twelve groups in a research project would be very unusual, mainly because nothing new would come out of a thirteenth one!

(d)   **Recruitment**. Usually on the basis of a quota sample: respondents are screened by a short questionnaire to see whether they are suitable. In order to persuade them to join in, the members are usually given an incentive plus expenses.

(e)   **Discussion topics**. These will be decided by the researcher with regard to the purpose of the group discussion, that is the data that are required. There should be a number of topics since the interviewer needs to be able to restart discussion once a topic has been fully discussed.

4.1 Discussion guide

A discussion guide (also known as a topic guide) is the guide prepared by a depth interviewer or focus group moderator to guide the topics under discussion. Topic guides can take many different forms, according to clients' preferences and the needs of the research, from looser lists of subject areas to be covered to more strictly structured lists of specific question areas.

The general format is to have three phases.

(a) **Introduction**, welcoming the group, explaining the purpose of the meeting and outlining the topics that will be discussed, and introducing the participants or getting them to do so themselves.

(b) **Discussion**, which may have several themed sub-phases and involve product trial.

(c) **Summary** and thanks.

 MARKETING AT WORK application

SAMPLE DISCUSSION GUIDE: HIGH FIBRE MICROWAVE PIZZA

Introduction

Introduce self, note ground rules and mention taping.

Warm up: Go around the table and state name and what types of pizzas you buy (briefly).

Discussion

Discuss pizza category: What's out there? What is most popular? What's changed in your pizza eating habits in the last five years?

When cooking pizza at home, what kinds do you make? (frozen, chilled, baked, microwaved, etc.) Any related products?

Probe issues: Convenience, costs, variations, family likes and dislikes

Probe issues: Any nutritional concerns?

Present Concept: Better nutritional content from whole wheat and bran crust, high in dietary fibre. Strong convenience position due to microwavability. Competitive price. Several flavours available. Get reactions.

Probe: Is fibre a concern? Target opportunity for some consumers?

Probe: Is microwave preparation appealing? Concerns about browning/sogginess/crispness?

Taste and discuss representative prototypes. Discuss pros and cons. Probe important sensory attributes. Reasons for likes and/or dislikes.

Review concepts and issues. Ask for clarification.

Ask for new product suggestions or variations on the theme.

Last chance for suggestions. False close (go behind mirror).

If further discussion or probes from clients, pick up thread and restart discussion.

Summary

Close, thanks, distribute incentives, dismissal.

 ASSIGNMENT TIP concept

The development of a discussion guide featured on the December 2009 assignment.

4.2 Moderator

Key to the success of a focus group will be the skill of the person running it, usually called the **moderator**.

(a) The moderator needs to be able to **build a rapport** between a group of people who have never met before.

(b)   He or she needs to make sure that **everyone gets an opportunity** to speak.

(c)   The moderator needs to ensure that the discussion **stays focused** on the topics at hand.

(d)   The moderator must be **sensitive to the mood** of the group throughout the discussion. It is likely to change a number of times even during a relatively short meeting.

Dillon et al (1996) believes that the moderator plays the same role as a therapist does in group therapy. As such they should discuss topics within a time period but not in any set order. The role of a moderator is not to lead or direct the discussion but to keep it focussed on the topic of interest.

Moderator discussion guides should be flexible enough to be altered as the discussion progresses.

  ACTIVITY 2  application

Next time you are in a meeting see if you can sense the changes in mood. You are most likely to notice a change when the meeting has gone on a bit too long and people start to want to leave! Look for tell-tale signs like body language and tone of voice, as well as changes in the quality of discussion.

Wilson (2006) draws attention to the typical thinking process of a focus group.

(a)   Initially there will be **anxieties and doubts**: participants won't know exactly why they are there and what is expected of them. The moderator needs to be aware of this and set their minds at rest: perhaps even ask them to share their doubts.

(b)   Participants will **wish to feel included** so it is important to get contributions from each member early on.

(c)   Especially because they are strangers, the group members are likely to want to **establish their own status**: what their experience of the matter under discussion is, why they should be listened to. This tends to die down after a while and participants are more interested in sharing and **relating to each other**. Depending on the individuals, however, intervention from the moderator may be required to prevent one or two people dominating the discussion.

(d)   People are keen to feel that their **opinions are valued**: the moderator needs good listening skills (good eye contact, asking for points made to be developed).

(e)   Sooner or later people will start to **wish to leave**, so the moderator needs to give indications of how much ground has been covered and what is left to be covered at regular intervals.

4.2.1 Advantages and disadvantages of focus groups

The **key advantages** of focus groups include the following.

(a)   The group environment with 'everybody in the same boat' can be **less intimidating** than other techniques of research which rely on one-to-one contact (such as depth interviews).

(b)   What respondents say in a group often **sparks off experiences** or ideas on the part of others.

(c)   **Differences between consumers** are highlighted, making it possible to understand a range of attitudes in a short space of time.

(d)   It is **easier to observe groups** and there is more to observe simply because of the intricate behaviour patterns within a collection of people.

(e)   **Social and cultural influences** are highlighted.

(f)   Groups provide a **social context** that is a 'hot-house' reflection of the real world.

(g)   Groups are **cheaper and faster** than depth interviews.

(h)   **Technology** may help to facilitate and add value to the process.

       (i)   Group discussions can be **video tape recorded** for later analysis and interpretation, or they may even be **shown 'live'** to the client via CCTV or webcam.

(ii)   In business-to-business situations it may be possible to use **video-conferencing**, enabling opinions to be sought from a wider variety of locations.

(iii)   **Forums** and **chat rooms** on the web can be used.

The principal **disadvantages** of groups are as follows.

(a)   Group processes may **inhibit some people from making a full contribution** and may encourage others to become exhibitionistic.

(b)   Group processes **may stall** to the point where they cannot be retrieved by the moderator.

(c)   Some groups may **take a life of their own**, so that what is said has validity only in the short-lived context of the group.

(d)   It is not usually possible to identify **which group members said what**, unless the proceedings have been video recorded.

  ACTIVITY 3    application

What are the advantages and disadvantages of group discussions and depth interviews?

4.3 The growth in online qualitative research

In less than a decade a third of US research agencies revenues has shifted to online research. Rather than the research industry being threatened by the new digital environment, Cooke and Buckley (2008) believed that if offers an opportunity to develop new research approaches. The researchers from agency GFK NOP identified Web 2.0 as one example of where innovative methods can be used to explore changing social environments. They clearly define Web 2.0 as:

> 'Web 2.0 refers to the new generation of tools and services that allow private individuals to publish and collaborate in ways previously available only to corporations with serious budgets, or to dedicated enthusiasts and semi-professional web builders.'

It is built around the concept of social software that enables people to collaborate and form online communities. Online communities combine one to one (email, instant messages), one to many (web pages, blogs) and many to many (social networking sites eg Wikis, Facebook, Second Life) communication modes.

The growth in social networking is significant for market researchers because within society a population is growing who are more willing to record and share their experiences with friends and other community members for evaluation. This evaluation forms the basis of individuals' reputations and possibly self concept. Social networks also highlight human tribal behaviour. Earls (2003) suggested that market researchers have in the past overlooked the most important part of what it means to be human; we are herd animals. He argued that market researchers should study the interaction between individuals to make informed decisions about consumer behaviour (Earls, 2003).

Social software which supports group interaction can include; blogs, wikis, podcasts, P2P file sharing, virtual worlds and social networks. Additional content is often generated following a 'mash up' where information is mixed from a number of disparate sources to create creative data. The key issue for researchers to grasp according to Cooke and Buckley (2008) is that social networks are formed voluntarily and sub groups develop as experiences are shared and reputations are built. Within these online environments, members set the agendas and conversations and therefore selectively only enter groups where there is a common interest.

For the market researcher, social networks can be created or existing networks used where community members are already interested in the subjects being investigated. Both qualitative and quantitative research is possible and provides a wealth of opportunity for not only increasing response rates as a result of precision sample selection and respondent interest but the ability to hold more sophisticated extended focus groups and interactive panels (although to describe social network research in these two traditional terms could be considered to undermine their true value and future opportunity).

ACTIVITY 4   application

Imagine you are investigating whether a new form of refrigerator which is highly environmentally friendly with a negligible carbon footprint. You know through secondary research that this would appeal to a growing group of ecologically aware consumers but because the production costs are high, you need to conduct some detailed research into the price that target consumers would be willing to spend.

How might social networks help with this research?

Research agencies with established online panels would be able to quickly and relatively cheaply form a social network of green consumers to discuss the product and the maximum prices that they would be willing to pay in different scenarios.

 MARKETING AT WORK   application

The virtual world Second Life has a growing number of established 'real-world' brands using it's communities to pilot test product launches, idea generation, concept testing and customer experience research. Second Life enables users to create alternative realities from scratch and so they could technically be living a double life, one within the real world with a virtual existence alongside. As lifestyles are built within these virtual lives, brands are entering the virtual marketplace for members to purchase and conspicuously use in order to develop their virtual self concept and reputation. Dell for example enables Second Life users to build their own bespoke computer to use in their virtual life and then to even buy the finished product in the real world if they wish.

Lego similarly through their own website enables member users to build their own models from over 500 pieces, this equates to a massive design team to assist with NPD.

Cooke, N. & Buckley, N. (2008) '*Web 2.0, social networks and the future of market research*' International Journal of Market Research, Vol 50 Issue 2.

5 Analysing qualitative data

The qualitative data you have collected from focus groups and depth interviews and the like will most probably be in the form of **transcripts** of tapes and interviewers' notes. A large volume of such data may seem unmanageable at first but there are a variety of techniques that you can use to make sense of it all. This is called **'content analysis'** (Miles and Huberman, 1994).

(a)   **Tabulation**. A table is created with columns for the different kinds of respondents and rows for the research objectives. Here is a very basic example.

	Men	Women
Attitude towards watching sports		
Attitude towards playing sports		

The comments and quotes from the transcripts are then entered into the appropriate box. This makes it much easier to make comparisons and can give rise to some quantitative data ('six out of ten women said ...').

Provided researchers are not allowed to add their own categories the task can be shared between several people with consistent results. On the other hand the method could be considered to be too inflexible: collected data that does not 'fit' anywhere might be discarded even though it is valuable.

(b)   **Cut and paste**. This is identical to the tabular method except that data is not entered afresh but simply 'lifted' from the original transcript, so preserving accuracy. A word processing package or a spreadsheet would be used.

(c) **Spider diagrams** or **mind maps**. The research issue is placed at the centre of a sheet of paper and the key themes that emerge and relevant quotes and comments from the transcripts responses are placed around it.

Factors influencing how customers assess price

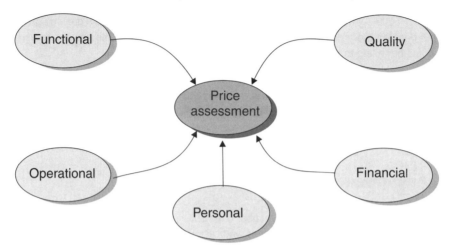

This makes it easier to include comments that don't 'fit' when using the tabulation method. The complexity of the interrelationships between items can be shown more clearly, via the placement of the comments and the use of interconnecting lines. Because the method is less rigid, there is no guarantee that two researchers would analyse the data in the same way, however.

(d) **Annotation.** As you might guess this entails the researcher categorising the items in a transcript by adding marginal comments, or perhaps using different coloured highlighter pens (or the equivalent in a word processor or spreadsheet). This leaves the actual data intact, so it is still possible to see how the full conversation flowed.

(e) **Computerised analysis** is possible with varying degrees of sophistication. Some programs might simply count the number of times a particular word or phrase appears; others can recognise patterns and related concepts.

Bradley (2006) has some very useful checklists which are relevant for this chapter. You may find them useful to refer to if you design qualitative research methods within your own assignment work. The tools inlcude 'considerations for qualitative group facilities' and 'checklist for projective techniques'.

Proctor (2005) has a number of useful case studies to demonstrate how qualitative research has helped to address research needs. The Avon, Muller and Brand Valuation case studies within his chapter on qualitative research are particularly good. ▮

To summarise our discussion about qualitative data collection:

- Qualitative research is particularly useful for new product research, marketing communications development and preliminary (exploratory) research prior to a more detailed, probably quantitative study.

- The main method of qualitative research is the interview.

- Projective techniques attempt to draw out attitudes, opinions and motives by a variety of methods.

- Focus groups concentrate on discussion of chosen topics in an attempt to find out attitudes. They do have limitations despite advantages such as the ability to observe a whole range of responses at the same time.

Learning objectives	Covered	
1 Identify and evaluate the techniques for collecting qualitative data	☑	Depth interviews, projective techniques, focus groups , online
2 Review in depth interviews	☑	Provides backdrop to primary research
	☑	Can be a substitute for primary research
	☑	Usually lasting approx 1 hour can be structured semi-structured or unstructured
	☑	Time consuming and expensive but offers deeper insights
3 Explain projective techniques	☑	Illicit subconscious responses
	☑	Useful when topic sensitive or respondents unsure of their own views
	☑	A range of projective devises
	☑	Used as part of another qualitative method eg interview, focus group
4 Describe the use of focus groups	☑	Designed to encourage open conversations between participants
	☑	A moderator not an interviewer
	☑	Discussion guides should be open and not include closed questions
	☑	The group needs to be carefully put together – 6-12 respondents recruited.
5 Explain how to analyse qualitative data	☑	Content analysis
	☑	Tabulation
	☑	Spider diagrams
	☑	Software to assist

1. Qualitative research is particularly appropriate in three cases. What are they?

2. If you are stopped in the street and asked a series of questions by someone with a clipboard you have taken part in qualitative research. True or false? Explain your answer.

3. Which of the following is most likely to be a question asked in a depth interview?

   A   How often do you buy this product?
   B   Which product do you prefer?
   C   Why do you like this product?

4. What projective technique is being described in each case?

   .... Fantasy situations
   .... Get someone talking about issues which do not interest them
   .... Sub-conscious thoughts may be revealed
   .... Underlying attitudes and opinions may be revealed
   .... What happens next
   .... What is happening in the picture
   .... What people think as opposed to what they say

5. List five factors that need to be considered when planning qualitative research using focus groups.

1. There is no definite answer, but people are more likely to be self-conscious about being captured on video than they are on tape and may even refuse to allow you to video them. If they are not comfortable it is less likely that you will get the information you require.

2. Don't forget to take part in the meeting, too!

3.

Group discussions	Depth interview
Advantages	
Less intimidating	Decision making *processes* can be analysed
Easily observed	Majority *and* minority opinion can be captured
Range of attitudes can be measured	Sensitive topics more easily discussed
Social aspect reflects real world	'Unusual' behaviour can be discussed
Dynamic and creative	
Cheaper	
Disadvantages	
Participants may not express what they really think – they may be inhibited or they may be showing off	Time consuming
	Less creative
Views may be unrealistic – meaningful in a group context but not for the individual	More expensive

4. There are a number of existing social networks which developed as individuals started to discuss their growing ecological concerns. The members of these online communities would be expected to be interested in debating and entering dialogue about such a refrigerator. These groups may also provide a strong referral market if the product finally was launched in the market

1   New product or service research, advertising and promotion research and exploratory research.

2   Probably not: the person with the clipboard will most likely be asking a series of pre-defined questions and asking you to choose between pre-defined options. Qualitative research is supposed to allow the respondents to say whatever they feel and think in response to flexible, 'prompting' questioning.

3   C. The other questions would be better asked as part of a questionnaire with pre-defined options, since there are only a limited number of possible answers.

4

Psychodrama	Fantasy situations
Third person or 'Friendly Martian'	Get someone talking about issues which do not interest them
Word association	Sub-conscious thoughts may be revealed
Sentence completion	Underlying attitudes and opinions may be revealed
Story completion	What happens next
Thematic apperception tests	What is happening in the picture
Cartoon completion	What people think as opposed to what they say

5   We only asked for a list, but see if you can add a comment to each item.

   (a)   Type of group
   (b)   Membership
   (c)   Number of groups
   (d)   Recruitment
   (e)   Discussion topics

References

Bradley, N. (2007) *Marketing research: tools and techniques,* Oxford University Press, Oxford.

Chisnall, P. (2004) *Marketing research,* 7th Edition, McGraw Hill, Maidenhead.

Cooke, N. & Buckley, N. (2008) '*Web 2.0, social networks and the future of market research*' International Journal of Market Research, Vol 50 Issue 2.

Dillon, W., Madden, T. & Firtle, N. (1994) *Marketing Research in a Marketing Environment,* 3rd Edition, Irwin, Illinois.

Earls, M. (2003) '*Advertising to the herd: how understanding our true nature challenges the ways we thing about advertising and market research*' International Journal of Market Research, Vol 45, Issue 3, pp 311-366.

Hague, P. *et al.* (2004) *Market Research in Practice: A guide to the basics,* Kogan Page, London.

Malhotra, N. (2004) *Marketing Research: an applied orientation* Pearson, New Jersey.

Miles, M. and Huberman, M. (1994) *Qualitative Data Analysis: An expanded sourcebook,* Sage, Thousand Oaks.

Proctor, T. (2005) *Essentials of marketing research* 4th Edition, Prentice Hall, Harlow.

Research (2007) '*MR challenged on 'cold calls*' Research, MRS, November 2007 edition, London.

Wilson, A. (2006) *Marketing Research An Integrated Approach* 2nd Edition, Prentice Hall, Harlow.

Chapter 9
Collecting quantitative data

Topic list

1. Quantitative data collection methods
2. Questionnaires and questionnaire design
3. Interviews and surveys

Introduction

The questionnaire is the most important means of collecting primary quantitative data, aside from information collected in the ordinary course of business. Observation and experimentation are also commonly used within research designs to collect quantitative data. Both of these approaches are covered in Chapter 10. It is fair to say however that these methods make extensive use of questionnaires and so it is appropriate for us to dedicate an entire chapter to discussing the use of alternative types of surveys and the questionnaires used in terms of their design, question formats and overall use.

KEY CONCEPT

concept

Quantitative research is structured to collect specific data regarding a specific set of circumstances.

As you probably know from personal experience many questionnaires are extremely **badly designed**. We begin this chapter by recommending a methodical approach and explaining and illustrating the **issues** that arise, and the **mistakes to avoid**.

ASSIGNMENT TIP

format

Within your assignment it is highly likely that you will have to design a questionnaire. .

Surveys may be **administered** face-to-face, by telephone, by post, on the web and each of these methods raises certain issues. Some forms of primary data collection will involve the customer trying out the product or service, as well as giving responses to questions.

Syllabus linked learning objectives

By the end of the chapter you will be able to:

Learning objectives	Syllabus link
1 Identify quantitative data collection methods	4.4
2 Design a basic questionnaire	4.6
3 Identify alternative survey types	4.4

1 Quantitative data collection methods

As we have just stated, questionnaires and surveys are key to collecting quantitative data. Surveys however can be administered in a number of different ways and the surveys that may be used therefore need to be produced in an appropriate style for that survey type. The following diagram highlights the alternative survey styles.

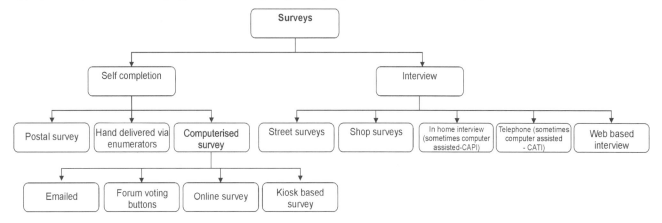

2 Questionnaires and questionnaire design

 KEY CONCEPT

concept

Questionnaire design (TAG) should be done methodically: develop question topics; select question and response formats and take care with wording; determine the sequence; design the layout and pilot test.

In the majority of research projects, the most critical technical issue is likely to be the **quality of the research techniques that have been used**. Where research findings are suspect, this is most commonly because there are fundamental **flaws in the design of the questionnaire**. In this section, therefore, we will spend some time looking at some of the key issues involved in designing an effective questionnaire.

Wilson (2004) recommends a methodical approach to designing questionnaires, with the following steps.

- Develop **question topics**: these will derive from the research **objectives** and may be refined by initial **qualitative research**. We have covered these topics in earlier chapters.
- Select question and response **formats and wording**
- Determine **sequence**
- Design **layout**
- **Pilot test**

2.1 Question and response formats and wording

 KEY CONCEPT

concept

Questions (TAG) need to be **worded with precision**, avoiding ambiguity and lack of clarity, not conflating multiple issues, not making unjustified assumptions, making it easy and clear for respondents to answer.

2.1.1 Precision

Even though most marketing research questionnaires explore comparatively straightforward issues, **precision** should always be a primary concern.

The principles set out in the following paragraphs may sound so obvious as to be **hardly worth stating** and yet, in many questionnaires, these apparently self-evident points are **routinely disregarded**. All too often, there is little clarity about the information that is required, there is woolliness and imprecision in the framing of questions and there are confusions both about the meaning of the question and about the interpretation of the response.

The potential causes of this imprecision are numerous, but there are a number of common pitfalls that are worth highlighting.

(a) **Ambiguity and uncertainty about language or terminology**. In framing a question, managers will often assume a common understanding of words or phrases, where no such commonality actually exists.

(b) **Lack of clarity about the information required**. Questionnaires are frequently weakened by a lack of clarity about the nature and detail of the information they are intended to collect. You should always stop and ask yourself some fundamental questions.

  - Why am I asking this question?
  - What is it intended to find out?
  - What exactly do I want to know?
  - Will this question give me the information I need?

These questions are often not explicitly addressed, with the result that the wrong question (or only part of the right question) is asked. In one employee survey, for example, the questionnaire asked:

> Which of the following do you feel are barriers to your undertaking further training or development in your own time?
>
> - Lack of spare time
> - Lack of motivation
> - Personal/domestic commitments
> - Cost

Not surprisingly, many respondents ticked most if not all of these options. The questionnaire designer really wanted to ask not **whether** these factors were seen as barriers, but **which** were the most significant barriers and **how** significant they were.

(c) **Conflation of multiple questions into one**. In one survey, for example, respondents were asked, 'How often does your workgroup meet to discuss performance, quality and safety issues?' The assumption behind this question – which was part of the evaluation of a team development programme – was that managers called workgroups together to discuss all three of these issues, as they were required to do. In fact, practice varied considerably across the organisation. Some workgroups did not meet at all, some met infrequently and many met relatively often but only discussed performance issues. However, this fact, which was crucial to evaluating the effectiveness of the programme, only emerged during subsequent focus group.

(d) **Making unjustified assumptions**. Similar problems can arise when the phrasing of the question implies an assumption of a preconception that is not justified by the evidence available to you. It is not uncommon, for instance, to encounter questions such as, 'In reviewing your performance, which of the following methods does your manager use?' The assumption here, of course, is that the manager reviews the respondent's performance at all.

2.1.2 Open and closed questions

Closed questions give people a choice of predetermined answers or can simply be answered with a 'Yes' or 'No' or a tick in a box or a very short factual answer. In conversation and information gathering they help to establish the basic facts.

Title	Mr ☐	Mrs ☐	Miss ☐	Ms ☐	Dr ☐	Other ☐
Would you like a sales representative to call you?				Yes ☐	No ☐	

- The advantage is that you will get short, relevant answers that are easy to analyse.
- The disadvantage is that the choices may be too restrictive to cover every possibility.

Open questions let people respond in their own words. Typically an open question begins with 'Why ...?' or 'How ...?' or a phrase like 'Could you describe...' or 'Tell me more about ..'.

(a) The advantage of this type of question is that it is less likely to lead people into giving the answer they think you want.

(b) The disadvantage is that you may end up collecting a large amount of subjective data. This may or may not be relevant, and you will need to spend time reading and interpreting it to find out.

For instance, suppose you design a questionnaire with the following (open) question and put a large blank box underneath for the answer.

What method(s) of communication did you use the last time you arranged to meet someone or a group of other people?

Some people would simply respond 'PHONE & E-MAIL', but (depending on the size of the blank box) others may be tempted to scribble you a little story about what the event was, who was there, how the initial idea for the event was a spontaneous conversation in the kitchen at work, how the news spread like wildfire by phone and e-mail - all of which you would have to decipher, read and interpret, but almost all of which you do not need to know!

A much better way to get the information you want is to offer a limited range of possible responses to the question, something along these lines.

Please indicate what methods of communication you used the last time you arranged to meet someone or a group of other people (✓ *Tick all boxes that apply*)			
E-mail	☐	I do not meet other people	☐
Telephone conversation	☐	Message pinned on notice board	☐
Post	☐	Website/chat-room	☐
Text message	☐	Face-to-face	☐
Other (please give brief details)			

The answers to this (almost closed) question will be much easier to analyse, and it will be much quicker for people to answer the question if they do not have to think up their own words.

(a) So far as possible you should avoid putting the choices in the order that you think reflects their popularity: note the two column layout, which tries to avoid this.

(b) Note that the text and the associated boxes to tick are closely aligned and shaded so that it is clear which box belongs to which option.

(c) It is also clear in this example that you want a tick, not a cross. Actually it probably doesn't matter what mark people use, but remember that lots of people are scared of forms: save them from worrying and make it clear for them.

(d) If the answer is 'Other' it is clear from the wording and the limited space for the answer that you do not want much detail.

2.1.3 Leading questions

Even when the question has been very carefully and precisely planned, it may still provide misleading or inaccurate data if it appears to be **leading the respondent towards a particular answer**. People may still feel **uncertain** about its outcomes and they may still feel **suspicious of your motives** for conducting it. In such cases, some may feel very keen to give the 'right' answer – the answer that they believe the organisation wants to hear. Regardless of your care in drafting the questionnaire, you may not be able to avoid this problem entirely.

This problem occurs most commonly when respondents are asked to **indicate their level of agreement or disagreement** with a particular statement. The preferences or prejudices of the questionnaire designer can appear too obvious to the respondent. It is prudent, therefore, to include a **mixture of positive and negative statements**, which do not suggest any intrinsic preference.

In some cases, the choice of statement can **significantly undermine the value of the information obtained**. In one questionnaire, for instance, respondents were asked to indicate their agreement or disagreement with the statement, 'The quality of work in my department is generally excellent'. If the respondent agreed with this statement the meaning was clear – that he or she thought the quality of work in the department was generally excellent. However, if the respondent **disagreed** with the statement, the meaning was less clear. Did they think the quality was moderate or even poor? From the information provided by the question, there was no way of telling.

2.1.4 Formats

KEY CONCEPT

concept

Question types include **Yes/No**, **multiple choice**, **ratings** and **scales**: the primary purpose is to facilitate statistical analysis. Two of the best known scales are the Likert scale and the Semantic Differential scale.

Apart from a simple **'Yes/No' closed question** format, there are various **other ways** of structuring questions. In general, the questions in a written questionnaire often contain **multiple choice** type, so providing the basis for quantitative analysis. The primary purpose of a written questionnaire is to facilitate **precise statistical analysis**. If the questionnaire includes too many narrative or open questions, analysis becomes very difficult. There is a fine balance when designing questionnaires in terms of the need to keep questions varied to avoid respondent boredom and also ensuring that the analysis is not overly complex. Open ended qualitative style questions can be used within surveys although they should be kept to a minimum.

Questions can be divided into two broad categories; those **exploring attitudes** or opinions and those **seeking some form of factual information**. In the former category would generally fall, for example, the 'agree/disagree' format, such as 'Safety is always a paramount concern for the organisation. Do you agree strongly/agree slightly/disagree slightly/disagree strongly'. In the latter category might fall questions about, say, the frequency of workgroup meetings or about recent experience of training.

ACTIVITY 1

application

You will often receive questionnaires, perhaps in the post, perhaps as door drops, perhaps when you purchase a new product. Don't throw them away, start collecting a file of them and make careful note of the styles of question used, use of graphics and symbols, layout. Some will be much better than others, of course, but it is worth keeping the bad examples too.

Within these two broad categories, a number of formats can be applied. Questions on attitude or opinion generally ask the respondent to indicate both the direction and the strength of feeling – say, 'strongly agree' to 'strongly disagree'. Alternatively, you might ask for the range of opinion relating to a given topic with a question like 'Do you think the quality of work in your department is generally excellent/good/fair/poor?' In such cases, where you are effectively asking respondents to commit themselves to a specific opinion, you need to be aware of what is sometimes called, in an experimental content, the 'error of the central tendency'.

BPP
LEARNING MEDIA

In other words, **respondents are commonly reluctant to give extreme responses** and prefer to hover around the middle ground. If you have an odd number of items in your scale, you may find that respondents disproportionately opt for the neutral option. There are benefits in forcing respondents off the fence by **offering only an even number of options**, so that the respondent has to choose between, say, 'agree slightly' and 'disagree slightly'. In this way, you gain a clearer perspective on the **true direction of opinion**.

Where you are asking to identify preferences from among a number of options, you may ask respondents to **rank the options against a given criterion**, such as 'Which of the following do you think are the most important contributors to high workgroup performance? (Please rank in order of importance.)'

(a)   If you use this format, you should remember to indicate **how the ranking should be applied**. Is number 1 the **most** or the **least** important factor? Ranking questions can seem **confusing** to respondents and are best used sparingly. In any cases, it is rarely worth asking respondents to rank more than the first three or four items. Beyond that, rankings usually become fairly arbitrary.

(b)   A more straightforward approach is to ask respondents simply to **select one item** – 'Which of the following do you think is the single most important contributor to high workgroup performance? (Please tick one only.)' Although slightly less detailed, this question is easier both to complete and to analyse.

In collecting **factual** information, you may again wish to **use scales** where the required information lies on a continuum. For example, 'How many days have you spent training in the past twelve months? Fewer than 3 days/4 – 6 days/6 – 10 days/more than 10 days.'

Where you are exploring more discrete items of information, you may simply ask respondents to **select the most relevant items**. For example, you might ask, 'Which of the following types of training have you undertaken in the last year? (Please tick any that apply.)' In this case, you are not asking respondents to evaluate the options against one another, but simply to make a choice between those that are and those that are not significant. This format can also be applied in cases of **opinions and attitudes**.

Name	Description	Example

CLOSED-END QUESTIONS

Dichotomous — A question with two possible answers.

'In arranging this trip, did you personally phone British Airways?'

Yes ☐   No ☐

Multiple choice — A question with three or more answers.

'With whom are you travelling on this flight?'

No one ☐	Children only ☐
Spouse ☐	Business associates/
Spouse and children ☐	friends/relatives ☐
	An organised tour group ☐

Likert scale — A statement with which the respondent shows the amount of agreement/

'Small airlines generally give better service

Strongly disagree 1	Disagree 2	Neither agree nor disagree 3	Agree 4	Strongly agree 5
☐	☐	☐	☐	☐

British Airways

Semantic differential — A scale connecting two bipolar words, where the respondent selects the point

Large _ _ _ _ _ _ _ _ _ _ _ _ _ _ _ _ _ Small
Experienced _ _ _ _ _ _ _ _ _ _ _ _ _ Inexperienced
Modern   Old-fashioned

Importance scale — A scale that rates the importance of some attribute.

Extremely important 1	Very important 2	Somewhat important 3	Not very important 4	Not at all important 5
☐	☐	☐	☐	☐

Rating scale — A scale that rates some attribute from 'poor' to 'excellent'.

Excellent   Very good   Good   Fair   Poor

Intention-to-buy scale — A scale that describes the respondent's intention to buy.

'If an inflight telephone was available on a long flight, I would'

Definitely buy 1	Probably buy 2	Not sure 3	Probably not buy 4	Definitely not buy 5
☐	☐	☐	☐	☐

OPEN-END QUESTIONS

Completely unstructured — A question that respondents can answer in an almost unlimited number of ways.

'What is your opinion of British Airways?'

Word association — Words are presented, one at a time, and respondents mention the first word that comes to mind.

'What is the first word that comes to mind when you hear the following'
Airline_____
British_____
Travel _____

Sentence completion — An incomplete sentence is presented and respondents complete the sentence.

'When I choose an airline, the most important _____ consideration in my decision is _____ '

Story completion — An incomplete story is presented, and respondents are asked to complete it.

'I flew B.A. a few days ago. I noticed that the exterior and interior of the plane had bright colours. This aroused in me the following thoughts and feelings.' Now complete the story.

Picture completion — A picture of two characters is presented, with one making a statement. Respondents are asked to identify with the other and fill in the empty balloon.

The inflight entertainment's good

Thematic Apperception Test (TAT) — A picture is presented and respondents are asked to make up a story about what they think is happening or may happen in the picture.

2.1.5 The Likert scale

This approach can be summarised in three steps.

Step 1. A list of statements is prepared about the topic being researched, and a test group of respondents is asked to rate each statement on a scale from strong agreement to strong disagreement.

Step 2. A numerical value is given to each response:

5	Strongly agree
4	Agree
3	Don't know
2	Disagree
1	Strongly disagree

Step 3. Each respondent's scores for all the statements are added up to give a total score for the topic, which may reflect overall positive or negative attitudes: responses to individual statements can also be analysed to get more meaningful information about the pattern of responses.

Likert scales are simple to prepare and administer. You may have been asked to complete such an inventory test over the telephone, or seen one in a magazine. However, again you should be aware that scale values have no absolute meaning, and are limited in their statistical uses, on an 'interval' scale.

2.1.6 The Semantic Differential scale

(a) Scales are constructed on a number of **'dimensions'** – pairs of opposite attributes or qualities, expressed as adjectives – valued on a continuum from +3 to –3.

Profile of Car Model X

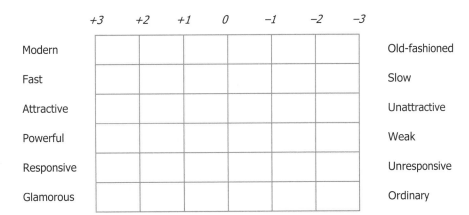

(b) Respondents are asked to **select the position of the object** being researched (in this case the car) on each continuum, according to the degree to which they think the adjective describes the object. (If the car is very powerful but not terribly responsive, say, it might rate +3 on the powerful-weak dimension, and +1 on the responsive-unresponsive scale.)

(c) A **'profile'** is thus built up by each respondent.

The main problem with Semantic Differential scales is the **subjectivity attached to language**. Words mean different things to different people. (The word 'old-fashioned' in our car profile above may mean 'old-hat' to some and 'classic' to others.)

The other problem of measuring responses to, and perceptions of, different attributes of the same thing is that **one attribute can influence our perception of other attributes** and some attributes bring clusters of other assumed attributes with them (stereotypes). Think, for example, about our model X car: if it looks sleek and attractive, we may perceive it as a fast car – whether it is or not – and if we think of old-fashioned cars as glamorous (because of stereotypes of 'classic' cars and the people who drive them) we might distort our glamour rating.

2.2 Sequence

The overall structure of the questionnaire can take a number of forms, depending on the purpose and nature of the research. As a general rule, when you are exploring a given topic, you should aim to be as systematic as possible in **progressing from the general to the specific**. Typically, your initial aim should be to gain an understanding of the **broad context** within which opinions are held. You can then progress to gaining an understanding of the **nature and strength of opinion** in a given area. Finally, you can move, step by step, towards identifying the **detail that underpins these**.

To illustrate this, let us take a specific example – and one where you can easily put yourself in the position of the customer, assuming you enjoy being paid by your organisation! This is a staff questionnaire (staff are **internal customers**, of course) designed to explore attitudes to reward and recognition. The questionnaire might begin, for example, by asking a question about perceptions of reward and recognition in the organisation generally.

> How satisfied are you with the level of recognition and reward you receive for your achievements at work?
>
> Very satisfied
> Fairly satisfied
> Fairly unsatisfied
> Very dissatisfied?

The **responses** to this question will help provide you with a **context** within which you can interpret the more detailed information you will obtain from subsequent questions.

Having defined the broad organisational context, you can begin to focus more precisely on the detail of the specific topic. The next question might be:

> If you feel that your work achievements are recognised, what form does this recognition generally take? (Please tick any that apply.)
>
> Increased basic pay
> Bonus payment
> Other financial reward
> Promotion
> Verbal congratulations
> Non-financial reward
> Other (please specify)

This will provide you with an understanding of the **current perceptions of the topic** – what respondents' perceptions of the rewards they typically receive for work achievements are. It is important not to make assumptions (in this case it would be all too easy to assume that **your** perceptions and perspective reflect those of the wider workforce, but that may not be the case). The broad rule, as in most aspects of research, is **do not make assumptions**. If you have any doubts at all about people's views or perceptions, test them out.

Having identified people's perceptions of the current state of play in the specific area, you can then move to the next level of detail and begin to explore, for example, internal customers' **preferences** for reward and recognition. You might ask:

> Which of the following forms of recognition for work achievements do you find most motivating? (Please tick one only.)
>
> Increased basic pay
> Bonus payment
> Other financial reward
> Promotion
> Verbal congratulations
> Non-financial reward
> Other (please specify)

As a general rule a questionnaire should **progress from the general to the particular** (funnelling). It may be helpful to avoid a pattern of negative responses by distributing questions about respective topics throughout the questionnaire rather than bunching them together.

Mapping these expressed preferences against the current perceived position should indicate very clearly **if or where there is gap between the current and the desired positions**. This, in turn, will enable the organisation to focus its future activities very precisely on these areas, where they are likely to bring maximum pay-back. Having identified the most important issues in this way, you can then, of course, move on to look in detail at specific aspects of the topic (Dillon, 1996).

This process of moving from the general to the specific is sometimes known as **'funnelling'**. Clearly, it is an important device for **ensuring precision in interpretation**. In addition, it may also help you to provide a meaningful interpretation of responses that may be influenced by extraneous factors, such as **self-interest**. The use of broad, contextual questions, however, will help you to interpret such responses against a range of other issues and concerns. You might, for instance, ask respondents, initially, to rank areas of potential dissatisfaction in order of significance. This will then provide you with a basis on which to evaluate any specific expression of dissatisfaction with the really important issue.

Other questionnaire structures can also be used, to **minimise the influence of external factors**. If you are exploring a range of issues, for example, it can be helpful to distribute questions about each respective issue throughout the questionnaire, rather than bunching them in discrete sections. This can help reduce what is sometimes known as the **'halo effect'**, which is when overall positive or negative feelings about a given issue influence responses to individual questions. For example, if customers generally feel unhappy about delivery times, they may feel inclined to give negative responses to **all** questions relating to delivery, even though they may actually be highly satisfied with, say, quality of packaging. Distributing questions about delivery throughout the questionnaire may help to prevent such respondents establishing a **pattern of negative responses**.

2.3 Questionnaire length and layout

Questionnaire **length** will depend on the circumstances, but **short is better than long**. Clear instructions and layout are vital.

One of the most common questions asked by those conducting or commissioning research is, 'What length of questionnaire is acceptable?' As with sampling, there is **no straightforward answer**. It depends on the nature and complexity of the **questions** being asked. It depends on the **population** being researched, and their familiarity and confidence with questionnaires. It depends on the **methods being used** to administer the questionnaire. It is also true that the appliance and format of the questionnaire may be just as important as its length. Everything else being equal, a well-designed and clearly laid out questionnaire can afford to be longer than a poorly constructed equivalent.

Above all, of course, there is generally a trade-off between questionnaire length and the level of response. The **longer and more detailed** the questionnaire, the **more likely** you are to encounter **resistance** from potential respondents. Ultimately, you will need to balance these two factors. In some cases, for instance, you may feel that a smaller response is justified by the need to obtain a higher level of detail from the questionnaire.

Despite these caveats, the following crude guidelines for different forms of questionnaire administration may be helpful.

(a)   **Cold surveys**. Where the questionnaire is being sent out with no preparation and where respondents have no particular incentive to respond, you should aim for an absolute maximum of 4 sides of paper and no more than 15 to 20 questions (including sub-questions), but in many cases, it will be preferable to aim for just 1 or 2 sides of paper and even fewer questions. The key issue here is likely to be one of presentation. You will want to suggest that the questionnaire is easy to complete and will involve comparatively little of the respondent's time. Therefore, simple, 'user-friendly' layout is likely to be an even more significant issue than the overall length.

(b)   **Postal questionnaires**. Where respondents have been briefed and prepared, but are nevertheless expected to complete the questionnaire entirely in their own time, you should generally aim for a questionnaire of some 6 to 8 sides of paper, ideally with no more than 30 to 40 questions. You will still need to ensure that the form is not unduly intimidating or off-putting and, ideally, respondents should feel encouraged to complete it immediately rather than delaying. If potential respondents put the questionnaire to one side, the chances are that a substantial proportion will not get around to completing it at all.

Some other general points about questionnaire design are also worth stressing. First, make sure that you provide **clear instructions** throughout, indicating precisely how the questionnaire should be completed. These should be simply phrased and as concise as possible. It is also a good idea to **provide some examples** of specific question types and how they should be completed. As always, one good example is worth several dozen words of explanation.

Try to **avoid over-complicated instructions**. In some cases, a degree of complexity may be inevitable – particularly where, for example, some respondents are required to skip a number of the questions. Nevertheless, the most effective questionnaires, in terms of ease of response, are those where all respondents are able to proceed straightforwardly through the questionnaire from the first question to the last.

2.3.1 Laying out the questionnaire

(a)   If respondents have to complete the questionnaire themselves, it must be approachable and as short as possible. Consider the use of **lines, boxes, different type faces and print sizes and small pictures**. Use plenty of space.

(b)   Consider the use of **tick boxes**. Is it clear where ticks go or how to respond in each case? For analysis, will it be easy to transfer responses from the forms to a summary sheet or a computer? Consider pre-coding the answers.

(c)   Explain the **purpose of the research** at the beginning of the questionnaire and where possible guarantee confidentiality. Emphasise the date by which it must be returned and where it should be returned.

(d)   At the end of the questionnaire, **thank the respondent** and make it clear what they should do with the completed questionnaire.

2.3.2 Showcards

Showcards are used to help respondents remember options read to them in face to face surveys. They are used as prompts and can include a list of scale points, phrases to select from, logos to recognise, lists of items, pictorial images or anything else that the researcher needs (Brace, 2004).

The increased use of computer assisted personal interviewing has meant that the researcher will not necessarily need to use physical cards (similar to children's flashcards) as previously but they can make use of more interactive computerised prompts.

 MARKETING AT WORK   application

Direct Marketing guru Drayton Bird believes that market researchers can learn a lot from tips he would give to a direct marketers. In an interview with Richard Young for Research magazine, Bird, outlines what he thinks about research and what he would change. He discussed research generally however also made specific points about data collection. The last two items in the list below outline his view of surveys. Bird's points can be summarised as:

(a)   Good research helps you to make better decisions that will lead to action.

(b)   The secret of good research is a good brief. Clients should understand what is going on in their market and so should help to write specific questions to help everyone come to a conclusion. The aim of the research should be expressed very simply. Researchers often ask the wrong question.

(c)   One of the roles of research is to help refine what you are doing- not to tell you where you should start. Bird recalls a line by Ogilvy '*Don't use research like a drunk clutching a lamppost - for support rather than illumination*'.

(d)   The biggest mistake that marketers make is that they don't talk to their customers.

(e) Researchers shouldn't be overly concerned with the number of questions they ask in surveys. Bird's own research shows that once you get beyond 12 questions people will keep going up to 70! This finding he equates to marketing copy where 75% of people who get past the first 250 words will read 2000 words.

(f) The copy in surveys is not conversational enough and should be more personal. Give someone a reason why they should and they are more likely to respond. Next flatter them, eg. why their opinions matter.   *Young (2008)*

2.4 Pilot tests

Finally, it is **vital** to pilot test questionnaires since mistakes, ambiguities and embarrassments in a questionnaire can be extremely expensive once the main data collection phase has been entered. The **conditions** for the test should be the **same as**, or as close as possible to, the intended conditions for **the real thing**: respondents of the type you really want to test, using interviewers or self-administered questionnaires.

2.5 Survey generating software

There are many IT packages available which help researchers and wannabe researchers to construct, design, select appropriate question formats and also analyse questionnaires for use as a paper versions, in a computer assisted surveying form or online.

 MARKETING AT WORK   application

Snap Solo is just one example of a growing number of survey creating software packages.

Alan Wilson's (2006) text comes with a student sample edition of software for you to try. The main package enables:

Questionnaire design

» Survey Constructor wizard
» WYSIWYG questionnaire design
» Questionnaire templates
» Set response types
» Access to SurveyPak question libraries
» Question routing
» Add images and logos

Data entry

» Four data entry modes
» Browsing of selected cases
» Verification of entered data
» Editing and cleaning

Results analysis

» Easy to read summary report
» Crosstabulations
» Frequency, grid and holecount tables
» 2D and 3D charts
» Statistical analysis
» Filtering / subsets
» Weighting
» Derived / recode variables
» Analysis of literals
» Templates for tables and charts
» Printed and electronic reports
» Volume batch reporting
» Exporting results

(www.snapsurveys.com)

3 Interviews and surveys

 KEY CONCEPT   concept

Interviews are **classified according to where they occur** (in the street, in a shop, in the home). Despite possible interviewer bias interviews can improve the quality and rate of responses.

Postal surveys are less costly and time consuming. Telephone surveys have some advantages, especially the ability to cover a wider geographical area, but have the disadvantage of lack of rapport and confusion with telesales.

Many surveys in UK market research take place as **face-to-face** interviews. The interviewers are often freelancers but can be employees of a market research organisation. An interview is a social encounter, where the personal interface between interviewee(s) and interviewer is crucial.

There are five main styles of interview, classified according to where they occur.

(a)   **Street surveys** take place typically in busy town centres, with the interviewer approaching individuals as they pass by. They need to be brief (5 minutes is too long for most people in their lunch break or going to or from work) and should not require too much concentration from the interviewees, so getting them to consider show material should be avoided. A survey taking place in a shopping centre requires the centre's manager's permission, and a fee may be payable.

(b)   **Shop surveys** take place inside or just outside a particular shop, obviously with the shop's permission.

(c)   **Hall tests** take place in a pre-booked location such as a hotel, where people are invited to attend to answer a few questions, usually being recruited from the street and being enticed by a give-away or refreshments. More complex tasks can be performed by the interviewee, for instance a display can be permanently set up and considered. Sometimes they may be carried out in a natural place for a particular product's consumption or usage: for example, a new brand of alcohol may be tested in pubs or restaurants. Hall tests will be discussed further in Chapter 10.

(d)   **Placement tests**. Respondents for these tests are recruited from omnibus surveys or street interviews, and are provided with the product to test in their own home, or whatever location is appropriate. Placement tests will be discussed further in Chapter 10.

(e)   **Home interviews** are held in the interviewee's home (or doorstep), with the interviewer recruiting simply by knocking on doors. They can be pre-arranged by phone or by dropping a note through the door. Larger, in depth interviews often result but they are time-consuming, expensive and prone to interruption. Many people are reluctant even to answer their doors let alone let an interviewer in so recruiting for home interviews is often frustrating for the interviewer.

(f)   **Business surveys** take place on the interviewee's business premises and are always pre-arranged. Again they are prone to interruption and/or last minute cancellation.

  ACTIVITY 2

application

The next time you see someone conducting interviews in the street don't cross the road or avert your eyes: volunteer to take part and (without being too obvious about it) try to take note of the way questions are phrased, how much depends on the skill of the interviewer, and how easy the interviewer (who may or not be well trained) finds it to record your responses. Don't forget to make notes when you get the opportunity.

It must always be remembered that people taking part in interview surveys are **doing the researcher a favour**, so the least one can do is ensure that the interviewer is well-prepared and does not make the interviewee feel that his or her time is being wasted. Good preparation will also save time in the long run and reduce the costs of hiring freelance interviewers. Finally, it will result in getting the data that is actually needed. It is vital, therefore, that the questionnaire or interview schedule is clear, unambiguous, and accurate.

The interviewer's other tasks are:

(a)   To **locate respondents** (stopping in street, calling house-to-house as instructed by the researcher)
(b)   To **obtain respondents' agreement** to the interview (no mean feat)
(c)   To **ask questions** (usually sticking strictly to the interview schedule/questionnaire's wording) and take down answers
(d)   To **complete records**

Since the desired outcome of the survey is useful data, it is important to consider whether **interviewer bias** may affect the outcome. This comes about in selection of respondents (stopping people who look 'nice' rather than a reasonable cross-section) and handling the interview (not annoying the respondent so his or her answers are affected).

The **advantages of interviews** as a survey method over telephone and postal surveys are as follows.

(a) Respondent **suitability can be checked** at the outset by asking quota questions but more effectively by assessment of the respondent (young man, woman shopping with children), so that the target number of interviews is achieved.

(b) Respondents can be **encouraged to answer as fully as possible** and the interview is usually completed.

(c) Questions are **asked in the right order**, and all relevant questions are asked.

(d) The **use of show material** is properly administered.

(e) **Response rates are higher** than for other forms of survey.

3.1 Postal surveys

Approximately 25% of market research questionnaires are completed by postal survey. We are using the term 'postal' survey to cover all methods in which the questionnaire is given to the respondent and returned to the investigator without personal contact. Such questionnaires could be sent by post but might also be left near a store exit or delivered via door drops.

Postal questionnaires have the following **advantages** over personal interviews.

(a) The **cost per person** is likely **to be less**, so more people can be sampled, and central control is facilitated.

(b) It is usually possible to **ask more questions** because the people completing the forms (the respondents) can do so in their own time.

(c) **All respondents are presented with questions in the same way**. There is no opportunity for an interviewer to influence responses (interviewer bias) or to misrecord them.

(d) It may be **easier to ask personal or embarrassing questions** in a postal questionnaire than in a personal interview.

(e) Respondents **may need to look up information for the questionnaire**. This will be easier if the questionnaire is sent to their homes or places of work.

 ACTIVITY 3   application

What are the advantages of personal interviews over postal questionnaires?

3.1.1 Enumerators

An **enumerator** will **deliver the questionnaire** and **encourage the respondent to complete it**. He will later visit the respondent again to collect the completed questionnaire and perhaps to help with the interpretation of difficult questions. This method results in a better response rate than for postal questionnaires.

 MARKETING AT WORK   application

The impact of technology on marketing research is demonstrated by the widespread use of CAPI and CATI.

First, the paper questionnaire-carrying clipboard is being rapidly replaced for many applications by the laptop computer. Computer assisted personal interviewing (CAPI) has become the norm for face-to-face interviews, according to BMRB International, one of the UK's biggest market research agencies.

Computer-assisted telephone interviewing (CATI) is already firmly established as an alternative to the more laborious written questionnaires that telephone interviewers used to complete.

For both CAPI and CATI, interviewers tap survey answers straight into a computer, cutting down on data processing time and improving accuracy. Surveys can be more complex and closely targeted because the computer automatically selects the interviewer's 'routing' – which question should follow on from a particular answer.

3.2 Telephone surveys

Surveys conducted over the phone rather than face-to-face have the following advantages.

(a) The response is **rapid**.

(b) There is a **standard sampling frame** – the **telephone directory**, which can be systematically or randomly sampled.

(c) A **wide geographical area** can be covered fairly cheaply.

(d) It may be **easier to ask sensitive or embarrassing questions**.

But there are considerable **disadvantages** as well.

(a) A **biased sample** may result from the fact that a large proportion (about 10%) of people do not have telephones (representing certain portions of the population such as old people or students) and many of those who do are ex-directory.

(b) It is not possible to use 'showcards' or pictures.

(c) Due to the reputation of telesales, the refusal rate is much higher than with face-to-face interviews, and the interview often cut short.

(d) It is not possible to see the interviewee's expressions or to develop the rapport that is possible with personal interviews.

(e) The interview **must be short**.

MARKETING AT WORK

application

'Do not call' was set up by the Federal Trade Commission in the United States in an attempt to stop unsolicited telemarketing calls to registered households.

Telephone surveys have been criticised by some pressure groups in their blogs such as plasticbag.org because market researchers are able to call consumers within the UK even though they have registered with the Telephone Preference Service. The TPS enables consumers to sign up to lists which prevents telemarketers then cold calling. The defence used within the market research industry is that because they are not directly selling anything, agencies are entitled to contact people without their permission. The view of the pressure groups has been that research agencies still make money and are infringing upon free time. Within the global market research industry a debate has been sparked about whether or not a national market research opt out list scheme should be initiated in order to remain a self regulating industry in most countries)

3.3 Web surveys

Web surveys are becoming more and more common. The Internet is ideal for surveys in some respects, but far less so in others.

(a) Questionnaires can be **generated dynamically** in response to the respondent's answers. For example if the respondent indicates no interest whatever in a particular topic then any questions relating to that topic can be skipped by the computer without the respondent even knowing the questions existed. Alternatively, if they indicate strong interest they may get additional questions that others would not see. This saves time for everybody.

(b) On the other hand **web users may not be typical** of the target market (not all of whom will have access to the Internet). **Design issues** are even more crucial than with paper-based questionnaires. All the same issues and pitfalls apply, but with several **additional factors** such as speed of processing, intuitive navigation through the questionnaire and security concerns.

Respondents can be recruited to participate in web based surveys either through

- self selection when they notice a link or a pop up on a website they have visited
- a email request with a link to the site
- a non electronic invitation to participate eg by letter

3.3.1 Voting buttons (forum voting)

Voting buttons are also popular in order to gather quick answers to just one or two key questions. Voting buttons can be sent by email or placed within a website. Clearly the use of voting buttons cannot be used where there are a number of complex research objectives but they are useful in quickly measuring a key issue .

3.3.2 Kiosk surveys

Kiosk surveys are essentially similar in terms of the look and design of the overall survey. The difference is that touch sensitive computer station are located in areas where sample respondents are likely to be passing. The kiosks are used frequently in research into exhibitions for example. Whereas previously footfall may have been measured and survey interviewers may have approached visitors as they left an exhibition, kiosks offer the opportunity for respondents to participate in research independently. Retailers and public services locations are also key users of kiosk based surveys.

3.4 Continuous research

The object of continuous research is to **take measurements regularly** so as to monitor **changes in the market**, either consumer, business or internally. Often syndicated because of the set-up costs, continuous research is usually undertaken by a large market research organisation. It can focus on the same consumers over time (panel research) or on a changing body of consumers.

Some research is continuous in the sense that measurement takes place every day, while in other cases measurements are taken at regular intervals.

3.4.1 Omnibus surveys

 KEY CONCEPT concept

Omnibus surveys may be a cost effective way of obtaining certain types of information.

An **omnibus survey** is a master questionnaire run by market research companies who 'sell' space on the questionnaire to marketing organisations who need data. Because the market research companies undertake the sampling, administration, processing and analysis, and spread the cost over the organisations needing data, it is a cost-effective method of research for all concerned. Like panel based surveys, omnibus surveys are increasingly popular because of the development of Web 2.0.

The master questionnaire usually contains some of the same questions (age, gender, occupation) every time, while the remainder of the questions are either continuous (the same questions in the same place on the questionnaire as were asked of a different group, say, one week earlier) or *ad hoc* (inserted on a first-come-first-served basis but in a sensible order).

 Look at the MRS's Research Buyers Guide spefically for Omnibus proviers. You will find that there are a many. Often there will be specialist omnibus surveys with particular groups of respondents such as children, students, business leaders etc. ■

 MARKETING AT WORK application

Opinion Research Corporation have launched 'Small Business Caravan' in the US, an omnibus service collecting the views of 500 small business owners each month on subjects including advertising awareness, brand awareness, purchase decisions and financial product needs. The sample is geared towards small firms in the financial, construction, transportation, communication and retail sectors.

Source: Research Magazine, May 2008

3.4.2 Market tracking surveys

Where the market research company designs the whole questionnaire seeking data on a particular market from regular samples of respondents, rather than a panel, there is a **market tracking survey**. The results are sold by the company to as many marketing organisations as possible. Sometimes information on product usage is combined with data on media exposure. These were also discussed in Chapter 7 because for the company purchasing this information really it is classified as secondary research.

3.4.3 In-store testing

Product testing in store may be a **relatively quick and inexpensive method** of gathering information about customer attitudes towards a particular product. In-store testing can be a useful, convenient way to gain insights into expected consumer behaviour before a full product launch is implemented. Selected stores can be chosen to test a product and gather information about likely buyer behaviour when the product is launched. In-store testing is also a way of promoting the product before, during and after a launch.

3.5 Incentives

It may be advisable to take active steps to **encourage better response rates** from questionnaires, surveys and telephone studies. Methods of achieving this include putting all respondents' names into a **prize draw** or offering a product or service **discount** to all respondents. A whole host of incentives exist and the key is to use an incentive which is valued by the respondents (Dillon, 1994). There is a lot of debate within marketing research about whether incentives work. A key issue to consider however is that it is probably fair to assume that respondents have come to expect some form of incentive in return for their time and opinions. It is probably not worth the risk of reducing response rates further by not including one.

To summarise our key discussions about collecting quantitative data:

- Questionnaire design should be done methodically: develop question topics; select question and response formats and take care with wording; determine the sequence; design the layout and pilot test.

- Questions need to be worded with precision, avoiding ambiguity and lack of clarity, not conflating multiple issues, not making unjustified assumptions, making it easy and clear for respondents to answer.

- Question types include Yes/No, multiple choice, ratings and scales: the primary purpose is to facilitate statistical analysis. Two of the best known scales are the Likert scale and the Semantic Differential scale.

- As a general rule a questionnaire should progress from the general to the particular (funnelling). It may be helpful to avoid a pattern of negative responses by distributing questions about respective topics throughout the questionnaire rather than bunching them together.

- Questionnaire length will depend on the circumstances, but short is better than long. Clear instructions and layout are vital.

- Interviews are classified according to where they occur (in the street, in a shop, in the home). Despite possible interviewer bias interviews can improve the quality and rate of responses. Postal surveys are less costly and time consuming. Telephone surveys have some advantages, especially the ability to cover a wider geographical area, but have the disadvantage of lack of rapport and confusion with telesales.

- Omnibus surveys may be a cost effective way of obtaining certain types of information.

Learning objectives	Covered
1 Identify quantitative data collection methods	☑ Questionnaire based
	☑ Can be through observation and experimentation
	☑ Surveys can be classified
	☑ Fast and relatively cheap to administer and analyse
2 Design a basic questionnaire	☑ Question and response formats
	☑ Types of scales
	☑ Sequence, layout and design
	☑ Software to assist
3 Identify alternative survey types	☑ Face to face vs self completion
	☑ Range of types within overall framework
	☑ Continuous surveys eg, tracking, omnibus

1   At what point in the questionnaire design process should you 'determine sequence'?

2   What four questions should you ask yourself when designing a question on a questionnaire?

3   Write an example of a closed question.

4   What is wrong with this question?

   A   BPP Study Texts are brilliant
   B   BPP Study Texts are very useful
   C   BPP Study Texts cover the syllabus very closely
   D   BPP Study Texts are user friendly

5   Rewrite option A in the previous question using a Likert scale

6   List four advantages of administering a questionnaire by means of a face to face interview.

7   Which of the following statements is NOT correct?

   A   Field tests should be carried out early in the product development cycle
   B   It is possible to buy space on an omnibus survey for your own organisation's question
   C   Web surveys allow questions to be generated dynamically depending on the answers to other questions
   D   Postal questionnaires are likely to be longer than interview questionnaires

8   It is not possible to measure feelings by observation. True or false? Explain your answer.

9   List four issues that need to be considered when devising mystery shopper research.

10   What does CAPI stand for?

---

1   This is a practical, ongoing exercise.

2   Don't forget to do this: it is not a waste of your time, it is a form of revision. And be sympathetic to the survey: you wouldn't want next year's CIM students wandering the streets giving frivolous answers to your carefully crafted questionnaire!

3   Large numbers of postal questionnaires may not be returned, may be returned only partly completed or may be returned very late. This may lead to biased results if those replying are not representative of all people in the survey. Response rates are likely to be higher with personal interviews, and the interviewer can encourage people to answer all questions. Low response rates are a major problem with postal questionnaires, but low response rates can be avoided by:

   (a)   Providing a stamped and addressed envelope or a box for the return of the questionnaire
   (b)   Giving a date by which you require the completed questionnaire
   (c)   Providing an incentive such as a lottery ticket for those who return questionnaires on time
   (d)   Using a good covering letter

   Misunderstanding is less likely with personal interviews because the interviewer can explain questions which the interviewee does not understand.

   Personal interviews are more suitable when deep or detailed questions are to be asked, since the interviewer can take the time required with each interviewee to explain the implications of the question. Also, the interviewer can probe for further information and encourage the respondent to think more deeply.

---

1   After you have determined the question topics, decided on question and answer formats and write the questions, but before final decisions are made about layout, pilot testing is carried out.

2   Why am I asking this question? What is it intended to find out? What exactly do I want to know? Will this question give me the information I need?

3   A closed question can be answered Yes or No or with a very short factual answer. For example, 'What is your date of birth?'.

4   This is intended to be an example of a very bad question. There is no indication of what to do (tick one or more options? Ring round one or more letters?). Option B in particular is far too vague: what does 'useful' mean? It is also a highly leading question, since there is no opportunity to do anything other than praise BPP Study Texts.

5   BPP Study Texts are brilliant

> 5   Strongly agree
> 4   Agree
> 3   Don't know
> 2   Disagree
> 1   Strongly disagree

6   (a)   Respondent suitability can be checked at the outset
     (b)   Respondents can be encouraged to answer as fully as possible
     (c)   Questions are asked in the right order, and all relevant questions are asked
     (d)   The use of show material is properly administered
     (e)   Response rates are higher than for other forms of survey

7   Option A is incorrect. Field tests are expensive and are usually carried out when a product is near to its final form.

8   False. Body language and eye movement in response to a stimulus can be revealing. However you cannot be completely sure without checking by some other means.

9   (a)   The shoppers should fit the profiles of consumers in the organisation's genuine target markets.
     (b)   Some observations made will be **subjective**.
     (c)   **Credibility** may be an issue
     (d)   Mystery shoppers may need to be trained in **data collection skills**

10   Computer Assisted Personal Interviewing.

Brace, I. (2004) *Questionniare Design: How to plan, structure and write survey material for effective market research*, MRS, Kogan Page, London.

Bradley, N. (2007) *Marketing research: tools and techniques*, Oxford University Press, Oxford.

Dillon, W., Madden, T. & Firtle, N. (1994) *Marketing Research in a Marketing Environment*, 3rd Edition, Irwin, Illinois.

Hague, P. *et al.* (2004) *Market Research in Practice: A guide to the basics*, Kogan Page, London.

Malhotra, N. (2004) *Marketing Research: an applied orientation*, Pearson, New Jersey.

Proctor, T. (2005) *Essentials of marketing research*, 4th Edition, Prentice Hall, Harlow.

Research (2007) 'Canadians Report Fall in sugging' Research, MRS, December 2007 Edition, London.

Research (2008) '*Business Wins Round up'*, MRS, May 2008 Edition, London.

Tarren, B. (2008) '*Agencies to feel pinch from DIY survey software, warns Forrester analyst*' Research, MRS, February 2008 Edition, p. 11, London.

Wilson, A. (2006) *Marketing Research An Integrated Approach*, 2nd Edition, Prentice Hall, Harlow.

Young (2008) 'Direct Speech' Research, MRS, February 2008 Edition, p. 32, London.

Chapter 10

Observation and experimentation

Topic list

Introduction

In this short chapter we look at the various procedures for observing behaviour and the techniques used for experiments and tests.

These research designs can use both qualitative and quantitative data collection methods although it is more common for a quantitative survey or some form of quantitative 'count' to be used (Malhotra, 2004).

We begin by giving an overview of the types of observation methods and then follow with experiments and tests. Much of the content contained within this chapter should be quite familiar by now as you have already covered research design and both qualitative and quantitative data collection.

Syllabus linked learning objectives

By the end of the chapter you will be able to:

Learning objectives	Syllabus link
1 Evaluate different methods of observing behaviour	4.2
2 Identify techniques for undertaking experiments	4.4

The diagram below shows the different forms of research observations and tests.

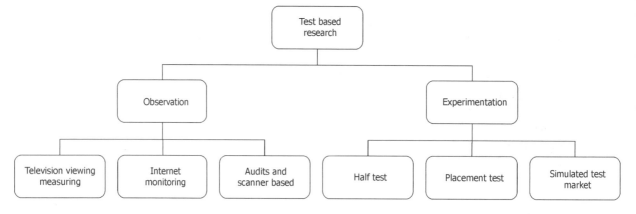

1 Observation

KEY CONCEPT

concept

Observation takes various forms: home audit, direct observation, and the use of physical and technological recording devices.

Interviews and questionnaires depend on respondents answering questions on behaviour and attitudes truthfully. Sometimes it is necessary to **observe behaviour**, not only because respondents are unwilling to answer questions but because such questions do not record behaviour and are therefore unable to provide the researcher with answers (Hague et al, 2006).

There are a number of decisions to make with regard to observations as outlined in the table below.

Categories of observation	
Natural In setting natural to the consumer / market setting eg a consumer using the new food to prepare a meal at home with a researcher present	**Contrived** Created specifically for the purposes of the observation eg a test kitchen to observe how consumers eat a new food product
Visible Respondents aware they are being observed	**Hidden** Respondent unaware that they are being observed
Structured There are pre-defined ideas about what the researcher is looking for	**Unstructured** The researcher observes respondents with no pre-defined ideas about what they are looking for
Mechanised Uses measuring and recording devises eg cameras, counters etc	**Human** The researcher conducts the observation for themselves
Participant The respondent is actively asked to carry out actions eg use a specific product	**Non participant** The respondent is not asked to behave in any specific way

1.1 Direct vs indirect observation

(a) **Indirect observation**. Also termed home audit, this involves the investigation of the respondent's home, office or premises so as to determine the extent of ownership of certain products/brands. (Note that the home audit and diary panels are termed **consumer panel** research.)

(b) **Direct observation**. This involves, not surprisingly, the direct observation of the behaviour of the respondent by the researcher. An event must meet three criteria to be a fit subject for direct observation.

    (i)   The event being observed must only occupy a **short period** of time.

    (ii)   It must be **frequently** performed.

    (iii) The event must be **visible** (and so feelings, beliefs and attitudes are not suitable topics for this technique).

1.2 Natural vs contrived

In **natural settings** video and movie cameras are used to record behaviour. In such settings there is an increased chance of observing real behaviour but the researcher might have to wait a long time until the behaviour occurs. Rather more prosaically, many retail outlets use **pressure mats** or automatic **sliding doors** to record basic information on number of shoppers.

Laboratory settings (contrived setting) are sometimes criticised on the grounds that consumers sometimes act differently when they are asked to respond within an unfamiliar setting. For some research projects this trait could actually be a positive feature especially for new product development projects.

Is the observation of shoppers in a store and their movements to different sections likely to be natural or contrived and visible or disguised?

1.3 Visible vs hidden

Sometimes the researcher can influence the findings of the research unintentionally simply by being present. Think about how you may act differently when you realise you are being watched or filmed. The researcher effect can sometimes have direct implications for the research results.

ACTIVITY 2

application

Imagine that you are a researcher and you need to observe the behaviour of a group of business professionals and their response to a new prototype. Should you conduct hidden or visible research and practically how would you observe them?

1.4 Structured vs unstructured

Structured (the researcher must know what is to be observed) or **unstructured** (the situation does not allow for the data requirements to be predetermined). Unstructured observation is more qualitative in nature and therefore more difficult to analyse. It is useful however because there may be behaviours that are discovered that the research had not expected prior to the fieldwork.

1.5 Mechanised vs human

Recording devices record micro behaviour in laboratory settings and macro behaviour in natural settings can be used in both direct and indirect forms of observation.

While questionnaires and diaries essentially record answers to direct questions, other devices are used to record **observations**, for instance of the order in which a consumer proceeds around a supermarket.

1.5.1 Manual recording systems

A consumer **diary** allows the consumer to record behaviour on or between different dates or even times of the day. The diary is completed every time a certain behaviour occurs, rather than behaviour being recalled at times specified by the researcher. It is thus an **accurate means of recording repetitive information** for, say, a consumer panel.

Diary-filling **can be very detailed and onerous** and it is rare that a household, even a member of a consumer panel, is asked to complete one for longer than two weeks. The problem is that the data recorded needs to be both accurate and up-to-date, whilst the room for error, with new brands on the market for instance, is vast.

During group discussion, **non-verbal communication** can be observed so as to assess the validity of a respondent's replies. This will rely on a researchers skill in interpreting behaviour and cannot be mechanised.

1.5.2 Electronic recording systems

An explosion in market research data has been made possible by the development of **electronic recording devices**.

(a) **EPOS** (electronic point of sale systems) with scanners of bar-codes provide fast and accurate records of sales, times and prices.

(b) **Electronic questionnaires** and diaries, discussed above, allow information to be input directly into a computer system, so results can be reviewed at any time in the survey and range and topical checks applied.

(c) **Audio and video recording devices** may be used to record interviews, especially depth ones, and camcorders can be used to record consumer behaviour.

A large range of measuring equipment is available such as:

(a) **Psychogalvanometers** measure a subject's response to, say, an advertisement by measuring the perspiration rate (which tends to increase when the subject is excited).

(b) **Eye cameras** are used to assess those parts of, for example, an advertisement which attract most attention and those parts which are neglected.

(c) **Pupilometric cameras** are used in assessing the visual stimulation derived from an image.

The key point about electronic recording devices is that **information recorded is complete**, so sampling and estimating are not required.

1.6 Participant vs non participant

Non participant observation is being used more because of the large scale use of observation to see how people behave online.

 MARKETING AT WORK

application

Technological developments are leading to the development of new research tools being used to collect primary research. Many of these examples use observation of online behaviour via tracking devises. The Market Research Societies Magazine titled 'Research' runs a regular feature called Roundup; New Product Development which reports on these advances. As an example:

UK internet analytics company Mobilestats has started offering a new service that sends website statistics in real time to mobile phones. Users will be able to track the number of visitors to their site, which pages they look at, peak traffic time and cost-per-click activity. The company also has a team of analysts to provide customers with in-depth written reports and analytics.

Coremetrics has released Explore, an analytics tool that allows users to track online search behaviour. Users will be able to track whether consumers searched, on a media site for example, for a specific author, genre or language. Consumer products can be filtered by brand, type, colour and size searches.

Starcom MediaVest Group has developed IntenTrack, a tool to predict consumers' purchase behaviour. The study surveys a panel of two million consumers weekly to gauge their purchase intent towards brands and products they have seen advertised in that time. IntenTrack covers 200 brands in 30 product categories in 28 countries. It was developed in partnership with research firms GMI and InsightExpress.

PopularMedia has released the Social Media Marketing Suite to allow marketers to create viral brand campaigns and track user actions, such as image and file sharing, across social media websites.

These developments are important not only from the respect of the technology being used to devise a new research tools but are indicative of the need for such tools in the first place. The explosion on online retailing, social networking, viral marketing and mobile communications generally has created a need for more sophisticated research.

1.7 Observation techniques

1.7.1 Retail audit

Retail audits are used by organisations to assess consumer demand for their products.

At set intervals **researchers visit a sample of shops**, audit (count) the stock in question and record the details of any deliveries since the last audit. Using the fact that

sales = original stock + deliveries – final stock

they are able to calculate the sales of the product since the last audit.

Shops are segmented according to their type (multiples, independent, department) and by the volume of business. Those shops which sell the largest range of products in which the organisation is interested are usually the ones upon which the auditors concentrate.

Retail audits **investigate product types** and hence the client of the research company can be provided with information on their competitors' product as well as their own.

Chisnall (2004) has a complete chapter dedicated to continuous research. It also finishes with a number of useful case studies. ■

1.7.2 Mystery shoppers

KEY CONCEPT

concept

There is a limit to the amount and type of information that can be captured by most forms of observation, although **mystery shopping** is one form that allows a wide range of marketing variables to be researched.

Mystery shopping my be carried out by researchers themselves or by specially recruited and trained members of the public. As the name suggests it involves a person posing as a genuine customer (not just in a shop, it could be **any sort of customer** for **any sort of business**) and reporting back on whatever aspect of the customer experience the researcher is interested in.

Issues in using mystery shopping as a research technique include the following.

(a) A **suitable number** of different shoppers must be used because the results may be affected by the **characteristics of the shopper** as well as of the organisation being researched. The shoppers should fit the profiles of consumers in the organisation's genuine target markets.

(b) Some observations made will inevitably be **subjective** and this must be taken into account.

(c) **Credibility** is an issue with certain types of purchase: for instance people do not buy several cars a week. Certain types of purchase, particularly in financial services, involve the selling organisation checking the credentials of the customer.

(d) Mystery shoppers may need to be trained in **data collection skills**: they will not be very 'mysterious' if they fill in a data sheet during a face to face encounter with a selling organisation!

MARKETING AT WORK

application

'The key to a successful mystery shopper program goes beyond design, administration or technology. It's about the quality of mystery shoppers actually performing the location observations and ensuring they have the resources required to conduct a thorough mystery shop/audit. Maritz' mystery shopping satisfaction services uses professional shoppers who have timely access to us via our bi-faceted communication approach. We take full advantage of technologies such as e-mail, message centers, and the internet for those instances where low-touch communication is needed. In those instances where a more high-touch approach is needed, Maritz' field operations office has over 200 telephone stations for supporting our nationwide mystery shopping service. This combination allows our shoppers access to quick answers and assures quality observations – providing you with reliable and actionable mystery shopping observational data.'

www.maritz.com – accessed 4 June 2010

1.7.3 Accompanied shopping

Researchers sometimes actually visit stores with respondents, go to their workplaces to shadow or even spend time in respondents homes in order to better appreciate how they behave. Related terms used are shadowing, consumer safari's and consumer buddying.

1.7.4 In-home scanning

Consumer panel research has traditionally relied on diaries or home audits to collect data. However, both Neilsen and AGB have now launched new panels based on in-home scanning, where each household is equipped with a **hand-held laser scanner** or light pen for reading the bar-codes on the products they buy. This has revolutionised the consumer panel process because it obviates the need for diary completion and, plausibly, generates much higher levels of accuracy and comprehensiveness.

All panellists need to do is run the scanner or light-pen over the **bar-code** as they unpack their shopping. The bar-code instantly records the country of origin, the manufacturer, the product, and the product variant if applicable. Other **information can be keyed in** at the same time using the number keys attached to the scanner, including price, source of purchase, date of purchase, promotions, and who made the purchase.

1.7.5 The value of observation techniques

Observation has the **advantage** over asking people questions of placing no reliance on respondents' memories, guesses or honesty – but it does have a number of **drawbacks**.

(a)   It may not be feasible. You can enjoy watching a customer pick your product, and no other, off the shelf, but you will have no idea why they did so.

(b)   It may be labour intensive (one observer can only observe a limited number of things). Timed video and CCTV are obviously of great assistance, and you can have several cameras, but you are unlikely to capture everything, and collating and interpreting the data may be highly time consuming.

(c)   Attitudes and feelings cannot be observed. If a customer approaches a store and then turns round and walks away without entering you have no way of knowing why, just by watching.

The use of observation as a data collection method has been stimulated by advances in electronics. **EPOS** systems allow firms to virtually 'observe' stock on hand, inflows, outflows and the speed at which stock items are moving through the store. **CCTV** is useful to combat shoplifting, but arguably much more so because of the behaviours it can reveal.

2   Experiments and tests

 KEY CONCEPT   concept

Testing may be carried out on promotional materials and messages and on products (field tests) or on samples of entire markets.

2.1 Laboratory tests

Laboratory experiments are most often used for measuring response to **advertisements**, to **product design** and to **package design**. They can take place before the item being tested is generally released (pre-testing), or after (post-testing).

In theory an **artificial environment** is set up by the researcher in which most of the crucial factors which may affect the outcome of the research are controlled. However, in pre-tests in particular it can be **difficult to design an experiment** which isolates the impact of one factor in a product or package from all the other factors which make up the proposed item, and which are likely to be the subjects of other experiments.

2.2 Hall tests

Hall tests were briefly discussed in Chapter 9. Generally they involve the prior recruitment of respondents who are then taken to a 'hall'. The hall test is most appropriate for a situation with **test materials** that can be **evaluated** quickly such as a new pack design or advertisement. They are most commonly used for **quantitative research**, but they can include observation and qualitative techniques alongside a structured questionnaire. They may include usage of a product and an interview during which a respondent is asked to give his or her opinions about a product and evaluate it, as well as make a future usage and purchase declaration. An individual test usually lasts about **20 minutes**, although the simplest versions may only involve tasting a product and evaluating it on a scale.

2.3 Field tests

With some products it is difficult for consumers to form an immediate opinion based on a short trial in unfamiliar surroundings. These include products such as domestic appliances, cars and some items of office equipment. These are better **tested over time** in the **place where they will be used**. Some products are only intended to work over a period of time (such as anti-ageing cream). Results are collated by the respondent in a diary or similar format and the results are then sent to the tester, by post or online. While they may be expensive and time consuming to conduct, these surveys have the advantage that extended testing can be carried out in realistic scenarios.

In a field test **a product is tested in realistic surroundings**, that is in the environment in which it will be bought and/or consumed once launched. Whilst the researcher has less control over extraneous variables, field experiments do give a more realistic idea of future behaviour. They are also known as product or **placement tests**.

Field tests are usually carried out for products in what the marketer hopes is their final form. They are therefore **expensive** as the product has to be made and marketed in small quantities, and they are **risky** in that competitors will inevitably get a good look. Laboratory experiments are often preferred but there are some elements of the marketing mix, such as distribution, which do not lend themselves to laboratory tests.

There are **three main types** of field test.

(a) A sample of consumers **try the product out at home** and report findings, usually by completing a questionnaire. The consumers are often members of a carefully selected **consumer panel**. Such in-home placement tests are often used for toiletry and other personal products.

(b) **Retail outlets** are used as the site for testing merchandising, packaging and point-of-sale material (**store tests**). There should be a reasonable cross-section of stores, both by size and by region, and ideally a control group. Results are measured primarily by changes in sales by store, but sometimes also by interview surveys of consumers.

(c) **Test marketing** is an expensive but often vital experiment in which one or more marketing actions (such as a new product) are **tried out in limited areas of the market** in order to predict sales volume, profitability, market share, consumer, retailer and distributor behaviour and regional variances. It is vital that the experiment be properly controlled since the prediction of a new product's success, or a successful change in the marketing mix of an existing product, very often depends on it. For example, the area chosen should be an accurate representation of the country as a whole. Mistakes can be expensive. The major drawback of test marketing is that it gives competitors a chance to see the new product – so it should be a short test!

Placement tests can be used for products that need to be tested over a period of time, such as household appliances or cosmetics.

Learning objectives	Covered
1 Evaluate different methods of observing behaviour	☑ Decisions to be taken when planning observation
	☑ Techniques for observations
2 Identify techniques for undertaking experiments	☑ Laboratory tests
	☑ Hall tests
	☑ Field tests

1   What is contrived observation?

2   Where are hall tests conducted?

3   What is a psychogalvanometer?

4   Are experiments and observation examples of qualitative or quantitative research?

5   What are we talking about when we refer to 'researcher effect'?

1 This is a natural setting. Ideally this should be hidden because there is the potential for consumers to behave differently if they know that they are being observed. Accompanied shopping however is a strategy used where consumers open shop with a researcher and discuss their behaviour.

2 In this scenario you probably would be fine to remain visible because these respondents are likely to appreciate why you need to consider their reactions. You could openly tell them at the beginning of a prototype launch that you are interested in their initial reactions and would like to record that part of the meeting.

1 Observation conducted in a setting which is not similar to the respondents usual environment

2 In a hall, meeting room- anywhere that can facilitate and will be self contained.

3 A mechanical observation measurement tool to measure perspiration and therefore is useful in advertising response research.

4 They are both qualitative and quantitative.

5 The effect on respondent response by having a researcher observe them. Often they will behave as they would like to be seen or think that people will expect them to.

Bradley, N. (2007) *Marketing research: tools and techniques*, Oxford University Press, Oxford.

Chisnal, P. (2004) *Marketing Research*, 7th Edition, McGraw Hill, Maidenhead.

Dillon, W., Madden, T. & Firtle, N. (1994) *Marketing Research in a Marketing Environment*, 3rd Edition, Irwin, Illinois.

Hague, P. *et al.* (2004) *Market Research in Practice: A guide to the basics*, Kogan Page, London.

Malhotra, N. (2004) *Marketing Research: an applied orientation*, Pearson, New Jersey.

Proctor, T. (2005) *Essentials of marketing research*, 4th Edition, Prentice Hall, Harlow.

Research (2008) '*Business Wins Round up*', MRS, May 2008 Edition, London.

Wilson, A. (2006) *Marketing Research An Integrated Approach*, 2nd Edition, Prentice Hall, Harlow.

Chapter 11
Reports and presentations

Topic list

Introduction

The final stage of the marketing research process is the presentation of findings to the client, either in the form of a written report or as an oral presentation, or more usually both.

There are differences in these methods of course – in particular a report is more formal and you cannot control the conditions in which it is read – but there are many similarities in the techniques that can be used.

 ASSIGNMENT TIP
 format

General points here about presentation may be familiar from your earlier studies, but it does no harm to be reminded: that is one of the principles of good communication! Please don't think that you will have an aural presentation within your assignment, you won't. You will however be expected to create professional slides and possibly even give advice about how to formally present for maximum effect.

Do not be intimidated or constrained by anything you read here. There are no hard rules about presentation and if you can think of a better way of organising a report or structuring a presentation than the standard way, then by all means use it.

Syllabus linked learning objectives

By the end of the chapter you will be able to:

Learning objectives	Syllabus link
1 Review the key formats when presenting marketing information to decision makers	1.4
2 Explain the relevance of the audience thinking sequence	1.4
3 Identify best practices when presenting information	1.4

1 The audience thinking sequence

KEY CONCEPT

concept

Whenever you are **communicating** in a **report** or in a **presentation** you should take into account the **audience's thinking sequence**: Respect the client's importance; Consider the client's needs; Demonstrate how your information helps the client; Explain the detail that underpins your information; Remind the client of the key points; Suggest what the client should do now.

We have mentioned the audience thinking sequence previously in this text but we return to it now because it is key to this chapter.

Wilson (2006) suggests that the researcher should take account of the typical 'thinking sequence' that people go through when you are communicating with them.

(a) **Respect the client's importance**: in other words don't waste their time with irrelevant, badly structured or presented, over-long information.

(b) **Consider the client's needs**: the client needs to make a marketing decision.

(c) **Demonstrate how your information helps the client**: relate the research findings to the original objectives

(d) **Explain the detail that underpins your information**: why should your findings be believed? Because you have evidence that 'Nine out of ten dogs prefer ...' or whatever. This is the place for tables and charts and apt quotes from respondents.

(e) **Remind the client of the key points**

(f) **Suggest what the client should do now**: there will usually be a variety of options. It is the client's decision, but it is usual to give recommendations.

The researcher knows more about the subject matter of the report or presentation than the report user. It is important that this information should be communicated impartially, so that the report user can make his own judgements.

(a) Any assumptions, evaluations and recommendations should be clearly signalled as such.

(b) Points should not be over-weighted (or omitted as irrelevant) without honestly evaluating how objective the selection is.

(c) Facts and findings should be balanced against each other.

(d) A firm conclusion should, if possible, be reached. It should be clear how and why it was reached.

The researcher must also **recognise the needs and abilities of the audience**.

(a) Beware of 'jargon', overly technical terms and specialist knowledge the user may not share.

(b) Keep your vocabulary, sentence and paragraph structures as simple as possible, for clarity (without patronising an intelligent user).

(c) Bear in mind the type and level of detail that will interest the user and be relevant to his/her purpose.

(d) The audience may range from senior manager to junior operational staff to complete layman (a non-executive director, say). Your vocabulary, syntax and presentation, the amount of detail you can go into, the technical matter you can include and the formality of your report structure should all be influenced by such concerns.

2 Research reports

A research report typically has the following elements: Title page; list of contents; executive summary; introduction/problem definition; research method (and limitations); research findings; conclusions; appendices.

Birn (2004) believes that the key to effectively presented research is to make managers want to use it. He argues that too much research is conducted only to be left to get dusty on the marketers shelf, the key to it being used he argues it to make it meaningful.

Various techniques can be used to make the content of a research report easy to identify and digest.

- The material in the report should be in a logical order
- The relative importance of points should be signalled by headings
- Each point may be numbered in some way to help with cross-reference
- The document should be easy on the eye, helped by different font sizes, bold, italics, capitals, spacing.

A typical report structure is shown on the next page.

(a) **Headings**. There is a 'hierarchy' of headings: there is an overall title and the report as a whole is divided into sections. Within each section main points have a heading in bold capitals, sub-points have a heading in bold lower-case and sub-sub-points have a heading in italics. (Three levels of headings within a main section is usually considered the maximum number that readers can cope with.) It is not necessary to underline headings.

(b) **References**. Sections are lettered, A, B etc. Main points are numbered 1, 2 and so on, and within each division paragraphs are numbered 1.1, 1.2, 2.1, 2.2. Sub-paragraphs inherit their references from the paragraph above. For instance the first sub-paragraph under paragraph 1.2 is numbered 1.2.1.

(c) **Fonts**. Word processors offer you a wealth of fonts these days, but it is best to avoid the temptation. It is often a good idea to put headings in a different font to the main text, but stop there: two fonts is quite enough!

The example on the next page is by no means the only way of organising a report, of course: you might choose to reference sub-paragraphs 1.2(a), 1.2(b). You might use roman numerals, although we advise against this. If your report turns out to be longer than you expected and you get up to paragraph XLVIII you are likely to confuse many of your readers.

# TITLE		Arial 48 pt Bold Capitals
## SECTION A		Arial 28 pt Bold Capitals
1 **HEADING STYLE 1**		Arial 18 pt Capitals Bold
1.1 Paragraph		Times New Roman 12 pt
Heading style 2		Arial 16 pt Bold
1.2 Paragraph		Times New Roman 12 pt
1.2.1 Sub-paragraph		Times New Roman 12 pt Indented

1.2.2 Sub-paragraph		Times New Roman 12 pt Indented
Heading style 3		Arial 14 pt Italic
1.3 Paragraph		Times New Roman 12 pt
Heading style 2		Arial 16 pt Bold
1.4 Paragraph		Times New Roman 12 pt
2 HEADING STYLE 1		Arial 18 pt Capitals Bold
2.1 Paragraph		Times New Roman 12 pt
etc.		
SECTION B		Arial 28 pt Bold Capitals
etc.		

A detailed report on an extensive research study may run to many pages, and may therefore require these elements.

(a) **Title page** (also giving contact information)

(b) A **list of contents**: the major headings and sub-headings. Most word processing software can produce these automatically.

(c) A **summary** of findings (to give the reader an initial idea of what the report is about). This is usually called the **executive summary**, the implication being that senior managers don't have time to read it all.

(d) **Introduction/problem definition**: this is likely to be very similar to the rationale and objectives set out in the research brief and proposal.

(e) **Research method (and limitations)**: again this is likely to be similar to the equivalent section in the proposal, although it must be updated if anything had to be changed during the implementation of the research or if the research did not go to plan (lower than expected response rates).

(f) **Research findings**: this is the main body of the report

(g) **Conclusions**: this section should point out the implications of the findings for the client with reference to the initial problem.

(h) Supporting **appendices**: these might include the questionnaire used or the original discussion document, more detailed tables of figures, lists of secondary sources used. Appendices contain subsidiary detailed material that may well be of interest to some readers, but which might lessen the impact of the findings if presented in full detail in the body of the report.

(i) Possibly, an **index**.

  ACTIVITY 1

application

You work in a marketing consultancy called The Brand Tracker Partnership. As marketing assistant you are involved in a variety of activities, ranging from marketing research on behalf of clients to assisting in the marketing of the Brand Tracker Partnership itself.

The firm has been commissioned to undertake research into the women's fragrance market by Sian Singh, the brand manager of Georgie, a perfume made by the leading cosmetics manufacturer Lanroche.

The raw data was collected by a colleague and is very disorganised. It needs to be analysed and put into an appropriate format for the client to read.

Marketing research data

Annual advertising spend	£'000
Georgie	955
Possession	1,870
Esta Lauda	877
Eternal	1,206
Ana	1,049
Charly Klein	698

Marketing research was conducted during December 201X. A sample of 300 women aged between 16-55, which was representative of the fragrance buying market, was questioned by means of a survey. Following a telephone survey, four focus groups were held in different hotels around the country to obtain further qualitative information.

Desk research, using secondary data sources published by MEAL and SalesMonitor, was analysed to produce advertising expenditure and industry sales figures. In addition, advertising in women's magazines and below the line promotional activity in retail outlets were monitored over a period between October to December 201X.

Reasons for purchase

	% saying
I tried it in the shop	55
It is the one I usually buy or wear	53
I wanted to try something new/different	32
I saw it advertised in a magazine	25
I smelt it on someone else	19
I smelt a scratch-and-sniff ad	16
I saw it advertised on television	14
Advice from the sales assistant	12
There was a money off offer	8
It was cheaper than the others	6

Thirty two fragrances were named as being bought or requested and received as gifts indicating that it is a fragmented market. However, eleven major brands had 73 per cent of total market share.

Of those mentioned, 64 per cent sell for more than £15 per 30 ml. Lady, Carlie and Max Maxa were ranked as the least expensive perfumes. ABC1s are no more likely to buy or receive premium priced fragrances than anyone else, with figures indicating that fragrances generally have a flat class profile. Charly Klein and Carlie draw more than two thirds of buyers from the 16-25 age group, with Cachet concentrated amongst those in their 30s. Ana, Georgie and Eternal appear to have popularity with all age groups. Channelle and Esta Lauda were popular amongst the older market – mainly those in the 40-55 age group.

Fragrances bought

Brand	*% market share*
Channelle	3.7
Max Maxa	2.0
Cachet	2.0
Possession	10.5
Georgie	8.8
Lady	7.2
Ana	13.0
Eternal	11.0
Charly Klein	5.5
Esta Lauda	5.0
Carlie	4.3

Price was not considered to be important except amongst buyers of Carlie. Of these, 34 per cent gave cheapness as the reason for purchase. Brand recognition levels were generally high for many fragrances. Newer entrants into the market such as, Cachet, Georgie and Possession, achieved high recall levels possibly influenced by the impact of point of sale and in-store promotional activity. Advertising expenditure was generally high amongst most brands.

Sampling is very important both on the counter and through scent strips in magazines.

Spontaneous ad recall	%
Ana	22
Possession	18
Eternal	12
Georgie	12
Channelle	9
Charly Klein	8
Max Maxa	7
Cachet	5
Esta Lauda	3
Lady	2
Carlie	2

Required

Write a short report for Sian Singh, using the market research data shown here.

3 Presenting findings

ASSIGNMENT TIP

format

Tables, **graphs**, **charts** and **illustrations** of various kinds can **greatly enhance** the **value** of a report because they make it easier to take in information at a glance.

3.1 Tables

Tables present data in rows and columns. This form of presentation makes it easier to understand large amounts of data. A railway timetable is a familiar example.

Charing Cross	15:38	16:08	16:18	16:28	16:37	16:45	16:58
Waterloo	15:41	16:11	16:21	16:31	16:40	16:48	17:01
London Bridge	15:49	16:19	16:29	16:39	16:48	16:56	17:09
New Cross	16:01	16:31	16:41	-	17:00	17:08	17:21
Lewisham	16:06	16:36	16:46	16:50	17:05	17:13	17:26

Suppose you arrive at London Bridge at 16:42 and you want to go to Lewisham. Using a table like the one above there are at least three things that this timetable tells you.

(a)   You can **look up a specific value** by seeing where rows and columns meet. Since you know it is 16:42 you can quickly see from the timetable that your next train is due in six minutes (at 16:48) and will arrive in Lewisham at 17:05.

(b)   You can work your way around the table from your original starting point and **test out other scenarios**. For instance, you can see that if you had arrived at London Bridge a few minutes earlier you could have got a fast train. If you are not sure that six minutes is long enough to buy a cup of coffee and a bar of chocolate you can get a slightly later train to Lewisham which will give you 14 minutes.

(c)   You can read across rows (or down columns) and **compare values**. For future reference you can note (by reading right across the London Bridge row) that from 16:19 onwards there is a train to Lewisham roughly every ten minutes.

Tables are a simple way of presenting numerical information. Figures are displayed, and can be compared with each other: relevant totals, subtotals, percentages can also be presented as a summary for analysis.

A table is two-dimensional (rows and columns): so it can only show two variables: a sales analysis for a year, for example, might have rows for months, and columns for products.

SALES FIGURES FOR 201X

	Product A	Product B	Product C	Product D	Total
Jan	370	651	782	899	2,702
Feb	718	312	748	594	2,372
Mar	548	204	585	200	1,537
Apr	382	616	276	359	1,633
May	132	241	184	223	780
Jun	381	216	321	123	1,041
Jul	679	612	733	592	2,616
Aug	116	631	343	271	1,361
Sep	421	661	868	428	2,378
Oct	211	158	653	479	1,501
Nov	306	243	676	404	1,659
Dec	898	759	796	394	2,847
Total	5,162	5,334	6,965	4,966	22,427

You are likely to present data in tabular form very often. Here are the key points to remember.

(a) The table should have a clear **title**.

(b) All columns and rows should be clearly **labelled**.

(c) Where appropriate, there should be **sub-totals** and a **right-hand total column** for comparison.

(d) A total figure is often advisable at the **bottom of each column** of figures also, for comparison. It is usual to double-underline totals at the foot of columns.

(e) **Numbers** should be **right-aligned** and they are easier to read if you use the **comma separator** for thousands.

(f) **Decimal points should line up**, either by using a decimal tab or by adding extra noughts (the latter is preferable, in our opinion).

(g) A grid or border is optional: see what looks best and is easiest to read. (In the above example we've used a grid to illustrate the alignment of numbers more clearly.)

(h) Tables should not be packed with too much data. If you try to get too much in the information presented will be difficult to read.

3.1.1 Columns or rows?

Often it will be obvious what information should go in the columns and what should go in rows. Sometimes, it won't matter too much which way round you have the rows and columns. Here are some points to remember.

(a) It is usually easier to read across a short line than a long one. That means that it is usually **better to have a long thin table** than a short wide one: lots of rows rather than lots of columns. If you had a price list of five hundred products each of which came in 3 different sizes. You would probably tabulate the information like this, without even considering the other possibility (it wouldn't fit on the paper or screen, anyway, if you had products in columns).

Product	Large	Medium	Small
A001	12.95	11.65	9.35
A002	14.50	12.50	10.50
A003	Etc.	Etc.	Etc.
A004			
A005			
Etc.			

(b) However, most people find it easier to compare figures by reading across than by reading down. For example in the previous version of the sales figures it is easier to compare product totals, but in the version below it is easier to compare monthly totals.

	Jan	Feb	Mar	Apr	May	Jun	Jul	Aug	Sep	Oct	Nov	Dec	Total
Product A	370	718	548	382	132	381	679	116	421	211	306	898	5,162
Product B	651	312	204	616	241	216	612	631	661	158	243	759	5,334
Product C	782	748	585	276	184	321	733	343	868	653	676	796	6,965
Product D	899	594	200	359	223	123	592	271	428	479	404	394	4,966
Total	2,702	2,372	1,537	1,633	780	1,041	2,616	1,361	2,378	1,501	1,659	2,847	22,427

(c)   If you are not sure what your audience will most want to compare it might be helpful to give them both versions, if practicable.

3.2 Line graphs

In business, line graphs are usually used to illustrate **trends over time** of figures such as sales or customer complaints.

Product A Sales in 201X

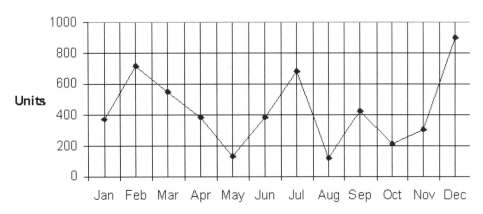

The figures are plotted on a grid and then joined by a line that reflects the 'ups and downs' of the figure, over a period of time. Note that it is conventional to show **time** on the **horizontal** axis.

Now the trend in sales is shown instantly, in a way that is probably not immediately apparent from a column or row of figures. This **encourages us to ask questions**: for instance why did sales drop in the early months of the year and suddenly shoot up in June and July?

By using different symbols for the plotted points, or preferably by using different colours, several lines can be drawn on a line graph before it gets too overcrowded, and that means that **several trends** (for example the sales performance of different products) can be compared.

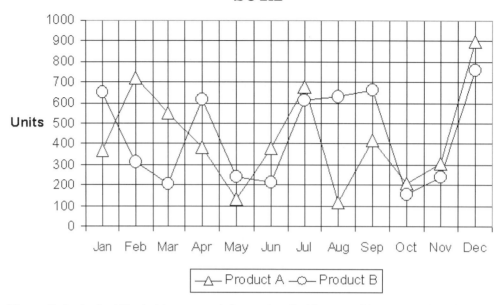

Sales of products A and B in 201X

The scale of the vertical axis should be just large enough for you to tell with reasonable accuracy the sales figure at any given point during the period. In the example above we have used a scale of 100 and you can tell, for instance that sales of product A in April were a little less than 400 (check in the table given above).

3.3 Charts

3.3.1 Bar charts

The bar chart is one of the most common methods of visual presentation. Data is shown in the form of bars which are the same in width but variable in height. Each bar represents a different item, for example the annual production cost of different products or the number of hours required to produce a product by different workteams.

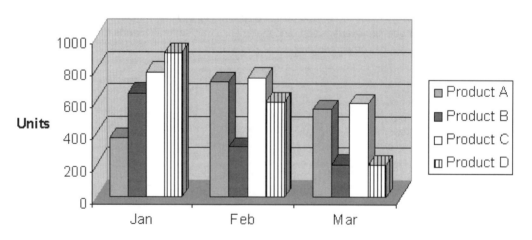

Sales in Quarter 1, 201X

As you can see, here we are more interested in comparing a few individual items in a few individual months (although you can still get a visual impression of trends over time).

Horizontal presentation is also possible.

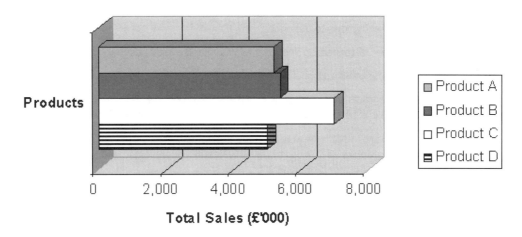

Sales by Product in 201X

Products

Total Sales (£'000)

Legend:
- Product A
- Product B
- Product C
- Product D

There are no hard and fast rules about whether you should use vertical or horizontal presentation. However, these guidelines may help.

(a)   If you are showing **trends over time** (for instance January to March) **vertical bars** look best

(b)   If you are showing **differences at a single point in time** (the end of 201X, for instance) you might prefer **horizontal** bars.

3.3.2 Pie charts

A pie chart shows the **relative** sizes of the things that make up a total.

Pie charts are most effective where the number of slices is small enough to keep the chart simple, and where the difference in the size of the slices is large enough for the eye to judge without too much extra information.

Share of total sales in 201X

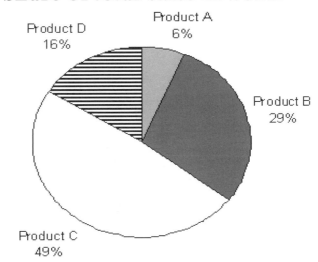

Product D 16%
Product A 6%
Product B 29%
Product C 49%

3.4 Flow charts, organisation charts and other labelled diagrams

Flow charts and organisation charts are useful ways of presenting and summarising information that involves a series of **steps** and **choices** and/or **relationships** between the different items.

On the following pages there are some examples of this type of presentation.

If you choose any of these forms of presentation here are some points to bear in mind.

(a) Be consistent in your use of layout and symbols (and colours, if used). For instance, in our flow chart example below a decision symbol is consistently a diamond with italic text; a YES decision consistently flows downwards; a NO decision consistently flows to the right.

(b) Keep the number of connecting lines to a minimum and avoid lines that 'jump over' each other at all costs.

(c) Keep the labels or other text brief and simple.

(d) Hand-drawn diagrams should be as neat and legible as possible. If they are likely to be seen by a lot of people (not just your team) it is better to use a business graphics programme like Microsoft Visio.

(e) Everyone can draw ... but only so well. If you are not expert you can waste an enormous amount of time playing with computer graphics. If it needs to be really beautifully presented and you are not an expert sketch it quickly by hand and then give it to a professional!

3.4.1 A flowchart

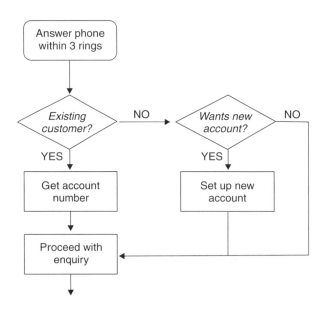

3.4.2 An organisation chart

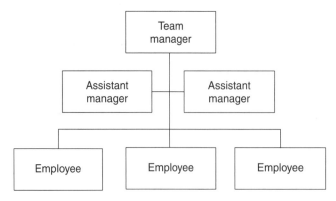

3.5 Pictograms

A pictogram is a simple graphic image in which the **data is represented by a picture or symbol**, with a clear key to the items and quantities intended. Different pictures can be used on the same pictogram to represent different elements of the data. For example a pictogram showing the number of people employed by an organisation might use pictures of … people!

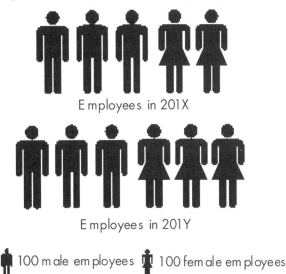

Employees in 201X

Employees in 201Y

100 male employees   100 female employees

You can see quite easily that the workforce has grown and that the organization employs far more female workers than before.

Pictograms present data in a simple and appealing way. They are **often used on television**. Watch out for them next time you are watching a news item involving numbers (number of trains late, number of new jobs created, and so on).

- The symbols must be clear and simple.
- There should be a key showing the number that each symbol represents.
- Bigger quantities are shown by more symbols, not bigger symbols.

Bear in mind, however, that pictograms are **not appropriate** if you need to give **precise** figures. You can use portions of a symbol to represent smaller quantities, but there are limits to what you can do.

 150 female employees

 Over 100 employees, mostly male. But how many others and what sex are they?

3.6 Drawings and graphics

A labelled drawing may sometimes be the best way of presenting a lot of information in a small space. Imagine how difficult it would be to explain all the information you get from the following diagram if you could only use words!

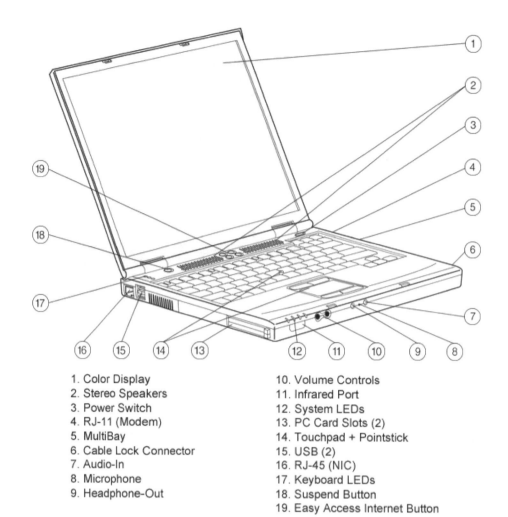

1. Color Display
2. Stereo Speakers
3. Power Switch
4. RJ-11 (Modem)
5. MultiBay
6. Cable Lock Connector
7. Audio-In
8. Microphone
9. Headphone-Out

10. Volume Controls
11. Infrared Port
12. System LEDs
13. PC Card Slots (2)
14. Touchpad + Pointstick
15. USB (2)
16. RJ-45 (NIC)
17. Keyboard LEDs
18. Suspend Button
19. Easy Access Internet Button

3.7 Product positioning maps

Although they may be called **'maps'** these are really a form of **scatter diagram**. **Two key attributes** of a product are taken and competing products are graded to fit between the extremes of possessing an attribute or not possessing it.

For example a package delivery service may be **fast** or **slow**, and it may deal with **large** or **small** packages.

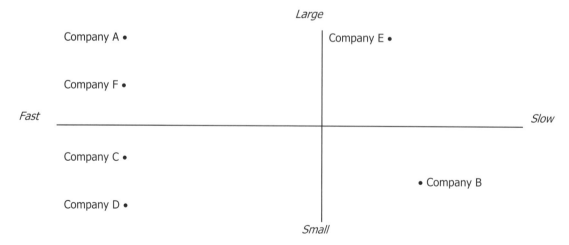

ACTIVITY 2

Interpret the diagram above.

4 Oral presentations

KEY CONCEPT

concept

An oral presentation would have the following structure: Introduction; Explanation of research methodology; Key findings; Conclusions/recommendations; Questions.

Wilson (2006) suggests the following outline structure for an oral presentation.

- Introduction
- Explanation of research methodology
- Key findings
- Conclusions/recommendations
- Questions

This is not unlike the structure of a report, and many of the same points apply. However, **live interaction** with the audience has its own issues.

ACTIVITY 3

application

What presentations, conferences, or speech-making occasions have you attended recently? For each, note:

- The style of speech (formal/informal etc)
- The length of the speech
- Any visual aids used

How effective was the speaker in targeting each of these elements to

(a) The purpose of the speech and
(b) The needs of the audience?

MARKETING AT WORK

format

In an effort to help people who aren't young anymore understand those who are, MTV and Microsoft commissioned OTX to conduct an 18-month research project to study 24,000 youngsters in their natural habitats. The researchers presented their findings in an exhibition in London's Brick Lane.

As interesting as the study itself is the fact that the findings have been presented in a fun, funky exhibition open to the public, as well as targeting clients of MTV and OTX. This approach was a much better way to grab clients' attention than even the most brilliantly crafted PowerPoint presentation.

OTX researcher and ex MTV employee Graham Saxton told Research: '*The point is to showcase a lot of insights about global youth culture that would be hard to present in more traditional ways. Researchers beat themselves up about adding value*

and getting findings in front of clients and yet most research is presented in the same old way, so we're trying to get away from that, and we'd love to do more of it.'

Saxton then planned to take the exhibition to the US, where he suggested that presentation of research tends to be 'more traditional' than in Europe.

'Clients are always looking for more engaging ways of research being communicated and this is one way of doing that – although it is an expensive way.'

The research findings identified that concerned parents might see kids retreating from the 'real world' into technology, but youngsters are actually just connecting with the world in a way that, to them, is just as 'real' as anything else.

The researchers also found that to think that young people 'like' technology is wrong. In fact, most don't even notice it. Mobiles, computers and social networks are just ways for them to stay in touch with their friends.

Adapted from: Bain, R (2008) *'MTV dissects the youth of today :London exhibition reveals findings of global youth culture study'* Research Magazine, MRS, October edition, London

---

 KEY CONCEPT

concept

Matters to consider when preparing and delivering presentations include **audience motivation**, **physical factors** in the presentation room, **content**, **clarity**, adding **emphasis and interest**, and **controlling nerves** and **body language**.

4.1 Audience

The audience's **motivations** and **expectations** in attending a presentation will, as we have seen, influence their perceptions of you and your message. Why might they be at your presentation?

(a) **They need specific information from the presentation**. An audience which is deliberately seeking information, and intending to use it to further their own objectives, is highly motivated. If their objectives match the speaker's (say, in a training seminar, where both trainer and trainees want improved job performance as the outcome), this motivation aids the speaker. It is therefore important to gauge, as far as possible, what this highly-motivated group **want** to hear from you, and **why**.

(b) **They are interested in the topic of the presentation**. The audience may have a general expectation that they will learn something new, interesting, or useful on a topic that they are pre-disposed to gather information about: it is up to the speaker to hold their attention by satisfying the desire for relevant information. They may also have some prior knowledge, on which the speaker can build: there will be a fine line to tread between boring the audience by telling them what they already know, and losing them by assuming more knowledge than they possess.

(c) **They are required to be there**.

   (i) Attendance may be **compulsory**, whether or not those attending are motivated or interested in the subject matter. In this case, you can at least find out the size and composition of your audience, but unless motivation and interest can be stimulated by the presentation, compulsory attendance may simply create resistance to the message.

   (ii) Attendance may be **recommended by a superior**, in which case even if the participants are not interested in the subject matter, they may be motivated to pay attention because they perceive it to be in their own interest to do so.

   This is known as a **captive audience**. Note that it is a double-edged sword: the audience may be compelled to listen to you, but they are actually **less** likely to listen attentively, co-operatively and with positive results, unless you can motivate them to do so once you have them in front of you.

(d) **They expect to be entertained**. The topic of the presentation may be entertaining or the audience may expect the speaker to put information across in an entertaining manner – perhaps using humour or illustration. The organisation culture may encourage the idea that attending meetings and conferences is equivalent to rest and recreation: a bit of a 'day out' for the participants, more useful for the networking in the coffee breaks than the technical content of the presentations. As a speaker, you will have to ensure that you do not fulfil such expectations at the expense of your primary objectives – but be aware that the entertainment-seekers are also a potential audience for your message: it may be possible to arouse more motivated interest.

Taking into account any **specific** audience needs and expectations, your message needs to have the following qualities.

(a) **Interest**. It should be lively/entertaining/varied or relevant to the audience's needs and interests, or preferably both.

(b) **Congeniality**. This usually means positive, supportive or helpful in some way (eg in making a difficult decision easier, or satisfying a need).

(c) **Credibility**. It should be **consistent** in itself, and with known **facts**; apparently **objective**; and from a source perceived to be **trustworthy**.

(d) **Accessibility**. This means both:

    (i) **Audible/visible**. (Do you need to be closer to the audience? Do you need a microphone? Enlarged visual aids? Clearer articulation and projection?)

    (ii) **Understandable**. (What is the audience's level of knowledge/education/ experience in general? Of the topic at hand? What technical terms will need to be avoided or explained? What concepts or ideas will need to be explained?)

4.2 Physical preparation

At the planning stage, you might also consider physical factors which will affect the audience's concentration: their ability and willingness to keep listening attentively and positively to your message. Some of these may not be in your control, if you are not planning the meeting or conference or arranging the venue, but as far as possible, give attention to the following.

(a) **Listening conditions**. Try and cut out background noise – conversations outside the room, traffic, loud air conditioning or rattling slide projector, say. (There may be a trade-off between peace and quiet, and good ventilation, also required for alertness: be sensible about the need to open a door or window or switch on a fan.)

(b) **Freedom from interruption and distraction**. Do not let the focus shift from the speaker and his message to outside views of people passing by. Arrange not to be disturbed by others entering the room. Announce, if appropriate, that questions and comments will be invited at the end of the session.

(c) **Ventilation, heating and lighting**. A room that is too stuffy, or draughty, too hot or cold, too bright or too dim to see properly, can create physical discomfort, which shifts attention from the speaker and his message to the listener.

(d) **Seating and desking**. Excessive comfort can impair alertness – but uncomfortable seating is a distraction. Combined with inadequate arrangements for writing (since many people may wish or need to take notes), it can cause severe strain over a lengthy talk.

(e) **Audibility and visibility**. Inadequate speaking volume or amplification is a distraction and a strain, even if it does not render the message completely inaccessible. Excessive volume and electronic noise is equally irritating. Visibility requires planning not just of effective visual aids (clear projection in suitable light, adequately enlarged) but also of seating plans, allowing unobstructed 'sight lines' for each participant.

(f) **Seating layout**. Depending on the purpose and style of your presentation, you may choose formal classroom-like rows of seating, with the speaker in front behind a podium, or informal group seating in a circle or cluster in which the speaker is included. The formal layout enhances the speaker's credibility, and may encourage attention to information, while the informal layout may be more congenial, encouraging involvement and input from the whole group.

(g) **Time**. Listeners get tired over time – however interesting the presentation: their concentration span is limited, and they will not be able to listen effectively for a long period without a break.

    (i) If you have the choice (and a limited volume of information to impart), a ten-minute presentation will be more effective than a one-hour presentation.

(ii)   If the volume of information or time allotted dictate a lengthy talk, you will need to build in reinforcements, breaks and 'breathers' for your listeners, by using repetition, summary, jokes/anecdotes and question-and-answer breaks.

(iii)   Bear in mind, too, that the time of day will affect your listeners' concentration, even if your presentation is a brief one: you will have to work harder if your talk is first thing in the morning, late in the day (or week), or approaching lunch-time.

(h)   **The speaker's appearance.** It should already be obvious that the appearance of the speaker may sabotage his efforts if it is uncongenial or unappealing, lacks credibility or the authority expected by the audience or is distracting in some way.

ACTIVITY 4

application

In what other research circumstances besides the final presentation might the researcher find it useful to think about physical factors that will affect his or her audience's concentration?

4.3 Content

Armed with your clearly-stated objectives and audience profile, you can plan the **content** of your presentation.

One approach which may help to clarify your thinking is as follows.

Prioritise	Select the **key points** of the subject, and a **storyline** or theme that gives your argument a unified sense of 'direction'. The **fewer** points you make (with the most emphasis) and the clearer the **direction** in which your thoughts are heading, the easier it will be for the audience to grasp and retain your message.
Structure	Make notes for your presentation which **illustrate** simply the **logical order** or **pattern** of the key points of your speech.
Outline	Following your structured notes, **flesh out** your message. • **Introduction** • **Supporting evidence, examples and illustrations** • **Notes** where **visual aids** will be used • **Conclusion**
Practise	Rehearsals should indicate difficult logical leaps, dull patches, unexplained terms and other problems: adjust your outline or style. They will also help you gauge and adjust the **length** of your presentation.
Cue	Your outline may be too detailed to act as a cue or **aide-memoire** for the talk itself. **Small cards**, which fit into the palm of the hand may be used to give you: • **Key words** for each topic, and the logical links between them • Reminders for when to use **visual aids** • The **full text** of any detailed information you need to quote

An effective presentation requires two key structural elements.

(a)   An **introduction** which:

•   Establishes your credibility

•   Establishes rapport with the audience

•   Gains the audience's attention and interest (sets up the problem to be solved, uses curiosity or surprise)

•   Gives the audience an overview of the **shape** of your presentation, to guide them through it: a bit like the scanning process in reading.

(b)   A **conclusion** which:

- **Clarifies and draws together** the points you have made into one main idea (using an example, anecdote, review, summary)

- **States or implies what you want/expect your audience to do** following your presentation

- Reinforces the audience's **recall** (using repetition, a joke, quotation or surprising statistic to make your main message **memorable**).

4.4 Clarity

Your structured notes and outline should contain cues which clarify the **logical order**, shape or progression of your information or argument. This will help the audience to **follow you** at each stage of your argument, so that they arrive with you at the conclusion. You can signal these logical links to the audience as follows.

(a)   **Linking words or phrases**

Therefore ...   [conclusion, result or effect, arising from previous point]
As a result ...

However ...   [contradiction or alternative to previous point]
On the other hand ...

Similarly ...   [confirmation or additional example of previous point]
Again ...

Moreover ...   [building on the previous point]

(b)   **Framework**: setting up the structure

'Of course, this isn't a perfect solution: There are advantages and disadvantages to it. It has the advantages of ... . But there are also disadvantages, in that ... '

(c)   You can use more elaborate devices which summarise or repeat the previous point and lead the audience to the next. These also have the advantage of giving you, and the listener, a 'breather' in which to gather your thoughts.

Other ways in which content can be used to clarify the message include the following.

(a)   **Examples and illustrations** – showing how an idea works in practice.

(b)   **Anecdotes** – inviting the audience to relate an idea to a real-life situation.

(c)   **Questions** – rhetorical, or requiring the audience to answer, raising particular points that may need clarification.

(d)   **Explanation** – showing how or why something has happened or is so, to help the audience understand the principles behind your point.

(e)   **Description** – helping the audience to visualise the person, object or setting you are describing.

(f)   **Definition** – explaining the precise meaning of terms that may not be shared or understood by the audience.

(g)   The use of **facts, quotations or statistics** – to 'prove' your point.

Your **vocabulary and style** in general should contribute to the clarity of the message. Remember to use short, simple sentences and non-technical words (unless the audience is sure to know them): avoid jargon, clichés, unexplained acronyms, colloquialisms, double meanings and vague expressions (like 'rather', 'good'). Remember, too, that this is **oral** communication, not written: use words and grammatical forms that you would **normally use in speaking** to someone – bearing in mind the audience's ability to understand you, and the formality of the occasion.

Visual aids will also be an important aspect of content used to signal the structure and clarify the meaning of your message. We discuss them specifically below.

4.5 Adding emphasis

Emphasis is the 'weight', importance or impact given to particular words or ideas. This can largely be achieved through delivery – the tone and volume of your voice, strong eye contact, emphatic gestures – but can be reinforced in the content and wording of your speech. Emphasis can be achieved by a number of means.

(a) **Repetition:** 'If value for money is what the market wants, then value for money is what this brand must represent.'

'One in five customers has had a quality complaint. That's right: one in five.'

(b) **Rhetorical questions:** 'Do you know how many of your customers have a quality complaint? One in five. Do you think that's acceptable?'

(c) **Quotation:** ''Product quality is the number one issue in customer care in the new millennium.' That's the conclusion of our survey report.'

(d) **Statistical evidence:** 'One in five of your customers this year have had a quality complaint: that's 10% more complaints than last year. If the trend continues, you will have one complaint for every two satisfied customers – next year!'

(e) **Exaggeration:** 'We have to look at our quality control system. Because if the current trend continues, we are going to end up without any customers at all.'

4.6 Adding interest

Simple, clear information often lacks impact, and will only be interesting to those already motivated by the desire for the information. The speaker will need to balance the need for clarity with the need to get the key points across. All the devices discussed so far can be used for impact.

Here are some further suggestions.

(a) **Analogy, metaphor, simile** etc – comparing something to something else which is in itself more colourful or interesting.

(b) **Anecdote or narrative** – as already mentioned, telling a story which illustrates or makes the point, using suspense, humour or a more human context.

(c) **Curiosity or surprise** – from incongruity, anticlimax or controversy. Verbatim quotes from customers can be very useful in this respect.

(d) **Humour**. This is often used for entertainment value, but also serves as a useful 'breather' for listeners, and may help to get them on the speaker's side. (Humour may not travel well, however: the audience may not be on the speaker's wavelength at all, especially in formal contexts. Use with caution.)

4.7 Controlling nerves

Stage-fright can be experienced before making a phone call, going into an interview or meeting, or even writing a letter, but it is considerably more acute, for most people, before standing up to talk in front of a group or crowd of people. Common fears are to do with **making a fool of oneself**, forgetting one's **lines**, being unable to answer **questions**, or being faced by blank incomprehension or **lack of response**. Fear can make vocal delivery hesitant or stilted and **body language** stiff and unconvincing.

A **controlled amount of fear**, or stress, is actually **good for you**: it stimulates the production of **adrenaline**, which can contribute to alertness and dynamic action. Only at excessive levels is stress harmful, degenerating into **strain**. If you can **manage your stress** or stage-fright, it will help you to be **alert** to feedback from your audience, to think 'on your feet' in response to questions, and to project vitality and enthusiasm.

(a) **Reduce uncertainty and risk**. This means:

(i) **Preparing thoroughly** for your talk, including rehearsal, and anticipating questions

(ii) **Checking** the venue and facilities meet your expectations

(iii)   **Preparing** whatever is necessary for your own confidence and comfort (glass of water, handkerchief, note cards)

(iv)   **Keeping your notes to hand**, and in order, during your presentation.

(b)   **Have confidence in your message**. Concentrate on the desired outcome: that is why you are there. Believe in what you are saying. It will also make it easier to project enthusiasm and energy.

(c)   **Control physical symptoms.** Breathe deeply and evenly. Control your gestures and body movements. Put down a piece of paper that is visibly shaking in your hand. Pause to collect your thoughts if necessary. Smile, and maintain eye contact with members of the audience. If you **act** as if you are calm, the calm will **follow**.

4.8 Non-verbal messages

Any number of body language factors may contribute to a speaker **looking confident and relaxed**, or nervous, shifty and uncertain. **Cues** which indicate confidence – without arrogance – may be as follows.

(a)   An upright – but not stiff – **posture**: slouching gives an impression of shyness or carelessness.

(b)   **Movement** that is purposeful and dynamic, used sparingly: not constant or aimless pacing, which looks nervous.

(c)   **Gestures** that are relevant, purposeful and flowing: not indecisive, aggressive, incomplete or compulsive. Use gestures **deliberately** to reinforce your message, and if possible keep your hands up so that gestures do not distract the audience from watching your face. In a large venue, gestures will have to be exaggerated – but practise making them look **natural**. Watch out for habitual, irrelevant gestures you may tend to make.

(d)   **Eye-contact** with the audience maintains credibility, maintains the involvement of the audience and allows you to gather audience feedback as to how well you are getting your message across. Eye-contact should be **established immediately**, and **re-established** after periods when you have had to look away, to consult notes or use visual aids.

The most effective technique is to let our gaze wander (purposefully) across the whole audience, **involving** them all, without intimidating anybody: establish eye-contact long enough for it to be registered, to accompany a point you are making, and then move on.

4.9 Visual aids

 KEY CONCEPT   concept

Visual aids include slides (acetates and PowerPoint), videos, flipcharts, handouts and props and demonstrations.

The term **visual aids** covers a wide variety of forms which share two characteristics.

(a)   They use a visual image.

(b)   They act as an aid to communication. This may seem obvious, but it is important to remember that visual aids are not supposed to be impressive or clever for their own sake, but to support the message and speaker in achieving their purpose.

A number of media and devices are available for using visual aids. They may be summarised as follows.

Equipment/medium	Advantages	Disadvantages
Slides: photographs, text or diagrams projected onto a screen or other surface	• Allow colour photos: good for mood, impact and realism • Pre-prepared: no speaker 'down time' during talk • Controllable sequence/ timing: pace content/audience needs	• Require a darkened room: may hinder note-taking • Malfunction and/or incompetent use: frustration and distraction
Film/video shown on a screen or TV monitor	• Moving images: realism, impact: can enhance credibility (eye witness effect)	• Less flexible in allowing interruption, pause or speeding up to pace audience needs
Overheads: films or acetates (hand drawn or printed) projected by light box onto a screen behind/above the presenter	• Versatility of content and presentation • Low cost (for example, if hand written) • Clear sheets: can be used to build up images as points added	• Require physical handling: can be distracting • Risk of technical breakdown: not readily adaptable to other means of projection
Presentation software: for example, Microsoft PowerPoint. PC-generated slide show (with animation, sound) projected from PC to screen via data projector	• Versatility of multi-media: impact, interest • Professional design and functioning (smooth transitions) • Use of animation to build, link and emphasise as points added	• Requires PC, data projector: expensive, may not be available • Risk of technical breakdown: not readily adaptable to other means of projection • Temptation to over-complexity and over-use: distraction
Flip charts: large paper pad mounted on frame – sheets are 'flipped' to the back when finished with	• Low cost, low-risk • Allows use during session (for example, to 'map' audience views, ideas) • Can be pre-prepared (for example, advertising 'story boards') • Easy to refer back	• Smaller, still, paper-based image: less impact • Hand-prepared: may lack perceived quality (compared to more sophisticated methods)
Handouts: supporting notes handed out for reference during or after the session	• Pre-prepared • Audience doesn't need to take as many notes: reminder provided	• Audience doesn't need to take as many notes: may encourage passive listening.
Props and demonstrations: objects or processes referred to are themselves shown to the audience	• Enhances credibility (eye witness effect) • Enhances impact (sensory solidity)	• May not be available • Risk of self-defeating 'hitches'

The following illustrations show two of the media discussed above, demonstrating some of their key features – and showing how a picture can be a helpful 'break' from reading or hearing lots of verbal content!

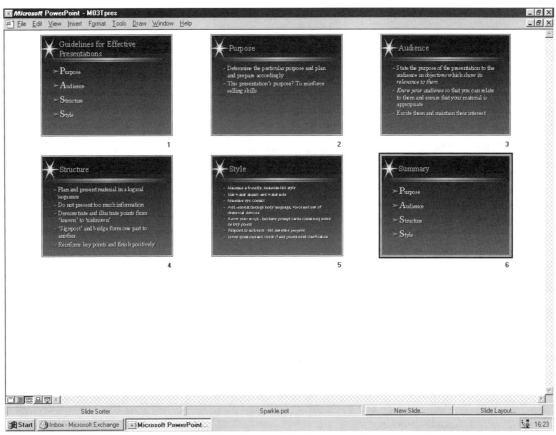

Whatever medium or device you are using, visual aids are **versatile** with regard to **content**: maps, diagrams, flowcharts, verbal notes, drawings and photographs.

When planning and using visual aids, consider the following points.

(a)   Visual aids are **simplified and concrete**: they are easier to grasp than the spoken word, allowing the audience to absorb complex relationships and information.

(b)   Visual aids are **stimulating** to the imagination and emotions, and therefore useful in gaining attention and recall.

(c)   Visual aids can also be **distracting** for the audience – and for the presenter, who has to draw/write/organise/operate them. They can add complexity and ambiguity to the presentation if not carefully designed for relevance and clarity.

(d) Visual aids impose **practical requirements**.

   (i) The medium you choose must be **suitable** for the needs of your **audience**. Demonstrations, or handing round a small number of samples, is not going to work for a large audience. A flipchart will not be visible at the back of a large room; a slide projector can be overwhelming in a small room. A darkened room, to show video or slides, will not allow the audience to take notes.

   (ii) **Skill, time and resources** must be available for any pre-preparation of aids that may be required in advance of the presentation.

   (iii) **The equipment, materials and facilities** you require must be available in the venue, and you must **know** how to **use** them. (No good turning up with a slide projector if there is no power source, or film when there is no overhead projector, or without proper pens for a particular type of board.)

The following are some **guidelines** for effective use of visual aids.

(a) Ensure that the aid is:

   • **Appropriate** to your message, in content and style or mood
   • **Easy to see** and understand
   • Only used when there is **support** to be gained from it

(b) Ensure that all **equipment** and materials are **available and working** and that you can (and do) operate them efficiently and confidently. This includes having all your slides/acetates/notes with you, in the right order and the right way up.

(c) Ensure that the aid does not become a **distraction**.

   (i) Show each image **long enough** to be absorbed and noted, but not so long as to merge with following idea.

   (ii) Maintain **voice and eye contact** with your audience, so they know that it is you who are the communicator, not the machine.

   (iii) **Introduce** your aids and what they are for, placing the focus on the verbal presentation.

   (iv) Hand out **supporting material** either well before the presentation (to allow reading beforehand) or at the relevant point: if you hand it out just before, it will distract or daunt the audience with information they do not yet understand.

   (v) **Write or draw**, if you need to do so during the presentation, as quickly and efficiently as possible (given the need for legibility and neatness).

The look of presentation slides (or other visual aids) is very important. Make sure that they are:

• Simple: not too many points
• Visually appealing: use graphics and type styles to create an effect
• Neat: especially if you are preparing them by hand

4.10 Handling questions

 KEY CONCEPT

concept

Questions are important to help clarify misunderstandings and overcome doubts. It is important that the speaker maintains **credibility**.

Inviting or accepting questions is usually the final part of a presentation.

(a) In informative presentations, questions offer an **opportunity to clarify any misunderstandings**, or gaps that the audience may have perceived.

(b)   In persuasive presentations, questions offer an opportunity to address and overcome specific doubts or resistance that the audience may have, which the speaker may not have been able to anticipate.

The manner in which you 'field' questions may be crucial to your **credibility**. Everyone knows you have prepared your presentation carefully: ignorance, bluster or hesitation in the face of a question may cast doubt on your expertise, or sincerity, or both. Moreover, this is usually the last stage of the presentation, and so leaves a lasting impression.

The only way to tackle questions effectively is to **anticipate** them. Put yourself in your audience's shoes, or, more specifically, in the shoes of an ignorant member of the audience and a hostile member of the audience and a member of the audience with a particular axe to grind: what questions might they ask and why? When questions arise, listen to them carefully, assess the questioner's manner, and draw the questioner out if necessary, in order to ascertain exactly what is being asked, and why. People might ask questions:

(a)   To **seek additional information** of particular interest to them, or to the group – if you have left it out of your talk

(b)   To seek **clarification** of a point that is not clear

(c)   To **add information** of their own, which may be relevant, helpful and accurate – or not

(d)   To **lead the discussion into another area** (or away from an uncomfortable one)

(e)   To display their **own knowledge or cleverness**

(f)   To **undermine** the speaker's authority or argument, to 'catch him out'

If you have anticipated questions of the first two kinds (a) and (b) in the planning of your talk, they should not arise: incorporate the answers in your outline.

The important points about **answering questions** are as follows.

(a)   You may **seek feedback** throughout your talk, as to whether your message is getting across clearly – and it is common to invite the audience to let you know if anything is unclear – but by and large, you should encourage questions only at the end of your presentation. That way, disruptive, rambling, hostile and attention-seeking questions will not be allowed to disrupt your message to the audience as a whole.

(b)   You should **add or clarify** information if required to achieve your purpose. An honest query deserves a co-operative answer.

(c)   You need to **maintain your credibility** and authority as the speaker. Strong tactics may be required for you to stay in control, without in any way ridiculing or 'putting down' the questioner.

      (i)   If a question is based on a **false premise** or incorrect information, **correct it**. An answer may, or may not, then be required.

      (ii)   If a question is **rambling**: interrupt, clarify what the question, or main question (if it is a multiple query) is, and answer that. If it is completely irrelevant, say politely that it is outside the scope of the presentation: you may or may not offer to deal with it informally afterwards.

      (iii)   If a question is **hostile or argumentative**, you may wish to show understanding of how the questioner has reached his conclusion, or why he feels as he does. However, you then need to reinforce, repeat or explain your own view.

      (iv)   If a question tries to **pin you down** or 'corner' you on an area in which you do not wish to be specific or to make promises, be straightforward about it.

      (v)   If a question exposes an area in which you do not know the answer, **admit your limitations** with honesty and dignity, and invite help from members of the audience, if appropriate.

      (vi)   Try and answer all questions with **points already made** in your speech, or related to them. This reinforces the impression that your speech was in fact complete and correct.

(d)   **Repeat** any question that you think might not have been **audible** to everyone in the room.

(e)   **Clarify** any question that you think is lengthy, complex, ambiguous or uses jargon not shared by the audience as a whole.

(f)   **Answer briefly**, keeping strictly to the point of the question (while relating it, if possible, to what you have already said). If your answer needs to be lengthy, structure it as you would a small talk: introduce what you are going to say, say it, then confirm what you have said!

(g)   Keep an eye on the **overall time-limit** for your talk or for the question-and-answer session. Move on if a questioner is taking up too much time, and call a halt, courteously, when required. 'I'll take one more question ... ' or 'I'm afraid that's all we have time for' is standard practice which offends few listeners.

To summarise our discussion about presenting research:

- Whenever you are communicating in a report or in a presentation you should take into account the audience's thinking sequence: Respect the client's importance; Consider the client's needs; Demonstrate how your information helps the client; Explain the detail that underpins your information; Remind the client of the key points; Suggest what the client should do now.

- A research report typically has the following elements: Title page; list of contents; executive summary; introduction/problem definition; research method (and limitations); research findings; conclusions; appendices.

- Tables, graphs, charts and illustrations of various kinds can greatly enhance the value of a report because they make it easier to take in information at a glance.

- An oral presentation would have the following structure: Introduction; Explanation of research methodology; Key findings; Conclusions/recommendations; Questions.

- Matters to consider when preparing and delivering presentations include audience motivation, physical factors in the presentation room, content, clarity, adding emphasis and interest, and controlling nerves and body language.

- Visual aids include slides (acetates and PowerPoint), videos, flipcharts, handouts and props and demonstrations.

- Questions are important to help clarify misunderstandings and overcome doubts. It is important that the speaker maintains credibility.

Learning objectives	Covered	
1 Review the key formats when presenting marketing information to decision makers	☑	Research reports
	☑	Research presentations
2 Explain the relevance of the audience thinking sequence	☑	Thinking sequence people go through when you communicate with them
	☑	Remain impartial as a researcher
	☑	Recognise the needs of the audience
3 Identify best practices when presenting information	☑	Formatting information
	☑	Structure of reports and presentations
	☑	Audience appreciation

Learning objective review

1 The use of a graph or bar chart illustrates that the writer or presenter is aware of what part of the audience thinking sequence?

2 Which part of a report contains a summary of findings?

3 A graphic aid used to show processes and relationships is a .... chart.

4 If 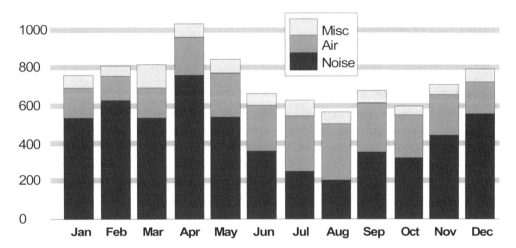 represents $100m, draw a pictogram for $550m.

5 The following is an example of multiple bar chart. True or false?

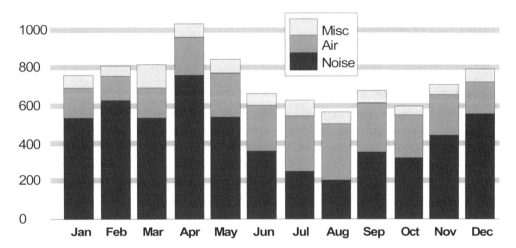

6 List five techniques that can be used to add emphasis.

7 List five reasons why people might ask questions when attending a presentation.

1   **REPORT ON THE WOMEN'S FRAGRANCE MARKET**

For the attention of: Sian Singh
                         Georgie Brand Manager
                         Lanroche

Completed by: Wanda Wen
                 Marketing Assistant

The Brand Tracker Partnership

Date of submission: 10 June 201X

I   INTRODUCTION

The Brand Tracker Partnership was commissioned by Sian Singh, Lanroche, to research the women's fragrance market and to investigate reasons for purchasing fragrance products and brand preferences.

II   RESEARCH METHODS

The research was conducted during October to December 201X. Secondary data sources were MEAL and Sales/Monitor. These provided industry-wide data and were used to produce advertising expenditure and industry sales figures. In addition women's magazines were analysed for advertising and sales promotion information.

During December primary data was collected by survey from a sample of 300 women aged between 16-55. This is a representative cross-section of the fragrance buying market. From this sample four focus groups were held across the country in order to capture possible regional variations.

III   FINDINGS

1.   Market size and share

The fragrance market is fragmented (32 fragrances were named). However just 11 brands have 73% of total market share.

Georgie, at fourth place, is one of the leading brands. It has 8.8% market share behind:

Ana – 13%
Eternal – 11%
Possession – 10.5%

The fifth placed brand is Lady with 7.2%.

2.   Customer profile

There is no correlation between customers and their socio-economic group. The class profile is flat. ABC1s do not stand out in terms of either buying or receiving premium priced products.

3.   Price

Price was only considered important by purchasers of Carlie which, along with Lady and Max Maxa, was at the cheapest end of the market.

64% of fragrances sold were priced at more than £15 per 30ml.

4.   Brands and brand recognition

All age groups are attracted to the four leading brands. There is a notable age-based differentiation amongst the others.

16 – 25 years – Charly Klein and Carlie
Thirty-somethings – Cachet
40 – 55 years – Channelle and Esta Lauda

Brand recognition is highest for those brands with the greatest advertising spend (per annum figures).

£1.57m – Possession
£1.2m – Eternal
£1.04m – Ana
£0.955m – Georgie

Note, however, that Esta Lauda with a spend of £0.877m only achieved a 3% spontaneous ad recall.

New entrants to the market may be achieving high recognition figures as a result of point-of-sale and promotional initiatives. Two other forms which these take are: counter samples and scent strips in magazines.

5. Buyer behaviour

The key factors for purchase are as follows (in descending order).

55% – 'tried it in the shop'
53% – 'usual one'
32% – 'something new'
25% – 'saw advertisement'

IV CONCLUSION

Georgie is well established in the market across the complete age range. It is not discriminated against in terms of price and its advertising strategies are effective.

However, Ana with only a slightly larger spend is the most widely recognised brand (22% against 12% for Georgie). This factor warrants further research.

2 Company A specialises in delivering quite large packages quickly
Company B delivers smaller packages fairly slowly
Company C delivers smaller packages quite quickly
Company D delivers fairly small packages slightly more quickly than average
Company E delivers very large packages very slowly
Company F delivers medium to large packages more quickly than average

3 The answer to this depends upon your own experiences.

4 We had in mind a situation when the researcher is conducting qualitative research, particularly focus groups and also when an agency first presents its proposal to a client in a beauty parade.

---

1 The writer or presenter is offering a means of taking in information at a glance therefore he or she is respecting the importance of the audience (not wasting their time).

2 Not the introduction or the conclusion! Remember this in your exam. The summary is contained where you would expect it, in the executive summary.

3 Flow chart

4 💰 💰 💰 💰 💰 💰

5 False: it is a stacked bar chart.

6 Repetition, rhetorical question, quotation, statistical evidence, exaggeration

7 To seek additional information, to seek clarification, to add information, to lead the discussion into another area, to display their own cleverness, to undermine the speaker.

Bain, R (2008) '*MTV dissects the youth of today :London exhibition reveals findings of global youth culture study*' Research Magazine, MRS, October edition, London.

Birn, R. (2004) *The effective use of Market Research: How to drive and focus better business decisions*, Kogan Page, London.

Wilson, A. (2006) *Marketing Research An Integrated Approach*, 2nd Edition, Prentice Hall, Harlow.

References

Key concepts

Attitude, 101

Audience thinking sequence, 22

Category management, 100

Cluster sampling, 120

CRM software, 30

Customer database, 39

Customer relationship management (CRM), 42

Data cleansing, 45

Data mining, 55

Data warehousing, 53

Database marketing, 39

Decision support systems, 29

Desk research, 130

Distribution research, 104

Environmental scanning, 139

Executive information system, 30

Extranet, 26

Focus groups, 155

Forum voting, 181

Groupware, 24

Intranet, 25

Knowledge assets, 4

Knowledge management, 4

Knowledge-based economy, 3

Market research, 113

Marketing decision support system, 29

Marketing information system, 26

Marketing intelligence system, 28

Marketing research, 113

Population, 117

Product life cycle, 97

Product testing, 100

Product research, 97

Qualitative research, 150

Quantitative research, 166

Reliable data, 20

Research brief, 87

Research proposals, 88

Sampling, 117

Secondary data, 130

Stratified sampling, 120

Systematic sampling, 120

Valid data, 20

Visual aids, 217

Index

Review form & Free prize draw

All original review forms from the entire BPP range, completed with genuine comments, will be entered into one of two draws on 31 January 2011 and 31 July 2011. The names on the first four forms picked out on each occasion will be sent a cheque for £50.

Name: _____   **Address**: _____

_____

_____

1.How have you used this Text?
(Tick one box only)

☐ Self study (book only)

☐ On a course: college_____

☐ Other _____

3. Why did you decide to purchase this Text?
(Tick one box only)

☐ Have used companion Assessment workbook

☐ Have used BPP Texts in the past

☐ Recommendation by friend/colleague

☐ Recommendation by a lecturer at college

☐ Saw advertising in journals

☐ Saw website

☐ Other _____

2. During the past six months do you recall seeing/receiving any of the following?
(Tick as many boxes as are relevant)

☐ Our advertisement in *The Marketer*

☐ Our brochure with a letter through the post

☐ Saw website

4. Which (if any) aspects of our advertising do you find useful?
(Tick as many boxes as are relevant)

☐ Prices and publication dates of new editions

☐ Information on product content

☐ Facility to order books off-the-page

☐ None of the above

5. Have you used the companion Assessment Workbook?   Yes ☐   No ☐

6. Have you used the companion Passcards?   Yes ☐   No ☐

7. Your ratings, comments and suggestions would be appreciated on the following areas.

	Very useful	Useful	Not useful
Introductory section (How to use this text, study checklist, etc)	☐	☐	☐
Introduction	☐	☐	☐
Syllabus linked learning outcomes	☐	☐	☐
Activities and Marketing at Work examples	☐	☐	☐
Learning objective reviews	☐	☐	☐
Magic Formula references	☐	☐	☐
Content of suggested answers	☐	☐	☐
Index	☐	☐	☐
Structure and presentation	☐	☐	☐

	Excellent	Good	Adequate	Poor
Overall opinion of this Text	☐	☐	☐	☐

8. Do you intend to continue using BPP CIM Range Products?   ☐ Yes   ☐ No

9. Have you visited bpp.com/lm/cim?   ☐ Yes   ☐ No

10.If you have visited bpp.com/lm/cim, please give a score out of 10 for it's overall usefulness   /10

Please note any further comments and suggestions/errors on the reverse of this page.

Please return to: Rebecca Hart, BPP Learning Media, FREEPOST, London, W12 8BR.

If you have any additional questions, feel free to email cimrange@bpp.com

Marketing information and research

Review form & Free prize draw (continued)

Please note any further comments and suggestions/errors below.

Free prize draw rules

1   Closing date for 31 January 2011 draw is 31 December 2010. Closing date for 31 July 2011 draw is 30 June 2011.

2   Restricted to entries with UK and Eire addresses only. BPP employees, their families and business associates are excluded.

3   No purchase necessary. Entry forms are available upon request from BPP Learning Media. No more than one entry per title, per person. Draw restricted to persons aged 16 and over.

4   Winners will be notified by post and receive their cheques not later than 6 weeks after the relevant draw date. List of winners will be supplied on request.

5   The decision of the promoter in all matters is final and binding. No correspondence will be entered into.

Marketing information and research